Microsoft®
Publisher 2013
ILLUSTRATED

Microsoft®
Publisher 2013
ILLUSTRATED

Elizabeth Eisner Reding

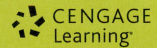
CENGAGE
Learning®

Australia • Brazil • Japan • Korea • Mexico • Singapore • Spain • United Kingdom • United States

Microsoft® Publisher 2013—Illustrated Introductory
Elizabeth Eisner Reding

Senior Product Team Manager: Marjorie Hunt

Associate Product Manager: Amanda Lyons

Senior Content Developer: Christina Kling-Garrett

Content Developer: Kim Klasner

Marketing Manager: Gretchen Swann

Developmental Editor: Susan Whalen

Project Manager: GEX Publishing Services

Copyeditor: GEX Publishing Services

Proofreader: Lisa Weidenfeld

Indexer: Rich Carlson

QA Manuscript Reviewers: Serge Palladino,
    John Freitas, Danielle Shaw, Jeff Schwartz

Cover Designer: GEX Publishing Services

Cover Artist: ©Alena P/Shutterstock

Composition: GEX Publishing Services

For product information and technology assistance, contact us at
Cengage Learning Customer & Sales Support, 1-800-354-9706

For permission to use material from this text or product, submit all
requests online at **www.cengage.com/permissions**
Further permissions questions can be emailed to
permissionrequest@cengage.com

Library of Congress Control Number: 2013949096
ISBN-13: 978-1-285-08271-4
ISBN-10: 1-285-08271-0

Cengage Learning
200 First Stamford Place, 4th Floor
Stamford, CT 06902
USA

Cengage Learning is a leading provider of customized learning solutions
with office locations around the globe, including Singapore, the United
Kingdom, Australia, Mexico, Brazil, and Japan. Locate your local office at:
www.cengage.com/global

Cengage Learning products are represented in Canada by
Nelson Education, Ltd.

For your course and learning solutions, visit **www.cengage.com**

Purchase any of our products at your local college store or at our
preferred online store **www.cengagebrain.com**

Printed in the United States of America
1 2 3 4 5 6 7 19 18 17 16 15 14 13

Brief Contents

Contents

Preface

Welcome to *Microsoft Publisher 2013—Illustrated*. This book has a unique design: Each skill is presented on two facing pages, with steps on the left and screens on the right. The layout makes it easy to learn a skill without having to read a lot of text and flip pages to see an illustration.

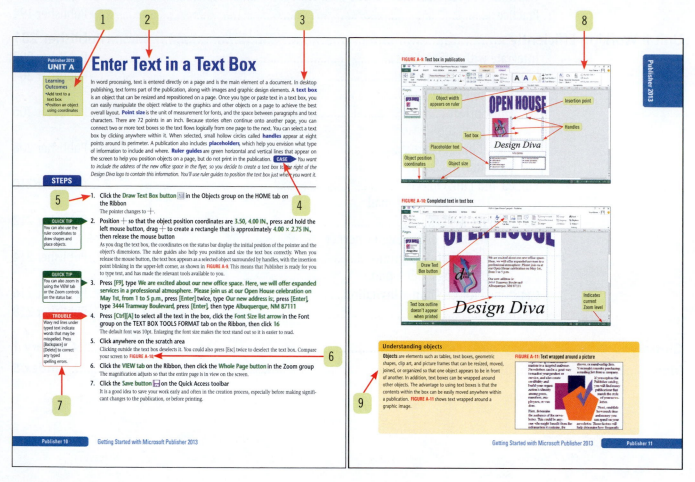

1 Red! Learning Outcomes box lists measurable learning goals for which a student is accountable in that lesson.

2 Each two-page lesson focuses on a single skill.

3 Introduction briefly explains why the lesson skill is important.

4 A case scenario motivates the steps and puts learning in context.

5 Step-by-step instructions and brief explanations guide students through each hands-on lesson activity.

6 New! Figure references are now in red bold to help students refer back and forth between the steps and screenshots.

7 Tips and troubleshooting advice, right where you need it—next to the step itself.

8 New! Larger screenshots with green callouts now keep students on track as they complete steps.

9 Clues to Use yellow boxes provide useful information related to the lesson skill.

This book is an ideal learning tool for a wide range of learners—the "rookies" will find the clean design easy to follow and focused with only essential information presented, and the "hotshots" will appreciate being able to move quickly through the lessons to find the information they need without reading a lot of text. The design also makes this a great reference after the course is over! See the illustration on the left to learn more about the pedagogical and design elements of a typical lesson.

What's New in this Edition

- **Coverage** — This book helps students learn essential skills using Microsoft Publisher 2013—including step-by-step instructions on creating a publication, working with text and graphics, enhancing a publication, working with multiple pages, and adding design elements. Reworked to cover the new features of Publisher 2013, including the updated user interface, new Start screen, new templates and new picture tools.

- **New! Learning Outcomes** — Each lesson displays a green Learning Outcomes box that lists skills-based or knowledge-based learning goals for which students are accountable. Each Learning Outcome maps to a variety of learning activities and assessments. (See the *New! Learning Outcomes* section on page xii for more information.)

- **New! Updated Design** — This edition features many new design improvements to engage students — including larger lesson screenshots with green callouts placed on top, and a refreshed Unit Opener page.

- **New! Independent Challenge 4: Explore** — This new case-based assessment activity allows students to explore new skills and use creativity to solve a problem or create a project.

Assignments

This book includes a wide variety of high quality assignments you can use for practice and assessment. Assignments include:

- **Concepts Review** — Multiple choice, matching, and screen identification questions.

- **Skills Review** — Step-by-step, hands-on review of every skill covered in the unit.

- **Independent Challenges 1-3** — Case projects requiring critical thinking and application of the unit skills. The Independent Challenges increase in difficulty. The first one in each unit provides the most hand-holding; the subsequent ones provide less guidance and require more critical thinking and independent problem solving.

- **Independent Challenge 4: Explore** — Case project that lets students explore new skills that are related to the core skills covered in the unit and is often more open ended, allowing students to use creativity to complete the assignment.

- **Visual Workshop** — Critical thinking exercises that require students to create a project by looking at a completed solution; they must apply the skills they've learned in the unit and use critical thinking skills to create the project.

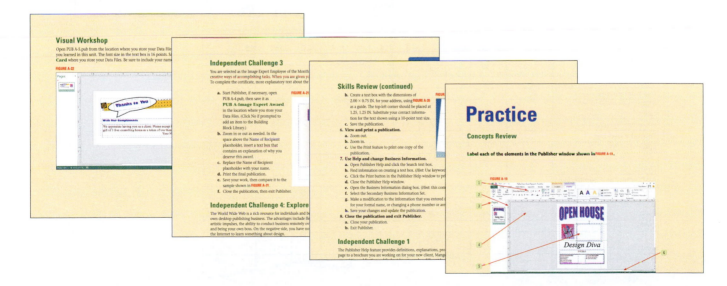

New! Learning Outcomes

Every 2-page lesson in this book now contains a green **Learning Outcomes box** that states the learning goals for that lesson.

- **What is a learning outcome?** A learning outcome states what a student is expected to know or be able to do after completing a lesson. Each learning outcome is skills-based or knowledge-based and is *measurable*. Learning outcomes map to learning activities and assessments.

- **How do students benefit from learning outcomes?** Learning outcomes tell students exactly what skills and knowledge they are *accountable* for learning in that lesson. This helps students study more efficiently and effectively and makes them more active learners.

- **How do instructors benefit from learning outcomes?** Learning outcomes provide clear, measurable, skills-based learning goals that map to various high-quality learning activities and assessments. A **Learning Outcomes Map**, available for each unit in this book, maps every learning outcome to the learning activities and assessments shown below.

Learning Outcomes Map to These Learning Activities:

- **Book lessons:** Step-by-step tutorial on one skill presented in a two-page learning format

Learning Outcomes Map to These Assessments:

1. **End-of-Unit Exercises: Concepts Review** (screen identification, matching, multiple choice); **Skills Review** (hands-on review of each lesson); **Independent Challenges** (hands-on, case-based review of specific skills); **Visual Workshop** (activity that requires student to build a project by looking at a picture of the final solution).
2. **Exam View Test Banks**: Objective-based questions you can use for online or paper testing.
3. **Extra Independent Challenges**: Extra case-based exercises available in the Instructor Resources that cover various skills.

Learning Outcomes Map

A **Learning Outcomes Map**, contained in the Instructor Resources, provides a listing of learning activities and assessments for each learning outcome in the book.

Learning Outcomes Map
Microsoft Publisher 2013 Illustrated Introductory
Unit C

KEY:
IC=Independent Challenge   EIC=Extra Independent Challenge
VW=Visual Workshop   CS=Capstone

	Concepts Review	Skills Review	IC1	IC2	IC3	IC4	VW	EIC 1	EIC 2	Test Bank	CS
Use layout guides											
Set up margin guides		✓	✓	✓	✓	✓	✓			✓	✓
Add a grid guide		✓	✓	✓	✓	✓	✓	✓		✓	
Use ruler guides											
Move horizontal and vertical rulers		✓	✓	✓					✓	✓	
Reposition the zero point		✓	✓	✓					✓	✓	✓
Format a text box											
Insert a text box		✓	✓	✓	✓	✓	✓			✓	
Change line color and weight		✓		✓	✓	✓	✓	✓			
Add bullets and numbering											
Create a numbered list		✓		✓				✓	✓	✓	✓
Modify the bullets in a bulleted list		✓		✓					✓	✓	
Check spelling								✓			
Check the spelling in a document	✓	✓	✓	✓	✓	✓	✓			✓	✓
Accept spelling suggestions											

Instructor Resources

This book comes with a wide array of high-quality technology-based, teaching tools to help you teach and to help students learn. The following teaching tools are available for download at our Instructor Companion Site. Simply search for this text at *login.cengage.com*. An instructor login is required.

- **New! Learning Outcomes Map** — A detailed grid for each unit (in Excel format) shows the learning activities and assessments that map to each learning outcome in that unit.

- **Instructor's Manual** — Available as an electronic file, the Instructor's Manual includes lecture notes with teaching tips for each unit.

- **Sample Syllabus** — Prepare and customize your course easily using this sample course outline.

- **PowerPoint Presentations** — Each unit has a corresponding PowerPoint presentation covering the skills and topics in that unit that you can use in lectures, distribute to your students, or customize to suit your course.

- **Figure Files** — The figures in the text are provided on the Instructor Resources site to help you illustrate key topics or concepts. You can use these to create your own slide shows or learning tools.

- **Solution Files** — Solution Files are files that contain the finished project that students create or modify in the lessons or end-of-unit material.

- **Solutions Document** — This document outlines the solutions for the end-of-unit Concepts Review, Skills Review, Independent Challenges and Visual Workshops. An Annotated Solution File and Grading Rubric accompany each file and can be used together for efficient grading.

- **ExamView Test Banks** — ExamView is a powerful testing software package that allows you to create and administer printed, computer (LAN-based), and Internet exams. Our ExamView test banks include questions that correspond to the skills and concepts covered in this text, enabling students to generate detailed study guides that include page references for further review. The computer-based and Internet testing components allow students to take exams at their computers, and also save you time by grading each exam automatically.

Key Facts About Using This Book

Data Files are needed: To complete many of the lessons and end-of-unit assignments, students need to start from partially completed Data Files, which help students learn more efficiently. By starting out with a Data File, students can focus on performing specific tasks without having to create a file from scratch. All Data Files are available as part of the Instructor Resources. Students can also download Data Files themselves for free at cengagebrain.com. (For detailed instructions, go to www.cengage.com/ct/studentdownload.)

System requirements: This book was developed using Microsoft Office 2013 Professional running on Windows 8. Note that Windows 8 is not a requirement; Publisher 2013 runs virtually the same on Windows 7 and Windows 8. Please see Important Notes for Windows 7 Users on the next page for more information.

Screen resolution: This book was written and tested on computers with monitors set at a resolution of 1366 x 768. If your screen shows more or less information than the figures in this book, your monitor is probably set at a higher or lower resolution. If you don't see something on your screen, you might have to scroll down or up to see the object identified in the figure.

Tell Us What You Think!

We want to hear from you! Please email your questions, comments, and suggestions to the Illustrated Series team at: **illustratedseries@cengage.com**

Important Notes for Windows 7 Users

The screenshots in this book show Microsoft Publisher 2013 running on Windows 8. However, if you are using Microsoft Windows 7, you can still use this book because Publisher 2013 (and all of the Office 2013 applications) run virtually the same on both platforms. There are only two differences that you will encounter if you are using Windows 7. Read this section to understand the differences.

Dialog boxes

If you are a Windows 7 user, dialog boxes shown in this book will look slightly different than what you see on your screen. Dialog boxes for Windows 7 have a light blue title bar, instead of a medium blue title bar. However, beyond this superficial difference in appearance, the options in the dialog boxes across platforms are the same. For instance, the screen shots below show the Font dialog box in Word 2013 running on Windows 7 and the Font dialog box running on Windows 8.

FIGURE 1: Font dialog box in Windows 7

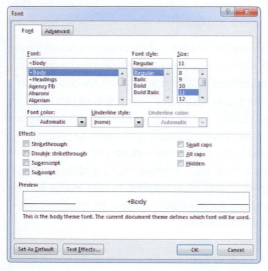

FIGURE 2: Font dialog box in Windows 8

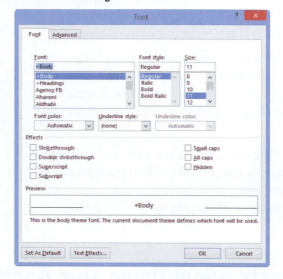

Alternate Steps for Starting an App in Windows 7

Nearly all of the steps in this book work exactly the same for Windows 7 users. However, starting an app (or program/application) requires different steps for Windows 7. The steps below show the Windows 7 steps for starting an app. (Note: Windows 7 alternate steps also appear in red Trouble boxes next to any step in the book that requires starting an app.)

Starting an app (or program/application) using Windows 7

1. Click the **Start button** on the taskbar to open the Start menu.
2. Click **All Programs**, then click the **Microsoft Office 2013 folder**. See Figure 3.
3. Click the app you want to use (such as **Publisher 2013**).

FIGURE 3: Starting an app using Windows 7

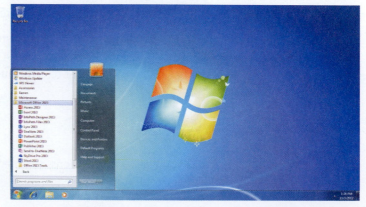

Acknowledgements

Author Acknowledgements

Elizabeth Eisner Reding - It takes a lot of dedicated professionals to take a manuscript and turn it into a book. It's just not possible to thank every person involved in this project, but I would like to take this opportunity to mention a few key members of the team: Marjorie Hunt, the Senior Product Team Manager, who made this team a reality; Susan Whalen, the Developmental Editor, Kimberly Klasner, the Content Developer and Christina Kling-Garrett, the Senior Content Developer; Heidi Aguiar, the Project Manager and manager of all aspects of the production process; John Freitas, Danielle Shaw, and Serge Palladino, the QA testers who were able to debug these lessons with style and class; and Michael Reding, my husband, whose unending patience and support is a constant joy.

Advisory Board Acknowledgements

We thank our Illustrated Advisory Board who gave us their opinions and guided our decisions as we redesigned all of our Illustrated Series products for Office 2013. They are as follows:

Merlin Amirtharaj, Stanly Community College

Londo Andrews, J. Sargeant Reynolds Community College

Rachelle Hall, Glendale Community College

Terri Helfand, Chaffey Community College

Sheryl Lenhart, Terra Community College

Dr. Jose Nieves, Lord Fairfax Community College

Getting Started with Microsoft Publisher 2013

CASE ▶ You work at Design Diva, a small advertising agency, as an assistant to Mike Mendoza, an account executive. Mike asks you to create a flyer announcing the location of the agency's new office. You decide to use Publisher to create this publication.

Unit Objectives

After completing this unit, you will be able to:

- Define publication software
- Start Publisher 2013
- Explore the Publisher window
- Open and save a publication
- Enter text in a text box

- View and print a publication
- Use Help and change Business Information
- Close a publication and exit Publisher
- Capstone Project: Study Abroad Flyer

Files You Will Need

PUB A-1.pub	PUB A-4.pub
PUB A-2.pub	PUB A-5.pub
PUB A-3.pub	

©Alena P/Shutterstock

Define Publication Software

Learning Outcomes
• Explore the uses of Publisher
• Define key desktop publishing terms

Publisher is a **desktop publishing program**, a software program that lets you combine text and graphics, as well as worksheets and charts created in other programs, to produce typeset-quality documents for output on a personal printer or for commercial printing. A document created in Publisher is called a **publication**. TABLE A-1 describes the types of publications you can create. CASE ▶ *You want to learn how to use Publisher so that you can generate a professional-looking flyer quickly and easily.*

DETAILS

The benefits of using Publisher include the ability to:

• **Create professional publications**

Publisher comes with a generous collection of templates, designs that let you choose the type of publication you want to develop. Publisher templates help you decide on the appearance, then suggest text and graphic image placement to complete the publication. Once you choose a template from the Featured Templates list, you can easily modify it to meet specific needs, using options on the PAGE DESIGN tab on the Ribbon.

• **Use artwork**

Artwork not only makes any publication appear more vibrant and interesting, but also helps to reflect and reinforce your ideas with visual images. Publisher comes with many pieces of artwork that can be incorporated into publications. In addition, other illustrations (from a variety of sources including Office.com), sound files, video art, and photographs can be imported into your publications.

• **Create logos**

Most organizations use a recognizable symbol, shape, color, or combination of these to attach to their name. This distinctive artwork, called a **logo**, can be created using resources such as the Publisher Page Parts Gallery or by designing your own artwork and text. FIGURE A-1 illustrates a sample flyer created in Publisher that contains a logo formed by combining clip art and text.

• **Make your work look consistent**

Publisher has many tools to help you create consistent publications that have similar design elements. You can use **designs** to create different types of stylized publications. When creating work from scratch, you might, for example, want to designate an area on the page that always displays the same information, such as a company name or mission statement. Using rulers and layout guides, you can create grids to help position graphics and text on a page. You can also save a publication as a **template**, a specially formatted publication of your own design with placeholder text that serves as a master for other, similar publications.

QUICK TIP
Text that flows from one page to another can be connected with "continued on" and "continued from" notices, sometimes called "jump lines."

• **Work with multiple pages**

Publisher makes it easy to work with multipage publications. Pages can be added, deleted, and moved within a publication.

QUICK TIP
Altering the appearance of text by using **bold**, *italic*, or underline formatting can emphasize its significance.

• **Emphasize special text**

Even great writing can be less than compelling if all the text looks the same. Use varied text styles to express different meanings and convey messages to add interest and help guide the reader's eye. You can use headlines to grab readers and lead them to stories of specific significance. You can use a sidebar to make a short statement more noticeable, or a pull quote to make an important point stand out and grab a reader's attention.

• **Publish to the Internet**

Publisher contains design elements specifically for Web sites, making it easy to include links and graphics. Page backgrounds and animated GIFs add color and motion to your pages. The Publish HTML command (in the Backstage view) helps you add common Web features to a print document and makes your Web site available to a local network drive, an intranet, or an Internet Service Provider for worldwide viewing.

FIGURE A-1: Sample Flyer

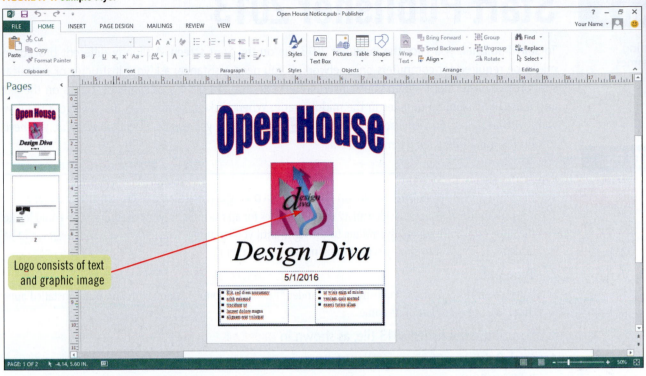

Logo consists of text and graphic image

TABLE A-1: Common publications you can create in Publisher

publication type	example
Informational	Brochures, signs, calendars, forms
Periodical	Newsletters, catalogs
Promotional	Advertisements, flyers, press releases
Stationery	Letterhead, labels, business cards, envelopes, postcards, invitations
Specialty	Banners, airplanes, origami, resumes, award certificates, gift certificates

© 2014 Cengage Learning

Creating branded publications

Branded publications are those that have a similar look to them, giving your company instant recognition. Branding may be as simple as putting your company logo on everything, or using a specific color in a special design. Common examples of branding are seen in the Nike swoosh and the Motorola 'M' logos.

When you use templates that have the same patterns, such as the Arrows and Brocade designs, or your own design, all your print and Web materials will have a similar look. This similar look will be associated with your company or brand.

Start Publisher 2013

To start Publisher, you click the Publisher 2013 tile on the Start screen. A slightly different procedure might be required for computers on a network. If you need assistance, ask your instructor or technical support person for help. When you start Publisher, the program displays recently used files on the left and a list of available templates in the middle pane. When clicked, some selections feature a preview window that helps you visualize your choices. **CASE** ▶ *Before you can create the publication, you need to start Publisher and open a new document.*

STEPS

> **TROUBLE**
> If you are running Windows 7, follow the steps at the bottom of this page.

1. **Press the Windows button ⊞ on the keyboard to go to the Start screen, if necessary**

   Your screen now displays a wide variety of colorful tiles for all the apps on your computer. You could locate the app you want to open by scrolling to the right until you see it, but if you have a lot of apps it could be difficult. It is easiest to simply type the app name to search for it.

2. **Type pub**

   Your screen now displays "Publisher 2013" under "Results for "pub"", along with any other installed apps that have "pub" as part of its name.

3. **Locate the Publisher 2013 tile, as shown in FIGURE A-2**

4. **Click Publisher 2013**

   Publisher 2013 launches, and the Publisher start screen appears, as shown in **FIGURE A-3**. The **start screen** is a landing page that appears when you first start an Office app. The left side of this screen displays recent files you have opened. (If you have never opened any files, then there will be no files listed under Recent.) The right side displays images depicting different templates you can use to create different types of documents. A **template** is a file containing professionally designed content that you can easily replace with your own. Using a template to create a document can save time and ensure that your document looks great. You can also start from scratch using the Blank Document option.

5. **Position ▷ over Blank 8.5 × 11" in the FEATURED list (in the right pane), but *do not click***

   The pointer is positioned over Blank 8.5 × 11". See **FIGURE A-3**. You can choose from a variety of page widths and dimensions. (If the size you want is not shown, click the More Blank Page Sizes button to see more options.)

6. **Click Blank 8.5 × 11"**

   A blank full-page publication appears in the workspace.

Starting an app using Windows 7

1. **Click the Start button 🏁 on the taskbar**
2. **Click All Programs on the Start menu, click the Microsoft Office 2013 folder, then click Publisher 2013**

Publisher 2013 launches, and the Publisher start screen appears, as shown previously in **FIGURE A-3**. The start screen is a landing page that appears when you first start an Office app. The left side of this screen displays recent files you have

opened. (If you have never opened any files, then there will be no files listed under Recent.) The right side displays images depicting different templates you can use to create different types of documents. A **template** is a file containing professionally designed content that you can easily replace with your own. Using a template to create a document can save time and ensure that your document looks great. You can also start from scratch using the Blank option.

FIGURE A-3: Blank page sizes

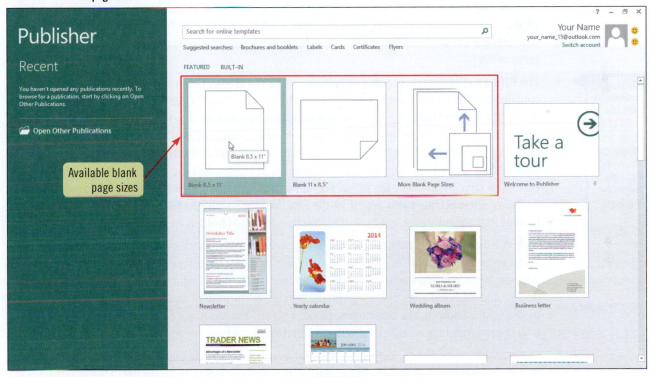

Creating a new publication

When you first open Publisher, the Featured Templates window displays in the center of the window. This window, which changes often, displays two tabs: FEATURED and BUILT-IN publications. The FEATURED tab displays blank (or empty) pages, commonly used publications, and publications such as advertisements, flyers, or letters. The BUILT-IN tab contains a variety of categories that are installed on your computer when the Publisher app is installed.

(These publications are also available if you *do not have* internet access.) Once you click a selection, you will be presented with a variety of options. Once your selections are made, Publisher will create the publication and it will open. If your computer is connected to the Internet, you can also choose a template from Office.com. These selections have been submitted by individuals and companies, and they change frequently.

Explore the Publisher Window

The area where a new or existing publication appears is called the **workspace**, which includes both the publication page and the scratch area. The workspace is where you actually work on a publication and view your work. The workspace is bordered above and on the left by horizontal and vertical rulers that help you position text and graphics in your publications. The workspace is also bordered by horizontal and vertical scroll bars that allow you to view different areas of the workspace. **CASE** ▶ *You decide to take some time to get familiar with the Publisher workspace and its elements before working on the flyer. Compare the descriptions below to FIGURE A-4.*

DETAILS

- The **title bar** is at the top of the window, and displays the program name (Publisher), and the filename of the open publication. In **FIGURE A-4**, the filename is Publication1, a default name, because the file has not yet been named and saved. The title bar also contains a Quick Access toolbar, Help button, a Close button, and resizing buttons. The Publisher Help feature can be accessed by pressing [F1] or by clicking ? at the right of the title bar.

- The **tab bar** contains tabs that contain buttons that are organized in task-based categories (such as PAGE DESIGN and VIEW). In Publisher, you can choose a tab by clicking it with the mouse, or by pressing [Alt], then pressing the displayed letter that appears beneath the tab name. (You can turn off the letter displays by pressing [Esc]).

- The **Ribbon** contains tabs grouped by Publisher tasks. The **HOME tab** is the first white tab on the left and contains buttons for the most frequently used Publisher commands. Place the pointer over each button to display the **ScreenTip**, a label that describes what each button does. To select a button, click it with the left mouse button. The faces of some buttons have a graphic representation of their function, while some have only text, or a combination of both. For example, the Shapes button displays a collection of shapes and the word Shapes. Buttons within each tab are organized in groups, and the group name is displayed at the bottom of each group. Some tab groups contain a launcher button indicating that additional options are available. **Formatting tools** appear in the Font and Paragraph groups of the HOME tab and contain buttons for frequently used text formatting commands such as **bold**, *italics*, or underlining.

- **Rulers** let you precisely measure the size of objects as well as place objects in exact locations on a page. They can be moved from the edge of the workspace to more convenient positions. Your rulers may have different beginning and ending numbers, depending on the size of your monitor, the resolution of your display, and the positioning of the page on the workspace. The units of measurement displayed in rulers can be changed to show inches, centimeters, picas, or points. You can modify the appearance and behavior of rulers by right-clicking on either the vertical or horizontal ruler.

- The workspace contains the currently displayed page and the scratch area. The **scratch area** is the gray area that surrounds the publication page, and can be used to store objects. To the left of the workspace is the **Pages pane**, which shows you how many pages are in the current publication and which pages are active, and allows you to navigate the pages. The Pages pane can be collapsed by clicking the Collapse Page Navigation Pane button (at the top-right edge of the pane); click the Expand Page Navigation Pane button to reopen the Pages pane. In a multi-page publication, an icon is displayed for each page; the icon for the current page is surrounded by a dark green outline. Click the thumbnail in the Pages pane for the page you want to view.

- The **status bar** is located at the bottom of the Publisher window. On the left side of the status bar are **page indicators**, which show you the number of pages in a publication and indicate which page is active. The left side of the status bar shows the object status, which includes the size and position of selected objects.

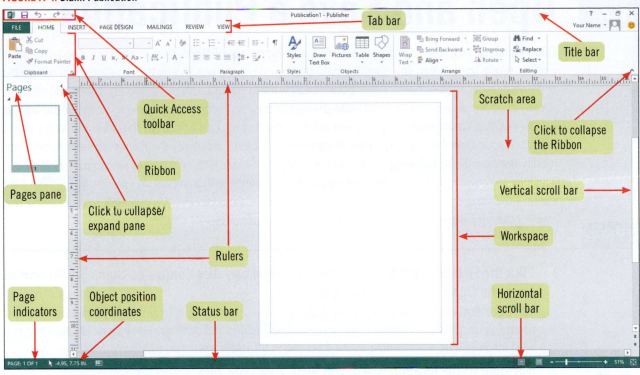

Tab bar

Title bar

Quick Access toolbar

Scratch area

Click to collapse the Ribbon

Ribbon

Pages pane

Click to collapse/ expand pane

Vertical scroll bar

Workspace

Rulers

Page indicators

Object position coordinates

Status bar

Horizontal scroll bar

Using panes and Building Blocks

A **pane** is an area of the Publisher window that is a visual gallery, which appears alongside your publication. In addition to the Pages pane, seen in **FIGURE A-5**, you can use panes for a variety of activities such as selecting and organizing clip art. Other tasks, such as adding important components to a publication, are done using Building Blocks. Located on the INSERT tab, Building Blocks let you add borders, accents, advertisements, and other elements that distinguish your publication and help make it unique.

FIGURE A-5: Pages pane

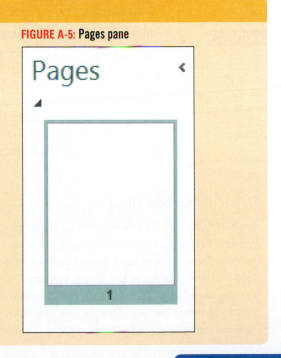

Open and Save a Publication

Learning Outcomes
• Open an existing Publisher file
• Save a file using a different name

Often a project is completed in stages: You start working on a publication, save it, and then stop to do other work or take a break. Later, you open the publication and resume working on it. Sometimes you open a file and save it under another name, either because you want to create a new publication by modifying one that already exists, or because you want to make changes to the document while preserving a copy of the original for safekeeping. Throughout this book, you will be instructed to open a file from the drive and folder where you store your Data Files, use the Save As command to create a copy of the file with a new name, then modify the new file by following the lesson steps. Saving the files with new names keeps your original Data Files intact in case you have to start the lesson over again or you wish to repeat an exercise. **CASE** ▶ *Mike started the Design Diva flyer and gives you the file to complete the document. You are ready to open the file and create a copy of it with a new name so that you can safely make changes.*

STEPS

1. **Click the FILE tab, click Open on the navigation bar, click Computer, then click Browse to open the Open Publication dialog box**

   The Open Publication dialog box opens. A dialog box is a window that opens when more information is needed to carry out a command. A list of the available folders and publications appears. The files that you need for these lessons are located on the drive and in the folder where you store your Data Files.

2. **Navigate to the location where you store your Data Files**

   A list of the Data Files appears, as shown in **FIGURE A-6**.

QUICK TIP
Use the Save As command to create a new publication from an existing one. Use the Save command to store any changes made to an existing file on your disk.

3. **Click PUB A-1.pub, then click Open**

   The file PUB A-1 opens. You could also double-click the filename in the Open Publication dialog box to open the file.

4. **Click the FILE tab, click Save As on the navigation bar, click Computer, then click Browse to open the Save As dialog box**

   The Save As dialog box opens.

5. **Make sure that the location where you store your Data Files appears in the Folders list**

   You should save all your files in the drive and folder where you store your Data Files unless instructed otherwise.

QUICK TIP
To save the publication in the future, you can click the FILE tab, then click Save, or click the Save button 💾 on the Quick Access toolbar.

6. **Select the current filename in the File name text box if necessary, then type PUB A-Open House Flyer**

   See **FIGURE A-7**.

7. **Click Save**

   The Save As dialog box closes, the file PUB A-1.pub closes, and a duplicate file named PUB A-Open House Flyer.pub is now open, as shown in **FIGURE A-8**. Changes made to PUB A-Open House Flyer will not be reflected in the file PUB A-1.pub.

Using dialog box views

You may notice that the information in the Open Publication and Save As dialog boxes varies depending on the view selected. There are eight views: Extra Large Icons, Large Icons, Medium Icons, Small Icons, List, Details, Tiles, and Content. Content view displays the folder content with icons and information about the type of file, the Tiles view shows the file type and the name of the file. List view displays the names of the contents of a given folder. The Details view displays the same information as List view, but includes the size, the last date and time the file was saved, and the file type. Extra Large, Large, Medium, and Small Icons views show the file type with the filename underneath. To select a different view, click the More Options list arrow in a File Explorer dialog box, then click the view you want.

FIGURE A-6: Open Publication dialog box

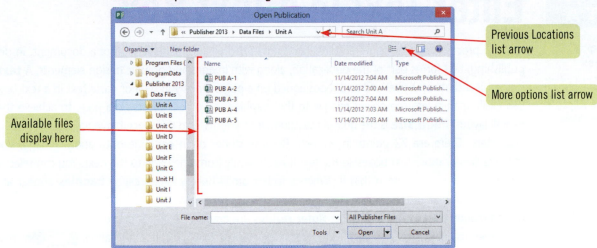

Previous Locations list arrow

More options list arrow

Available files display here

FIGURE A-7: Save As dialog box

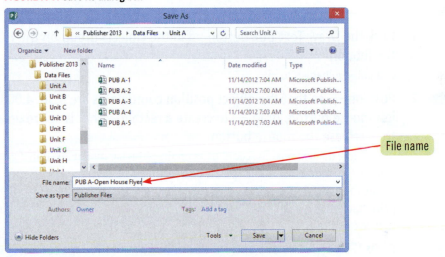

File name

FIGURE A-8: Open House Flyer publication

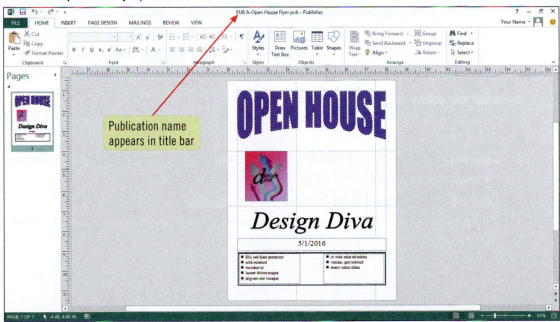

Publication name appears in title bar

Enter Text in a Text Box

Learning Outcomes
- Add text to a text box
- Position an object using coordinates

In word processing, text is entered directly on a page and is the main element of a document. In desktop publishing, text forms part of the publication, along with images and graphic design elements. A **text box** is an object that can be resized and repositioned on a page. Once you type or paste text in a text box, you can easily manipulate the object relative to the graphics and other objects on a page to achieve the best overall layout. **Point size** is the unit of measurement for fonts, and the space between paragraphs and text characters. There are 72 points in an inch. Because stories often continue onto another page, you can connect two or more text boxes so the text flows logically from one page to the next. You can select a text box by clicking anywhere within it. When selected, small hollow circles called **handles** appear at eight points around its perimeter. A publication also includes **placeholders**, which help you envision what type of information to include and where. **Ruler guides** are green horizontal and vertical lines that appear on the screen to help you position objects on a page, but do not print in the publication. **CASE** *You want to include the address of the new office space in the flyer, so you decide to create a text box to the right of the Design Diva logo to contain this information. You'll use ruler guides to position the text box just where you want it.*

STEPS

1. **Click the Draw Text Box button** [A] **in the Objects group on the HOME tab on the Ribbon**

   The pointer changes to +.

   QUICK TIP
   You can also use the ruler coordinates to draw shapes and place objects.

2. **Position** + **so that the object position coordinates are 3.50, 4.00 IN., press and hold the left mouse button, drag** + **to create a rectangle that is approximately 4.00 × 2.75 IN., then release the mouse button**

   As you drag the text box, the coordinates on the status bar display the initial position of the pointer and the object's dimensions. The ruler guides also help you position and size the text box correctly. When you release the mouse button, the text box appears as a selected object surrounded by handles, with the insertion point blinking in the upper-left corner, as shown in **FIGURE A-9**. This means that Publisher is ready for you to type text, and has made the relevant tools available to you.

   QUICK TIP
   You can also zoom in using the VIEW tab or the Zoom controls on the status bar.

3. **Press [F9], type We are excited about our new office space. Here, we will offer expanded services in a professional atmosphere. Please join us at our Open House celebration on May 1st, from 1 to 5 p.m., press [Enter] twice, type Our new address is:, press [Enter], type 3444 Tramway Boulevard, press [Enter], then type Albuquerque, NM 87111**

   TROUBLE
   Wavy red lines under typed text indicate words that may be misspelled. Press [Backspace] or [Delete] to correct any typed spelling errors.

4. **Press [Ctrl][A] to select all the text in the box, click the Font Size list arrow in the Font group on the TEXT BOX TOOLS FORMAT tab on the Ribbon, then click 16**

   The default font was 10pt. Enlarging the font size makes the text stand out so it is easier to read.

5. **Click anywhere on the scratch area**

   Clicking outside the text box deselects it. You could also press [Esc] twice to deselect the text box. Compare your screen to **FIGURE A-10**.

6. **Click the VIEW tab on the Ribbon, then click the Whole Page button in the Zoom group**

   The magnification adjusts so that the entire page is in view on the screen.

7. **Click the Save button** [💾] **on the Quick Access toolbar**

   It is a good idea to save your work early and often in the creation process, especially before making significant changes to the publication, or before printing.

FIGURE A-9: Text box in publication

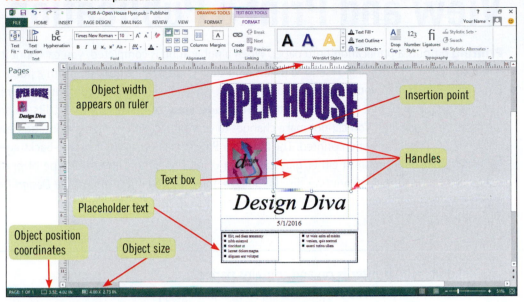

Object width appears on ruler

Insertion point

Handles

Text box

Placeholder text

Object position coordinates

Object size

FIGURE A-10: Completed text in text box

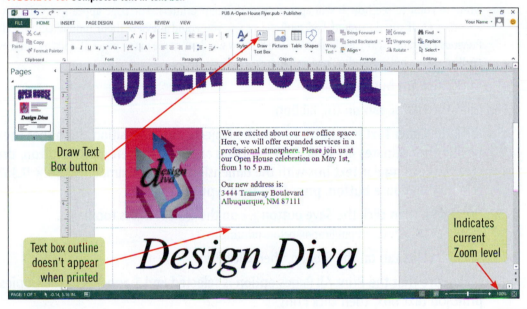

Draw Text Box button

Indicates current Zoom level

Text box outline doesn't appear when printed

We are excited about our new office space. Here, we will offer expanded services in a professional atmosphere. Please join us at our Open House celebration on May 1st, from 1 to 5 p.m.

Our new address is:
3444 Tramway Boulevard
Albuquerque, NM 87111

Design Diva

Understanding objects

Objects are elements such as tables, text boxes, geometric shapes, clip art, and picture frames that can be resized, moved, joined, or organized so that one object appears to be in front of another. In addition, text boxes can be wrapped around other objects. The advantage to using text boxes is that the contents within the box can be easily moved anywhere within a publication. **FIGURE A-11** shows text wrapped around a graphic image.

FIGURE A-11: Text wrapped around a picture

to provide specialized information to a targeted audience. Newsletters can be a great way to market your product or service, and also create credibility and build your organization's identity among peers, members, employees, or vendors.

First, determine the audience of the newsletter. This could be anyone who might benefit from the information it contains, for

shows, or membership lists. You might consider purchasing a mailing list from a company.

If you explore the Publisher catalog, you will find many publications that match the style of your newsletter.

Next, establish how much time and money you can spend on your newsletter. These factors will help determine how frequently

View and Print a Publication

Learning
Outcomes
• Print using
Backstage view

Printing outputs a publication onto paper. When a publication is completed, you can print it to have a paper copy to reference, file, or send to others. You can also print specific pages from a publication that is not complete so that you can review it or work on it when you are not at a computer. Before you print a publication, you should examine it in the **Backstage view** to make sure that it fits on a page and looks the way you want. You cannot make changes to your publication when in Backstage view; you can only see how it will look when printed. The Publisher Preview feature is visible in the Backstage view and will show your publication in either grayscale or in color, depending upon the type of printer that is selected. **TABLE A-2** provides printing tips. **CASE** ▸ *You want to print a copy of the Design Diva flyer to show Mike. First you want to preview the document to check its overall appearance and see how it will look when it is printed.*

STEPS

1. **Make sure the printer is on and contains paper**
   If a file is sent to print and the printer is off, an error message appears.

TROUBLE
If your selected printer is not a color printer, the Preview in the Backstage view will appear only in grayscale.

2. **Click the FILE tab, then click Print**
   If your printer allows both black and white and color printing, you can change the display from black and white to color to see how it will appear using different printers. The page appears in color, as shown in **FIGURE A-12**. If the document had multiple pages, you could preview them individually by clicking the Previous Page and Next Page buttons in the Preview window, or see many pages at once by clicking the View Multiple Pages button in the Preview window.

3. **Click the Print button**

4. **Click the HOME tab on the Ribbon**

5. **Click the Draw Text Box button** ▣ **in the Objects group, position** + **so that the object position coordinates are 0.50, 8.00 IN., press and hold the left mouse button, drag** + **to create a rectangular text box with the dimensions of approximately 2.00 × 0.35 IN., release the mouse button, press [F9], then type your name**

6. **Press [F9], then click the Save button** ▤ **on the Quick Access toolbar**
   You should always save a publication before printing it.

7. **Click the FILE tab on the Ribbon, then click Print**

QUICK TIP
If the Quick Print button has been added to the Quick Access toolbar, you can print your publication using the default settings by clicking it. (Click the Customize Quick Access toolbar button to add buttons to this toolbar.)

8. **Make sure that the Print All Pages option is selected and 1 appears in the Copies of print job text box, then click Print**
   Review the publication to see if it printed as expected.

9. **Click the Save button** ▤ **on the Quick Access toolbar**

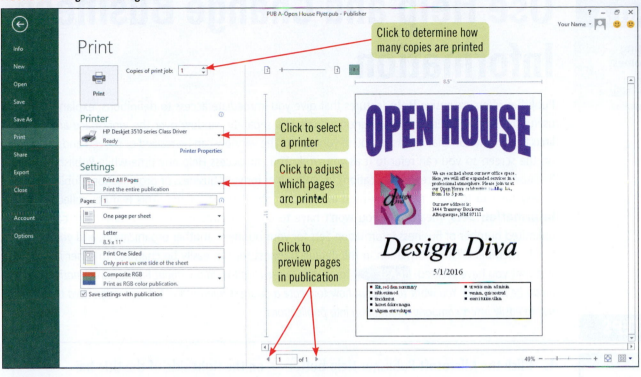

TABLE A-2: Publication printing tips

before you print	recommendation
Check the printer	Make sure that the printer is turned on and connected to the computer, that it has paper, and that it displays no error messages or warning signals.
Check the printer selection	In the Print command in Backstage view, select the correct printer from the Printer name list arrow to make sure that the correct printer is selected.

Using Backstage view

Microsoft Backstage view offers "one stop shopping" for many commonly performed tasks, such as opening and saving a file, printing and previewing, defining document properties, sharing information, and exiting a program. Backstage view opens when you click the FILE tab, and while the Ribbon, Mini-toolbar, and Live Preview all help you work *in* your documents, Backstage view helps you work *with* your documents.

Once you click Print in Backstage view, you can use the Print Settings to select a specific page size, or create a custom page size for a publication. Once you specify the dimensions of the page, any design template you select will be perfectly positioned on the page. To view the Print Settings, click the FILE tab, then click Print. Select a page size from the choices listed.

Use Help and Change Business Information

Publisher offers extensive **Help** features that give you immediate access to definitions, explanations, and useful tips. When open, the Help window floats in a separate window over the workspace and contains links to information that can assist you in your work. The window can be resized or moved and can remain on the screen so you can refer to it as you work. You can access Help any time while Publisher is open. Because you probably create publications for yourself or for your business or organization, Publisher makes it easy for you to store frequently used information about these entities. This feature, called **Business Information Sets**, means that you won't have to enter this information each time. You can store an unlimited number of Business Information Sets for your business, another organization, and your home or family members. The information in the default business set can easily be changed to other information sets that you have created. **CASE** *You decide to use Help to find out about Business Information and how it can be modified. You want to find out how to create a Business Information Set for Design Diva that you can use to easily insert company information into publications.*

STEPS

QUICK TIP
You can print the information in any Help window by clicking the Print button on the Publisher Help window toolbar.

1. Click the **Microsoft Publisher Help button** ? on the right side of the title bar

2. Click the search text box, type **business information**, then press **[Enter]**
   The Publisher Help window opens displaying topics about business information, as shown in **FIGURE A-13**.

3. Click **Edit Business Information,** then read about making modifications

4. Click the **Keep Help on Top button** 📌, then drag the Help window to the right edge of the screen

5. Click the **INSERT tab** on the Ribbon, click the **Business Information button** in the Text group, click **Edit Business Information**, then click **New** in the Business Information dialog box
   Any Business Information set can be modified, and the changes can be used in future publications.

QUICK TIP
If you are sharing a computer with other users, you may find another person's name in the Business Information Set. To add a new set, click New in the Business Information dialog box to open the Create New Business Information Set dialog box.

6. Press **[Tab]** three times to select the name in the Individual name text box, type **Your Name**, press **[Tab]**, then refer to **FIGURE A-14** to enter the rest of the information in the Create New Business Information Set dialog box including job title, phone numbers, and e-mail

7. Select the contents of the **Business Information set name text box**, then type **Secondary Business Information Set**
   The information in the dialog box is for the current secondary business.

QUICK TIP
You can also edit the Business Information from the Info command in Backstage view.

8. Click **Save**, confirm that the information you entered is correct, then click **Update Publication**
   Clicking Update Publication confirms your changes to the information set.

9. Click the **Don't Keep Help on Top button** 🖈, then click the **Close button** to close the Publisher Help window

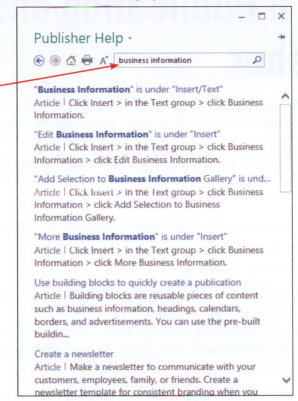

Search topic

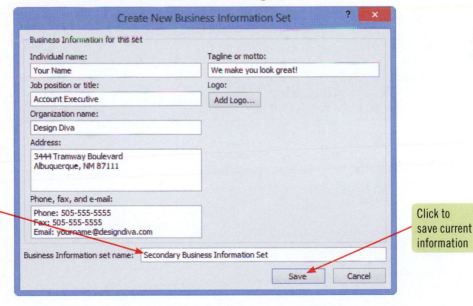

Information displayed is for the Secondary Business Information Set

Click to save current information

Close a Publication and Exit Publisher

When you finish working on a publication, you should save the file and close it. Closing a file puts away a publication so you can no longer work on it, but leaves Publisher running so you can work on other publications. When you complete all your work in Publisher, you want to exit the program. Exiting puts away any open publication files and returns you to the desktop, where you can choose to run another program. **CASE** ▶ *You finished adding the information to the Design Diva flyer and need to attend a meeting, so you close the publication and then exit Publisher.*

STEPS

1. **Click the FILE tab**

   Backstage view opens. See **FIGURE A-15**.

QUICK TIP

To exit Publisher and close the open publication, click the Close button on the upper-right corner of the window. Publisher prompts you to save any unsaved changes before closing.

2. **Click Close, then click Save if a dialog box opens asking if you want to save your changes**

   The file closes and Backstage view remains open.

   When viewing a publication, you can also double-click the program icon 📄 on the Quick Access toolbar to exit the program. Publisher closes, and computer memory is freed up for other computing tasks.

Opening a file with a single click

You can quickly open a recently used publication with a single click using the Recent list. When you click the FILE tab, then click Open, with Recent Publications selected you see a list of recently used Publisher files. To open a file in this list, simply click the name of the file you want.

You can get even more information about Microsoft Publisher by accessing the Microsoft Office Publisher Web site. This site is updated frequently, and offers tips, upgrades, sales promotions, and information on new developments in Publisher. By clicking on the blue underlined links, you'll be able to find additional information on the Microsoft product line. **FIGURE A-16** shows the Web site for Microsoft Publisher. It may look different on your screen because the site changes often. To find even more information, you can use your favorite search engine to search the Internet for any sites about Microsoft Publisher. To visit the Publisher Web site, click the Help button, then verify that you are connected to Office.com. When the Web site opens, click the Publisher link that matches your interest.

FIGURE A-16: Microsoft Publisher 2013 Web site

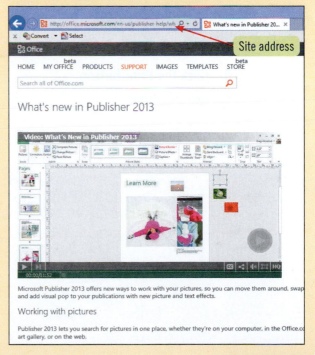

Capstone Project: Study Abroad Flyer

You have learned the basic skills necessary to modify an existing publication. You can open a file and save it under a different name. You know how to create a text box, insert text, zoom, and increase the font size to add emphasis. Once your work is complete, you can preview the flyer in both black and white and in color, then print it. **CASE** *Using a template, Mike started a flyer for the Community College Council that advertises a one-credit course in Mexico. He asks you to complete the project by adding contact information and then reviewing and printing the document.*

STEPS

1. Start Publisher, click Open Other Documents in Backstage view, open PUB A-2.pub from the location where you store your Data Files, then save the publication as PUB A-Study Abroad Flyer

QUICK TIP
In this book, ruler coordinates are given as follows: 1¼"H / 9" V refers to the intersection of 1¼" on the horizontal ruler and 9" on the vertical ruler.

2. Click the Draw Text Box button ⬚ in the Objects group on the HOME tab on the Ribbon, then use ✛ to create a rectangular text box from approximately **1.25" H / 9" V** with the approximate dimensions of **4 × 1 IN**

3. Press [F9] to zoom in to the text box

4. Type For more information, contact: press [Enter], type Your Name, press [Enter], then type Extension 5750

5. Press [Ctrl][A], click the Font Size list arrow ⬚ in the Font group, click 16, then press [Esc]

   Compare your publication to **FIGURE A-17**.

6. Press [Esc], press [F9] to zoom out, then click the Save button 💾 on the Quick Access toolbar

   The overall design of the publication looks good.

7. Click the FILE tab, then click Print

   The publication appears on the screen as it will look when printed. You cannot see the text box outlines or other nonprinting characters. Compare your publication to **FIGURE A-18**.

8. Click the Print button

9. Exit Publisher

FIGURE A-17: Contact information inserted in Study Abroad flyer

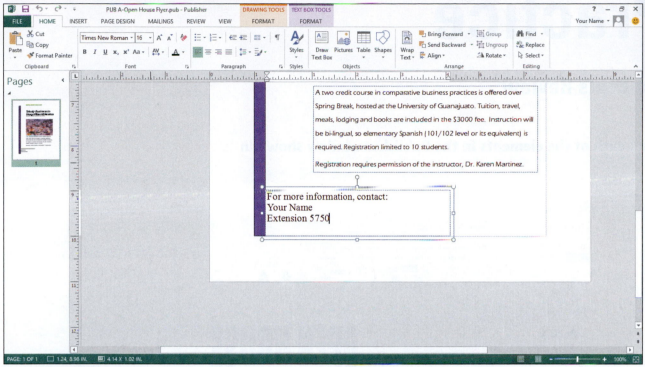

Image of village © Digital Vision/Getty Images

FIGURE A-18: Preview of Study Abroad flyer

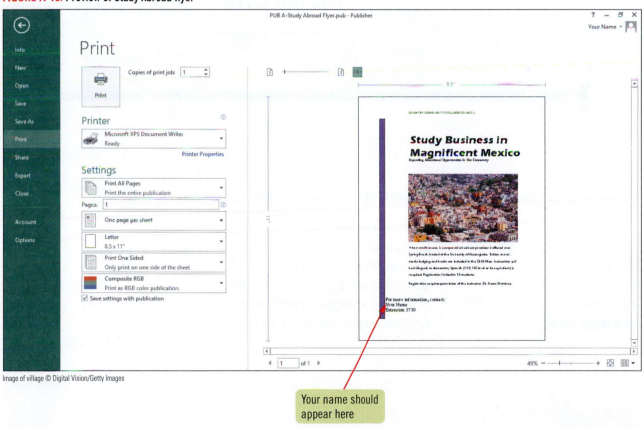

Image of village © Digital Vision/Getty Images

Practice

Concepts Review

Label each of the elements in the Publisher window shown in FIGURE A-19.

FIGURE A-19

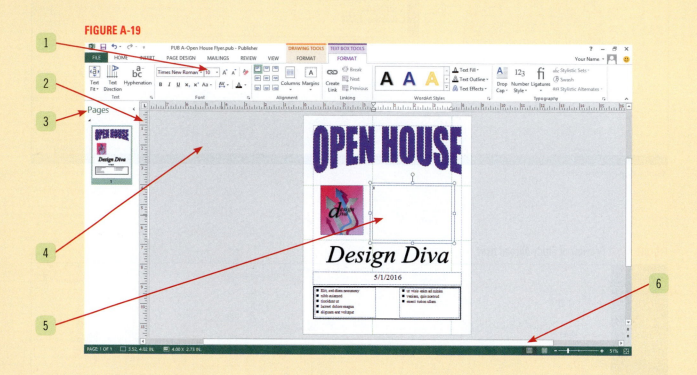

Match each of the terms or buttons with the statement that describes its function.

7. **Handles**

8. 💾

9. **Text box**

10. `10  ▼`

11. **Status bar**

12. **Backstage view**

a. Shows size and position of selected object

b. Contains typed text

c. Small hollow circles surrounding an object

d. Used to save a publication to a disk

e. Allows you to open a publication

f. Allows you to change the font size

Select the best answer from the list of choices.

13. A document created in Publisher is called a _____.
    - **a.** publication
    - **b.** notebook
    - **c.** booklet
    - **d.** brochure

14. Which of the following is considered an object?
    - **a.** Text box
    - **b.** Pictures
    - **c.** Tables
    - **d.** All of the above

15. Which of the following statements about text boxes is false?
    - **a.** They can be connected to other text boxes.
    - **b.** They can be resized.
    - **c.** They aren't very useful.
    - **d.** They can be moved.

16. Which key is pressed to zoom into a selected area?
    - **a.** [F8]
    - **b.** [F9]
    - **c.** [F6]
    - **d.** [F2]

17. A template is a(n) _____.
    - **a.** distinctive shape in a publication
    - **b.** short statement placed off to the side to grab a reader's attention
    - **c.** online artwork organizer
    - **d.** publication that serves as a master for other publications

18. Each of the following is found in the status bar, except _____.
    - **a.** a selected object's position
    - **b.** the name of the current publication
    - **c.** the currently selected page
    - **d.** a selected object's size

19. Which button is used to create a text box?
    - **a.**
    - **b.**
    - **c.**
    - **d.**

20. Which feature is used to magnify the view?
    - **a.** Magnify
    - **b.** Amplify
    - **c.** Enlarge
    - **d.** Zoom In

21. Which type of information is *not* included in the Business Information Set?
    - **a.** Address
    - **b.** Tagline or motto
    - **c.** Type of business
    - **d.** Job position or title

Skills Review

1. **Define publication software.**
   - **a.** Identify five advantages of using a desktop publishing program.
   - **b.** Name three Publisher features that you can use to create a publication.

2. **Start Publisher 2013.**
   - **a.** Start Publisher.
   - **b.** Open a new blank publication of any size.

3. **View the Publisher window.**
   - **a.** Identify as many elements in the Publisher window as you can without looking back in the unit.
   - **b.** Which Ribbon tabs are displayed?

4. **Open and save a publication.**
   - **a.** Open PUB A-3.pub. (Click No if prompted to add an item to the Building Block Library.)
   - **b.** Save the publication as **PUB A-Sample Business Card** in the location where you store your Data Files.

5. **Enter text in a text box.**
   - **a.** Create a text box with the dimensions of 2.00 × 0.50 IN. for your name, using **FIGURE A-20** as an example. The top-left corner should be placed at 1.25, 0.50 IN. (ruler guides were inserted to make this placement easier). Type your name using a 16 point font size or larger.

Skills Review (continued)

b. Create a text box with the dimensions of 2.00 × 0.75 IN. for your address, using **FIGURE A-20** as a guide. The top-left corner should be placed at 1.25, 1.25 IN. Substitute your contact information for the text shown using a 10-point text size.

c. Save the publication.

6. View and print a publication.

a. Zoom out.

b. Zoom in.

c. Use the Print feature to print one copy of the publication.

7. Use Help and change Business Information.

a. Open Publisher Help and click the Search text box.

b. Find information on creating a text box. (*Hint*: Use keywords "text box," then read several of the search result topics.)

c. Click the Print button in the Publisher Help window to print the information you find.

d. Close the Publisher Help window.

e. Open the Business Information dialog box. (*Hint*: this command is found on the INSERT tab.)

f. Select the Secondary Business Information Set.

g. Make a modification to the information that you entered (it can be a small change, such as substituting a nickname for your formal name, or changing a phone number or area code).

h. Save your changes and update the publication.

8. Close the publication and exit Publisher.

a. Close your publication.

b. Exit Publisher.

FIGURE A-20

Independent Challenge 1

The Publisher Help feature provides definitions, explanations, procedures, and other helpful information. You need to add a page to a brochure you are working on for your new client, Mangez!, a French importer of baked goods and cheeses. Open any existing publication and find out how to apply a different business information set. Print out the information.

a. Using the Help feature, find out how you can apply a different Business Information Set to a publication.

b. Print the information you found in step a.

Independent Challenge 2

Publisher can be used in many ways in business and education. If you were teaching a class, how could you use Publisher as a teaching aid?

a. Think of three types of publications you could create with Publisher that would be effective in a classroom.

b. Sketch a sample of each publication.

c. Open a blank publication for each sample. Using text boxes, re-create your sketches. (These publications do not need to be fancy; they can just contain text boxes.) Your three publications should be named **PUB A-Suggestion 1**, **PUB A-Suggestion 2**, and **PUB A-Suggestion 3**.

d. In a separate blank publication, use text boxes to explain why each of your suggestions would be an effective use of Publisher. Name this publication **PUB A-Explanations**.

e. Be sure to include your name in a text box in each publication, then print all three suggestion publications.

f. Save and close the publications, then exit Publisher.

Independent Challenge 3

You are selected as the Image Expert Employee of the Month. You're being honored because you always come up with creative ways of accomplishing tasks. When you are given your award, you are asked for ways to improve the certificate. To complete the certificate, more explanatory text about the recipient is needed.

a. Start Publisher, if necessary, open PUB A-4.pub, then save it as **PUB A-Image Expert Award** in the location where you store your Data Files. (Click No if prompted to add an item to the Building Block Library.)

b. Zoom in or out as needed. In the space above the Name of Recipient placeholder, insert a text box that contains an explanation of why you deserve this award.

c. Replace the Name of Recipient placeholder with your name.

d. Print the final publication.

e. Save your work, then compare it to the sample shown in **FIGURE A-21**.

f. Close the publication, then exit Publisher.

FIGURE A-21

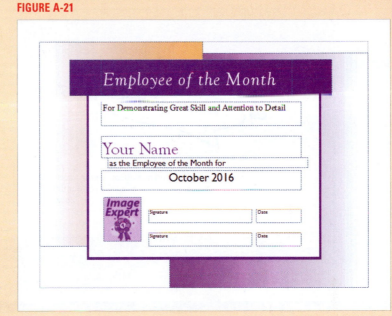

Independent Challenge 4: Explore

The World Wide Web is a rich resource for individuals and businesses. You examine the possibility of starting your own desktop publishing business. The advantages include flexible hours, low start-up costs, having an outlet for artistic impulses, the ability to conduct business remotely over the Internet, contact with other business people, and being your own boss. On the negative side, you have no formal education in design. You decide to look on the Internet to learn something about design.

a. Start Publisher, if necessary, then open a new blank publication.

b. Save the publication as **PUB A-Graphic Ideas** in the drive and folder where you store your Data Files.

c. Connect to the Internet, then use a search engine to find information on design basics.

d. Click the topics listed to find articles on design basics.

e. Create text boxes in the blank publication and type brief descriptions of some of your findings.

f. Disconnect from the Internet, if necessary.

g. Complete your publication. Be sure to include a title and your name.

h. Print the publication, then exit Publisher.

Visual Workshop

Open PUB A-5.pub from the location where you store your Data Files, and add the text shown in **FIGURE A-22** using the skills you learned in this unit. The font size in the text box is 16 points. Save the publication as **PUB A-Design Diva Gift Card** where you store your Data Files. Be sure to include your name. Print the publication.

FIGURE A-22

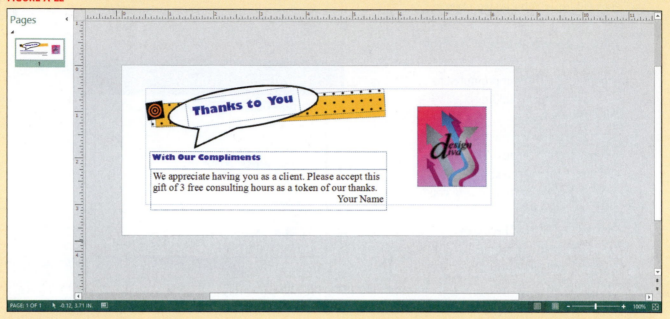

Creating a Publication

CASE ▶ Mike Mendoza, your boss at Design Diva, has assigned you the task of designing a company newsletter. You decide to use Publisher to create this publication.

Unit Objectives

After completing this unit, you will be able to:

- Plan a publication
- Design a publication
- Create a publication using a template
- Replace existing text
- Add a graphic image
- Add a sidebar
- Use Building Blocks
- Group objects
- Capstone Project: College Brochure

Files You Will Need

PUB B-1.docx
Design Diva logo.jpg

PUB B-2.docx
PUB B-3.docx
PUB B-4.docx

©Alena P/Shutterstock

Plan a Publication

Learning Outcomes
- Plan a successful publication
- Develop design skills

To create an effective publication, you should start with a planning session. Planning a publication involves at least three steps: determining what you want to achieve, deciding what information to include, and figuring out how to best present it. Knowing the goals of your publication helps you determine what form it should take. Keeping in mind the content of the message and your audience helps you to decide how the publication should be written and how it should look. While there are many approaches to planning, the best strategy is to start by determining the purpose of your publication. See **FIGURE B-1**. **CASE** ▶ *Your assignment is to create a one-page newsletter. Before starting, you answer these questions: Who is the audience? What is the message? What form should the message take?*

DETAILS

Answering the following questions is the key to planning a successful publication:

- ### What is the purpose of the publication?

  Are you trying to inform, motivate, sell, inspire confidence, raise morale, solicit a vote, or solicit a contribution of time or money?

  In your discussions with Mike and other managers at Design Diva, you learn that the purpose of the newsletter is to inform employees of news within the company and to publicize business and personal achievements.

- ### What type of response do you want?

  Do you intend this to be a one-way communication, or do you want a response? If you do want a response, what form should it take? Do you want volunteers, attendance at an event, and/or inquiries for additional information via phone or e-mail? For example, do you want visits to a Web site, registrations and RSVPs, contracts signed and returned, or payments by check, cash or credit card?

  The Design Diva newsletter is intended to make employees feel important and included. It is primarily a one-way communication.

- ### What are you going to do with the responses you receive?

  If you solicit inquiries for additional information via mail or e-mail, but don't prepare a polite, informative response to send, you risk alienating your audience. If you solicit information but neglect to gather, interpret, or use it, you waste time and effort, and lose an opportunity.

- ### Who is the target audience?

  The more accurately you can define the characteristics of your target audience, the more you can tailor the content and appearance of the message to appeal to that group. For instance, a colorful comic book publication would be right for trying to educate fourth graders, but not appropriate for informing cardiologists of newly identified risk factors for heart disease.

  Some of the possible ways to identify a group are by age, gender, geography, reading level, educational background, first language, hobbies, nationality, ethnicity, religion, culture, political affiliation, employment, income level, taste in music and art, home ownership, and health.

  The Design Diva newsletter has a narrow audience. It will be read by employees and clients of the company. While their demographics vary, all share an interest in the Design Diva agency and its core service, advertising.

FIGURE B-1: Planning process

Image of office (c) Blend Images/Getty Images

Developing design sense

Designing publications is a skill that can be learned through thoughtful practice and critical observation. Just as artists gather ideas from trips to museums, and musicians gather ideas from attending concerts, you can sharpen your design skills by looking at publications created by others. Start with a visit to a library or a magazine stand, observing the overall design of the publications.

Gauge your overall reaction to a publication, and judge for yourself what you find appealing and what you find distracting or offensive. Concentrate on how your eye moves across a page. What combinations of design elements (balance, color, consistency, contrast, and white space) are you drawn to, and what do you find unappealing?

Including the facts

Probably the most daunting part of creating a new publication is the notion of what information is essential and what is not. Space, of course, is a factor, but you should consider the following criteria:

- What information will the reader want? What questions is the reader likely to have? Your text should answer questions, not raise them.
- How much time does the reader have? Make sure the content is easy to read and scan, and that text is presented in 'bite-sized' chunks.

- Are there others in your organization who can provide guidance and ideas as you complete the planning stage?

There are many aspects to consider, and you should certainly get a consensus from your teammates. Take the time to hold one or more brainstorming sessions with all who will be involved in developing the publication. It's easier to incorporate valuable feedback before beginning the design process, and it saves time in the long run.

Design a Publication

Learning Outcomes
- Explore design elements
- Identify good and bad designs

Just as form follows function in the old adage, planning should always precede design. The elements of design—unity, balance, color, consistency, contrast, and white space—should be combined to support the objectives of the publication. This is why design follows planning, because it must support the goals identified in the planning stages. **CASE** ▷ *After planning, you know that you want the newsletter to catch the eye of potential readers, be easy to read, and look professional to clients. You decide to include the company logo to identify the newsletter as belonging to Design Diva, and you want to call attention to specific text to be sure it is seen and understood. You also want the newsletter to display a tasteful sense of humor, so that it entertains readers and keeps them looking forward to the next issue.*

DETAILS

- ### View the document as a whole
  The publication needs enough contrast and variety to be interesting, but must be consistent and logical so the reader can find the meaning without confusion or unnecessary effort.

- ### Use placeholders for text and graphics to create an effective layout
  Placeholder text and graphics are objects that are inserted into a publication to illustrate how the finished product will appear when replaced with more significant materials at a later time. Publisher uses placeholder text boxes and graphics extensively in its templates to demonstrate how the combined design elements in a finished publication will look.

- ### Use graphics to add interest and present ideas
  Use of artwork not only adds interest, but also is a means to communicate ideas and feelings that can reinforce text in a publication.

- ### Use white space liberally
  White space, also known as negative space, describes the open space between design elements. It can exist between elements of text (letters or paragraphs), in between and surrounding graphics, and between all other objects on the page. It is crucial for establishing spatial relations between visual items, and actually guides the reader's eye from one point to another. Without sufficient white space, text is unreadable, graphics lose emphasis, and there is no balance between the elements on a page. White space tells you where one section ends and another begins.

- ### Prominently feature the company logo
  The Design Diva logo appears on all its print material—letterhead, envelopes, business cards, and advertisements—to reinforce the identity of the company. It boosts morale for employees and associates to see the logo displayed with pride, and enhances clients' perception of the firm.

- ### Emphasize certain text
  Some text on a page should stand out. See **FIGURE B-2**. For example, **sidebars** are text related to the main story but not vital to it. They are placed adjacent to the story to add emphasis and pique the interest of readers. Usually sidebars have a different background color, font, or point size to set them apart from the story.

Work with the Design Diva

Volume 17, Issue 7   May 1, 2016

Date and Issue Number   Masthead

New Location Opens Soon

Graphic
Image

Design Diva is opening its new location at 3444 Tramway Boulevard on May 1, 2016. Besides being centrally located, our office space will more than double. Twice as many parking spaces are allotted as we have employees. Childcare is available too, just four doors down at Bonnie Billy's Kid Care.

We won't have our own recording/video studio but an enhanced computer network is planned, so in addition to preparing print advertising we will do on site audio/video editing of radio and TV

We make you look great!

ads.
Those of us who have scavenged space in the conference room to prepare layouts in the

past will be jazzed at the prospect of a work area that won't have to be vacated for meetings. Each full-time employee will have an office. Telecommuters may be in cubicles during their visits but all FTEs will have ample work space. We are growing fast!

Pull quote text is taken from an article

Sidebar is a related story with formatting to add emphasis

"Larger, more spacious facilities, with room for childcare, audio-video editing, and much more PARKING!"

College Campaign Wins Recognition

The Community College Action campaign generated renewed interest in expanding programs at the Community College.

At an awards banquet held graduation week Dean Debbie Picazolo credited Image Magic for boosting enrollment by a whopping 16.3% during the spring semester.

Mendoza Helps International Education Opportunities

Mike Mendoza has helped to create an international education opportunity through his volunteer work with the Community College Council. Using his fluency in Spanish and insights into Mexican history and business practices,

Mike was able to help establish ties between the Community College and the University at Guanajuato. The fruit of this relationship is a one-week course that will take local students "South of the Border" to study

Mexican business practices and culture. Dean Wallace agreed that Mike deserves full credit for making this program a reality.

Recognizing bad design

Thoughtful practice and critical observation are the keys to learning good design. But how can you recognize bad design? First, look at a publication from the reader's point of view, and try to identify what interesting elements (such as images) are in the publication. If you don't spot something of interest right away, do you think the typical reader is going to pursue it or set it aside? Nothing discourages a reader more than long columns of dull gray type, unless it is long columns of dull gray type that are hard to read. Ornate type that might look stylish on the sample sheet in a well-lighted print shop may be very hard to read elsewhere. Is the artwork carefully chosen and well placed to generate interest, or is the publication too cluttered with fluff that will only distract the reader from the information you are trying to present? In a nutshell, "bad" design is anything that fails to capture or sustain a reader's interest.

Create a Publication Using a Template

Learning
Outcomes
• Use a template
  to create a
  publication
• Apply a scheme to
  a publication

It's easy to create new publications using Publisher **templates**, specially formatted publications containing placeholder text that serves as a master for other publications. Publisher offers a wide variety of publication templates that meet the needs of different audiences and provide information in different ways. The Available Templates section organizes templates by category and is accessed by clicking the New command in Backstage view. Templates are arranged by popularity and purpose categories. The categories range from common types of publications, such as Flyers, Calendars, and Envelopes, to the not-so-common types, such as Gift Certificates and Paper Folding Projects. Some categories include design schemes such as Arrows, Bounce, Brocade, Color Band, Marker, and so on. The choices you select help create the initial publication, and you take it from there. **CASE** ▶ *You use a Publisher template to create a newsletter.*

STEPS

TROUBLE
If Publisher is already open but you do not see the Microsoft Publisher templates, click the FILE tab, then click New.

1. **Start Publisher**

   The Microsoft Publisher window opens with Featured Templates, displaying FEATURED and BUILT-IN Templates in the center pane.

2. **Click BUILT-IN in the right panel, scroll down, then click Newsletters in the right pane**

   The Newsletters category displays different newsletter templates that have been installed with Publisher.

TROUBLE
If you are not connected to the Internet while using Publisher, your template choices may be different.

3. **Scroll down to More Installed Templates, then click Borders**

   A thumbnail of the Borders newsletter layout appears in the right pane in the window, with options for customizing it, as shown in **FIGURE B-3**. You can keep the default settings or choose from the available options.

4. **Click CREATE in the far-right pane**

   Publisher creates the publication and displays it on the screen.

5. **Click the PAGE DESIGN tab on the Ribbon, click the More button ▼ in the Schemes group, then click Metro in the Built-In section**

   The existing color scheme is immediately replaced with the Metro color scheme, as shown in **FIGURE B-4**. You now have a clear view of the newsletter in the workspace.

6. **Click the Save button 🖫 on the Quick Access toolbar, navigate to the location where you store your Data Files, select the text in the File name text box if it is not highlighted, type PUB B-Design Diva Newsletter, then click Save**

Using templates

Have you ever stared at a blank piece of paper or a blank screen and just not known where to begin? You can use a template as a starting point, particularly if you are just beginning in design. Browsing through the templates can spark your creativity and get you started down the path to creating your own masterpieces. Believe it or not, there are occasions when even the best designers use templates. You can use a template if you just need a routine expense form or an invoice, if your client can't afford a "one-of-a-kind design," or to save time. The important thing to remember about using a template is to choose one that is appropriate to the publication. A bad choice will require too many alterations, and the advantages of using a template will be lost.

FIGURE B-3: Built-in Templates pane

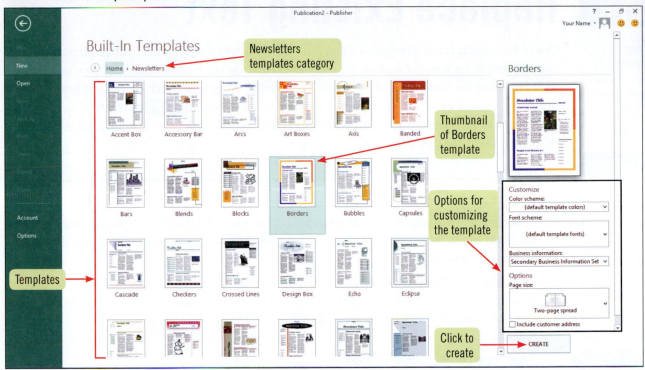

FIGURE B-4: Newsletter with the Metro color scheme

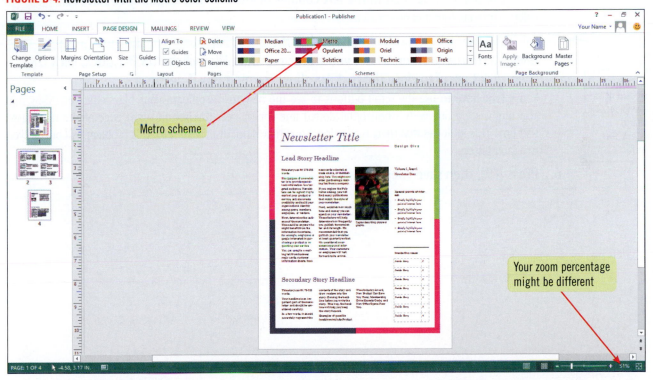

Understanding template options

The New command in Backstage view of the Publisher window is a visual directory that contains a large number of templates, which are organized into categories in the BUILT-IN Templates section of the window. Each category offers a variety of choices. Brochures, for example, are available in many different styles and layout schemes. Labels can be created for computer disks, binders, and CD and DVD case liners. Publications created using templates can be easily modified.

Replace Existing Text

Learning Outcomes
- Zoom in and out of a publication
- Replace placeholder text
- Insert a text file

One of the benefits of using templates is that your new document contains preformatted placeholders that suggest content for your publication. In order to replace these placeholders with your own content, you must first select the existing text in a text box. You can then either type directly in the text box or insert a document created with a word processor, such as Microsoft Word. **CASE** *You need to replace the placeholders in the newsletter with text for the Design Diva newsletter. Mike Mendoza has provided you with a Word document to use for the lead story.*

STEPS

1. **Press [F9]**

   Zooming into the selected text can help you get a closer look at specific objects. You can zoom by clicking the Zoom button, which always displays the Zoom Level factor, or clicking the Zoom In and Zoom Out buttons on the status bar.

2. **Click the Lead Story Headline text at 3" H / 3" V on the ruler, as shown in FIGURE B-5**

   Handles surround the selected text box, and its position and size appear on the status bar. Two additional tabs are displayed on the ruler: the DRAWING TOOLS FORMAT tab and the TEXT BOX TOOLS FORMAT tab.

3. **Type New Location Opens Soon**

   The placeholder text is deleted with the first keystroke of the new text.

4. **Click the placeholder text in the left column below the new heading to select it**

   Clicking placeholder text selects all the text.

5. **Click the INSERT tab on the Ribbon, click the Insert File button in the Text group, navigate to the location where you store your Data Files, click PUB B-1.docx, click OK, then click Cancel to close the text Autoflow warning box if necessary**

   You might have to use the scroll buttons to see the new text. Compare your newsletter to **FIGURE B-6**. You might see a box with a horizontal dotted line appear near the bottom right edge of the right-most text box. This indicates that there is additional text that is not displayed. If so, this problem will be resolved in a later lesson.

6. **Press [F9], then save your work**

FIGURE B-5: Selected text box

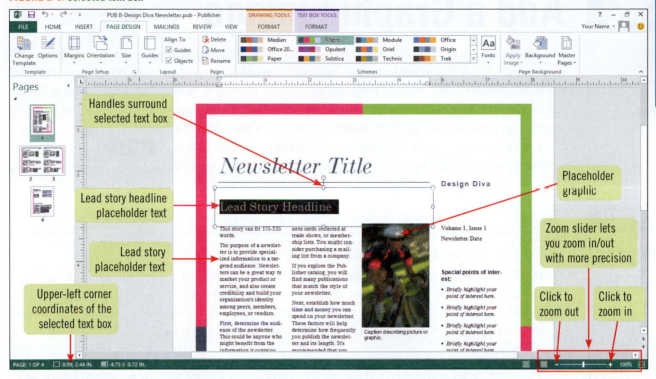

Handles surround selected text box

Lead story headline placeholder text

Lead story placeholder text

Upper-left corner coordinates of the selected text box

Placeholder graphic

Zoom slider lets you zoom in/out with more precision

Click to zoom out

Click to zoom in

FIGURE B-6: Word document text in newsletter

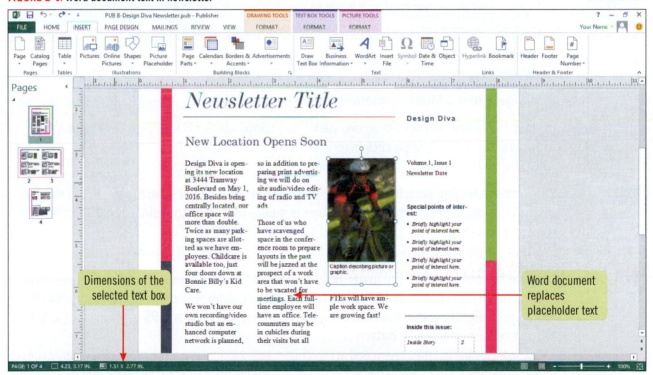

Dimensions of the selected text box

Word document replaces placeholder text

Resizing a frame

A frame—whether it is a text box or contains an object—can be resized. Once a frame is selected, you can change its size by placing the mouse pointer over a handle, then dragging the handle. The pointer may change to ⟷, ↕, ⤡, or ⤢ depending on which handle you place the pointer on. If, for example, the Text in Overflow button ⋯ appears at the end of a selected frame, it may be possible to resize the frame, enabling the text to fit.

Add a Graphic Image

Learning Outcomes
- Delete placeholder clip art
- Insert a picture

Artwork can express feelings and ideas that words just can't capture. A picture, a piece of clip art, a graph, or a drawing is called a **graphic image**, or simply a **graphic**. Artwork can also be scanned into your computer, created using drawing programs or a digital camera, or purchased separately on a disk or online. **Clip art** is a term for graphic images that can be used free of charge or for a fee. Clip art is usually supplied on a disk or over the Web. Publisher comes with thousands of pieces of clip art. **TABLE B-1** lists some of the common graphic image formats that can be used with Publisher. **CASE** *You have decided to include the Design Diva logo in the newsletter. Luckily, you already have this image in electronic format. You decide to place this logo near the graphic image placeholder of the bicyclist, so first you need to delete that placeholder.*

STEPS

QUICK TIP

Use the ruler and the horizontal and vertical coordinates, like the ones given in Step 1, to help you locate the correct placeholders throughout this unit.

1. **Click the graphic image placeholder at 5" H / 5" V**

   Handles surround both the placeholder clip art and the caption beneath it, indicating that although there are two objects, they are grouped and displayed as a single object. If you were to click on the PICTURE TOOLS FORMAT tab, you would see that the Ungroup button 🔳 is visible in the Arrange group, which indicates that the selected object has been grouped so it can be treated as one unit.

2. **Press [Delete]**

   The graphic image and caption text box placeholders disappear, and the text box expands to replace them, including the truncated text. If the graphic image was inserted here without first deleting the placeholder, it would replace the current graphic. It would be placed in roughly the same location.

QUICK TIP

You can change the view in the Insert Picture dialog box to Extra Large Icons by clicking the More options list arrow (to the right of the Change your view button) so that it shows you a sample of images available in the folder.

3. **Click the INSERT tab on the Ribbon, then click the Pictures button in the Illustrations group**

   The Insert Picture dialog box opens.

4. **Navigate to the location where you store your Data Files**

5. **Click the More options list arrow, click Extra Large Icons, click Design Diva logo.jpg as shown in FIGURE B-7, then click Insert**

   The Design Diva logo is inserted in the publication.

QUICK TIP

As you drag the object, the object alignment technology displays vertical and horizontal guides to help you get the right position.

6. **Select the Design Diva logo graphic image if it is not already selected, use ⬚ to drag it until the upper-left corner of the image is *approximately* at coordinates 4.23, 3.89 in., then press [F9]**

   The repositioned image is near the upper-left portion of the column, as shown in **FIGURE B-8**.

7. **Place the pointer over the lower-right handle of the image so it turns to ⬌, press and hold [Shift], press and hold the left mouse button, drag ✛ up and to the left until the image is slightly wider than the column (approximately 1.6 × 1.93 in.), release [Shift], then release the mouse button**

   The top-left corner of the image is now at coordinates 4.23, 3.89 in. (approximately), and has dimensions of approximately 1.6 × 1.93 in., as shown in **FIGURE B-9**. Placing the pointer over a handle and then dragging the frame edge resizes an image. As you drag the pointer, the status bar reflects the object's size and position, using the ruler coordinates. To preserve an image's scale while increasing or decreasing its size, press and hold [Shift] while dragging the frame edge.

8. **Press [F9], then click the scratch area to deselect the logo**

9. **Save your work**

FIGURE B-7: Insert Picture dialog box

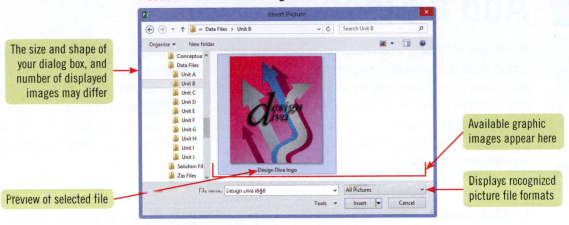

The size and shape of your dialog box, and number of displayed images may differ

Available graphic images appear here

Preview of selected file

Displays recognized picture file formats

FIGURE B-8: Repositioned graphic image

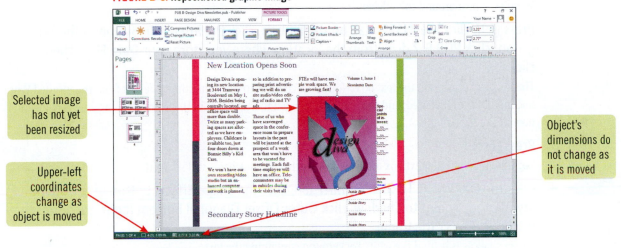

Selected image has not yet been resized

Object's dimensions do not change as it is moved

Upper-left coordinates change as object is moved

FIGURE B-9: Resized graphic image

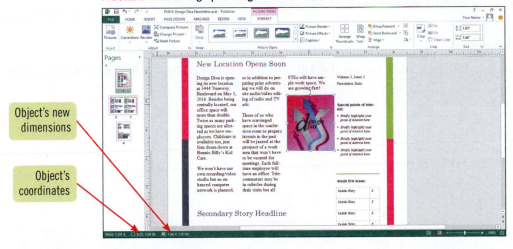

Object's new dimensions

Object's coordinates

TABLE B-1: Common graphic image formats

graphic image	extension	graphic image	extension
Bitmap	.BMP	Tagged Image File Format	.TIF or .TIFF
PC Paintbrush	.PCX	Joint Photographic Experts Group Picture Format	.JPG or .JPEG
Graphics Interchange Format	.GIF	Windows Metafile	.WMF
Encapsulated PostScript	.EPS	Portable Network Graphics	.PNG

Add a Sidebar

Learning Outcomes
• Select the contents of a sidebar
• Apply a shadow effect

Information not vital to a publication can make interesting reading when placed in a sidebar. A **sidebar** is a short news story containing supplementary information. You can place it alongside or below a feature story. It can use the same font size as regular body text, but it may look better in a larger size or a different font. Adding a border or shading can help to emphasize sidebars. **CASE** *You want to add a brief story to the newsletter about the success of a recent Design Diva ad campaign. You decide to use the sidebar placeholder in the third column to insert this existing text. You want to experiment with some formatting effects to draw attention to the sidebar. You also want to change the color scheme.*

STEPS

1. **Click inside the sidebar placeholder, then press [Ctrl][A] to select all the text inside the sidebar, as shown in FIGURE B-10**
   Handles appear around the sidebar.

2. **Press [F9], click the INSERT tab on the Ribbon, click the Insert File button in the Text group, click PUB B-2.docx from the location where you store your Data Files, then click OK**
   The new text appears in the text box. Notice the changes to the formatting. The text from the inserted Word document is not italicized, and the font size changed to fit the text in the frame. The heading is bold, and is now in the Arial font.

3. **Press [Esc]**
   Both the text and the text box are now not selected; the sidebar is still selected.

4. **Click the DRAWING TOOLS FORMAT tab, click the Shape Effects button in the Shape Styles group, point to Shadow, click Outer Offset Diagonal Bottom Right, then press [Esc] to deselect the frame**
   A gray shadow is behind the white background containing the text.

5. **Click the scratch area to deselect the sidebar**
   The sidebar is deselected.

6. **Press [F9]**

7. **Click the PAGE DESIGN tab on the Ribbon, then click Concourse in the Schemes group**
   The color scheme is changed. Compare your work to **FIGURE B-11**.

8. **Save your work**
   Looking at the full-page image, you can see that all the text fits nicely inside the frame.

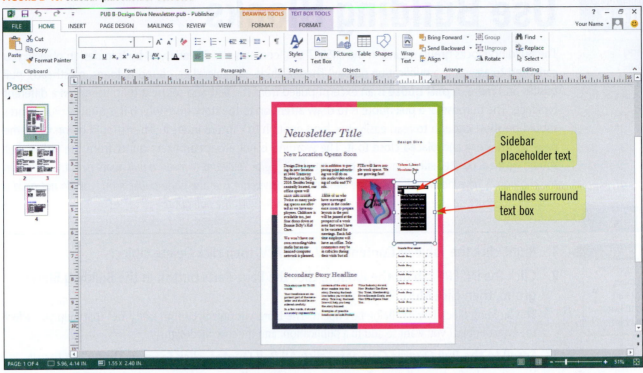

Sidebar placeholder text

Handles surround text box

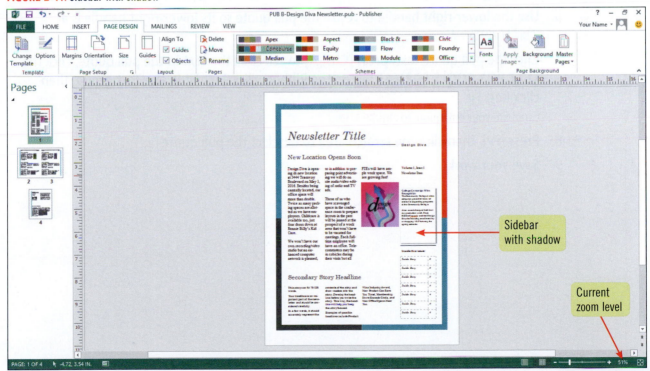

Sidebar with shadow

Current zoom level

Use Building Blocks

Learning
Outcomes
• Delete an object
• Insert a pull quote
• Fit text

The Building Blocks group (found in the INSERT tab) contains a wide variety of built-in design objects you can insert to assemble a publication quickly. These include ads, calendars, coupons, logos, mastheads, pull quotes and more. A **pull quote** is an excerpt pulled from the text and set next to it, usually in a different typeface. The purpose of a pull quote is to draw attention to the story from which it is quoted. Pull quotes should be short enough to read easily, but long enough to capture interest. They should be on the same page as the story and placed close to it. The wording is not always an exact quote from the article, but should be an accurate reflection of the content. **CASE** *You want to insert a pull quote near the article on the company's new location. Because the Design Diva newsletter is a one-page publication, you do not need a Table of Contents, so you decide to replace that placeholder with the pull quote.*

STEPS

1. **Right-click the Table of Contents at 7" H / 7" V, then click Delete Object**

2. **Click the INSERT tab on the Ribbon, click the Page Parts button in the Building Blocks group, then click More Page Parts**
   The Building Block Library dialog box opens. The Library is organized into categories that help you select the type of object you want to add to a publication, and the specific design.

3. **Scroll to the Pull Quotes Category, click All Pull Quotes, click Frames, then click Insert**
   You select the Frames pull quote because you want the pull quote to have a plain design. It is often best to use less ornate design elements, to avoid distracting the reader. The pull quote placeholder appears on the first page of the publication, as shown in **FIGURE B-12**.

4. **Place the pointer over the left edge of the pull quote so it changes to ⚡, drag the object until the coordinates read 5.79, 7.00 IN., then press [F9]**
   The pull quote sits just below the sidebar. Compare your pull quote text box to **FIGURE B-13**.

5. **Click the pull quote text to select it, then type "Twice as many parking spaces are allotted as we have employees. Childcare is also available."**
   When the pull quote is selected, the horizontal ruler becomes active, just as with any text box.

6. **Use the lower-right handle to resize the pull quote so its lower-right handle is at 7¾" H / 9¾" V**

7. **Click the pull quote text, press [Ctrl][A] to select all the text in the pull quote, click the TEXT BOX TOOLS FORMAT tab on the Ribbon, click Text Fit in the Text group, then click Best Fit**
   Compare your pull quote to **FIGURE B-14**.

8. **Press [F9], then click the scratch area to deselect the pull quote**

9. **Save your work**

FIGURE B-12: Pull quote added

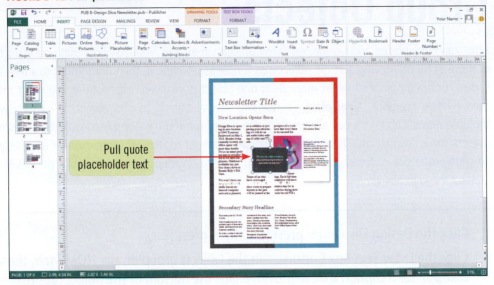

Pull quote placeholder text

FIGURE B-13: Repositioned pull quote

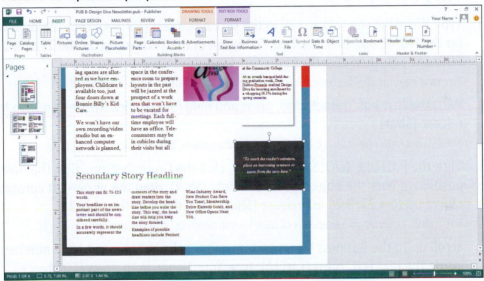

FIGURE B-14: Pull quote after Best Fit

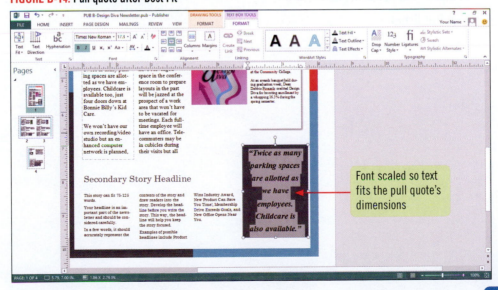

Font scaled so text fits the pull quote's dimensions

Group Objects

Learning Outcomes
• Add a caption to an object
• Group objects

After you have placed and positioned many objects on a page, you may find that you want to move one or more of them. Moving a single object is as simple as selecting it, then dragging it to a new location. But it gets more complicated when more than one object is involved, especially if you want them to retain their relative positions. **Grouping**, or defining several objects as one object, is an easy way to move multiple items. Later, you can always ungroup them, turning the combined objects back into individual objects for individual modifications. **CASE** *You want to place a caption under the Design Diva logo. To change the size of the caption text box, you need to ungroup the objects, make the modifications, then regroup the logo and caption.*

STEPS

1. Click the Design Diva logo, press [F9], then press [Esc]

2. Click the Draw Text Box button ▣ in the Objects group on the HOME tab, then draw a text box for a caption that slightly overlaps the bottom of the object (approximate suggested starting point coordinates: 4.23, 5.54 in., with dimensions of approximately 1.66 × 0.25 in.)

QUICK TIP
You can triple-click as an alternative to pressing [Ctrl][A] to select all the text.

3. Type We make you look great! in the text box, press [Ctrl][A], click the Bold button **B** on the HOME tab, click the Text Fit button in the Text group on the TEXT BOX TOOLS FORMAT tab, then click Best Fit

   The new caption appears beneath the logo and is in a Century Schoolbook font.

4. With the text box still selected, press and hold [Shift], click the Design Diva logo, then release [Shift]

   Notice that both objects have handles surrounding them, as shown in **FIGURE B-15**.

QUICK TIP
Pressing and holding [Shift] while moving an object retains the vertical or horizontal positioning.

5. Click the PICTURE TOOLS FORMAT tab, click the Group button ▣ in the Arrange group, position ▨ over the object, press and hold [Shift], drag the upper-left corner of the object up to 4.23, 3.25 in., release [Shift], then deselect the object

   The handles change to a single set of handles surrounding both the combined objects.

6. Scroll up to the Business Name text box above the Volume and Issue number, click inside the text box, press [Ctrl][A], type Your Name, then press [Esc] twice

7. Press [F9], save your work, then submit your work to your instructor

   Compare your newsletter to **FIGURE B-16**.

8. Exit Publisher

FIGURE B-15: Preparing to group objects

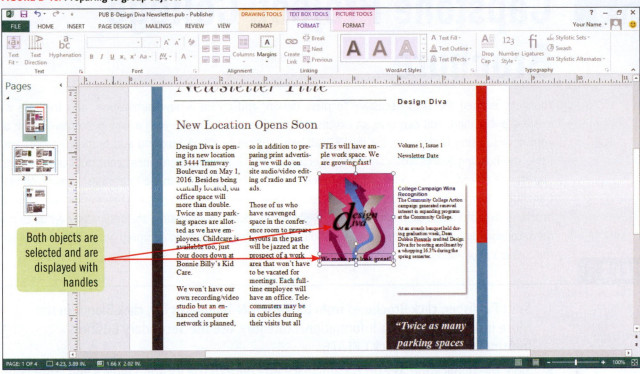

Both objects are selected and are displayed with handles

FIGURE B-16: Publication with grouped and repositioned objects

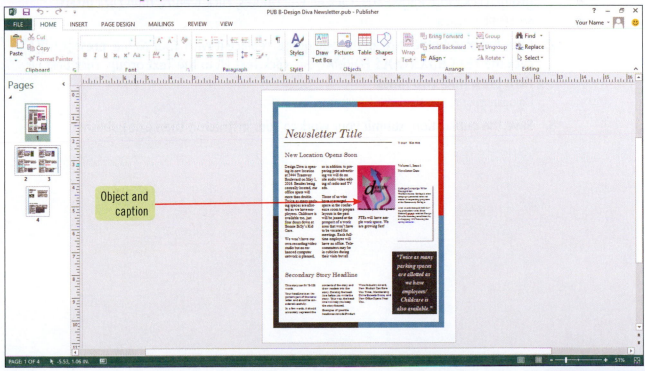

Object and caption

Capstone Project: College Brochure

You have learned the skills necessary to plan, design, and create a new publication, and to open an existing publication. You can save an existing publication or a template with a new descriptive name of your choice. Using buttons on the INSERT tab, you can create a text box and add graphic images, and using the Building Blocks, you can insert objects such as a sidebar that enhances your publication. Once objects are placed in your publication, you can group them so they can be treated as a single object. Camelback Community College is one of Design Diva's local clients. You have been asked to create a brochure that promotes their courses. **CASE** ▸ *For the purposes of drafting the design, you decide to use the Secondary Business Information Set as placeholder text. Once it has been approved, you can update it with the college's information.*

STEPS

1. Start Publisher, click Brochures from the BUILT-IN Templates list, click Blends in the More Installed Templates Informational category, use the Secondary Business Information Set, then click CREATE

2. Save the publication as PUB B-Camelback Brochure to the location where you store your Data Files, then change the color scheme to Cherry

3. Click the Product/Service Information placeholder, type Camelback University, then press [Esc] twice

4. Click the placeholder beneath the Camelback University text box, press [Ctrl][A] to select the text, then type An Education You Can Use!

5. If a logo placeholder displays, select it, then delete it

6. Click the INSERT tab on the Ribbon, click the Page Parts button in the Building Blocks group, click More Page Parts, click All Pull Quotes, click Blends, then click Insert
   See FIGURE B-17.

7. Click the placeholder text in the pull quote, replace it with Your Name, press [Ctrl][A], click the TEXT BOX TOOLS FORMAT tab, click Text Fit in the Text group, click Best Fit, then press [Esc] two times
   Compare your publication with FIGURE B-18.

8. Save the publication, submit your work to your instructor, then exit Publisher

FIGURE B-17: Inserted Building Blocks object

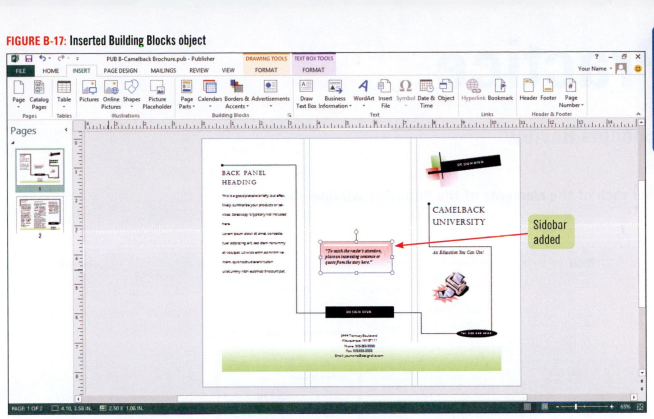

FIGURE B-18: Completed brochure

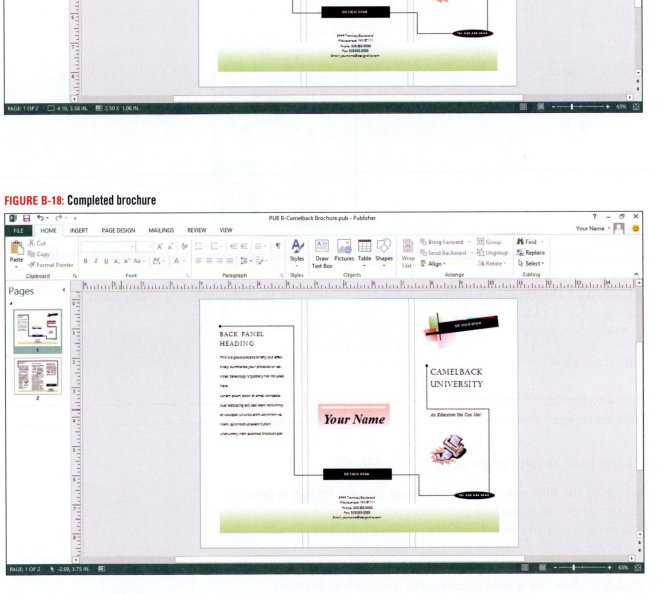

Practice

Concepts Review

Label each of the elements of the Publisher window shown in FIGURE B-19.

FIGURE B-19

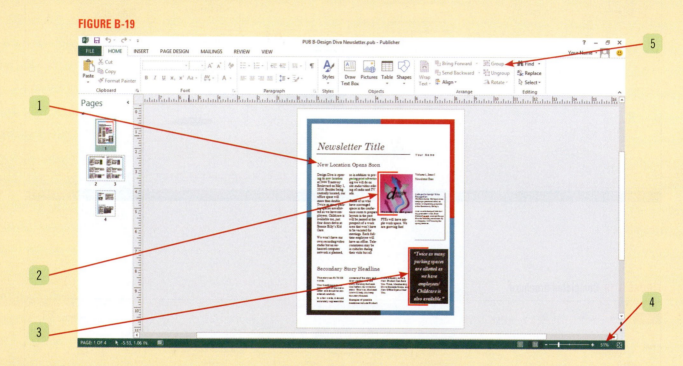

Match each of the terms or buttons with the statement that describes its function.

6. [image]
7. [image]
8. Backstage view
9. [image]
10. Building Blocks
11. Graphic image

a. Contains a directory of categorized templates
b. Resizes a frame vertically
c. Artwork stored in an electronic file
d. Can be used to create an ad or logo, for example
e. Creates a text box
f. Displays different shadows

Select the best answer from the list of choices.

12. Which of the following statements about graphic images is false?
   a. Scanned artwork can be used in Publisher.
   b. Artwork created in drawing programs can be used in Publisher.
   c. You can use only the artwork that comes with Publisher.
   d. You can use any electronic artwork in Publisher, as long as it's saved in a format that Publisher recognizes.

13. Which Ribbon tab is used to access the AutoFit text feature?
   a. EDIT
   b. TEXT BOX TOOLS
   c. INSERT
   d. WHOLE PAGE

14. **Which Ribbon tab is used to change a template?**
   a. INSERT
   b. PAGE DESIGN
   c. HOME
   d. VIEW

15. **Group objects by holding and pressing [Shift], clicking each object you want to add, then clicking _____.**
   a.
   b. the TOOLS tab on the Ribbon, then Group Objects
   c.
   d. the OBJECTS tab on the Ribbon, then Group

16. **Maintain the scale of a graphic image while resizing it by pressing _____.**
   a. [Esc]
   b. [Shift]
   c. [Alt]
   d. the right mouse button

17. **Paraphrased information that invites you to read a story is called a _____.**
   a. placeholder
   b. sidebar
   c. pull quote
   d. side quote

18. **Which pointer is used to change the location of an object?**
   a.
   b.
   c.
   d.

19. **Which of the following extensions does *not* indicate a common graphic image format?**
   a. .GFX
   b. .JPG
   c. .BMP
   d. .GIF

20. **Which of the following statements about a pull quote is false?**
   a. It should entice you to read the article.
   b. It should be short and easy to read.
   c. It does not have to be identical to the text in the article.
   d. It should be on a different page from the actual text.

Skills Review

1. **Plan a publication.**
   a. Name the three steps involved in planning a publication.
   b. Identify the questions you should ask as part of planning a publication.

2. **Design a publication.**
   a. Name as many elements of design, such as consistency, as you can.
   b. Identify at least three guidelines of good design, such as viewing the document as a whole.

3. **Create a publication using a template.**
   a. Start Publisher, then select Newsletters from the BUILT-IN templates.
   b. Create a publication (from the More Installed Templates category) that has the following options: Marble design, two-page spread, and does not include the customer address. Use the Business Information Set you created in Unit A, or enter information for address, phone number, and other pertinent information.
   c. Change to the Clay color scheme. Change the number of columns to 2. (*Hint*: You can change the number of columns by clicking the PAGE DESIGN tab, clicking the Options button in the Template group, then clicking the 2 option from the Columns list arrow.)
   d. Save this publication as **PUB B-Mock-up Newsletter** to the location where you store your Data Files.

4. **Replace existing text.**
   a. Click the Lead Story Headline placeholder, then zoom in.
   b. Replace the placeholder text with the following text: **Making the Most of Your Workspace**.
   c. Select the lead story text, then delete it.
   d. Insert the Word file PUB B-3.docx from the location where you store your Data Files.
   e. Read the article, zoom out, then save the publication.

5. **Add a graphic image.**

    a. Select the grouped graphic image placeholder and its caption, then delete them.

    b. Insert the picture file **Design Diva logo.jpg** from the location where you store your Data Files.

    c. Press and hold [Shift], resize the image to *approximately* 2.0 × 2.3 in., then reposition it so that the upper-left corner of the image is at approximately 6" H / 5" V, then save the publication.

6. **Add a sidebar.**

    a. Select the sidebar placeholder (Special points of interest) in the left column at the bottom of the page, then select all text within it.

    b. Zoom in to view the sidebar, then delete all the text within it.

    c. Insert the Word file PUB B-4.docx from the location where you store your Data Files.

    d. View and read the sidebar, use Best Fit to fit the text, zoom out so you can see the entire publication, then deselect the sidebar.

    e. Save the publication.

7. **Use Building Blocks.**

    a. Click the Page Parts button in the Building Blocks group on the INSERT tab, then click More Page Parts.

    b. Click All Pull Quotes, insert the Marble pull quote, then zoom in to view the pull quote.

    c. Move the pull quote so the upper-right corner is at the right margin and the top of the pull quote meets the bottom of the text box containing the Design Diva logo.

    d. Replace the placeholder with: **"Work shouldn't hurt. If you feel pain while sitting at your workstation, stop what you are doing."**

    e. Select the Best Fit command using the TEXT BOX TOOLS FORMAT tab.

    f. Zoom out so you can see the entire publication, deselect the pull quote, then save the publication.

8. **Group objects.**

    a. Press and hold [Shift], then select both the volume and newsletter date text boxes in the right column.

    b. Group the two selected objects.

    c. Ungroup the objects, deselect the objects, then replace the Newsletter Date text with **Your Name**.

    d. Save your work, submit your work to your instructor, then exit Publisher.

Independent Challenge 1

You volunteered to help the local Rotary Club design a flyer for its upcoming Fun Run fundraiser. The organization is trying to raise money for victims of earthquakes in Central America. The funds will go toward medicine, building materials, food, clothing, and transportation costs for the material and some volunteers.

    a. Start Publisher if necessary, then create a flyer using the Charity Bazaar flyer design (found in the Other section of the All Event Flyer group).

    b. Change the Color Scheme to Garnet, then accept the default options.

    c. Save the publication as **PUB B-Fun Run Flyer** in the folder where you store your Data Files.

    d. Modify the Charity Bazaar text placeholder to read **Rotary Fun Run**, replace the five bulleted items with five of your own good reasons to attend this event, then include your name somewhere on the flyer.

    e. Make up the necessary information, such as the location of the fundraiser, the address of the Rotary Club, and the date and time of the event, to make sure all the text in the flyer relates to the Fun Run event.

    f. Try resizing at least two of the frames within the flyer.

    g. See how the pointers change during resizing, and how the text reflows.

    h. Save the publication, submit it to your instructor, then close the publication and exit Publisher.

Independent Challenge 2

You are a regular at the Come and Get It Luncheonette. They ask you to help create a menu for their new take-out division. Use a template to create this menu, and replace the existing text with your own.

a. Start Publisher if necessary, then create a take-out menu by choosing the Gingham Take-Out Menu from the BUILT-IN templates.

b. Change the Color Scheme to Parrot, and accept the default options.

c. Save the publication as **PUB B-Take-Out Menu** to the location where you store your Data Files.

d. Modify the placeholder company name and information for the Come and Get It Luncheonette.

e. Replace the placeholder text under the restaurant's name with a description of the food served at this establishment.

f. Include your name as the contact person for take-out orders.

g. Make sure all the text in the flyer relates to the take-out menu.

h. Make up at least two menu items. (*Hint*: Click the Page 2 icon to access the second page.)

i. Group two objects on the menu and move them.

j. Save the publication, submit it to your instructor, then exit Publisher.

Independent Challenge 3

The tenants in your rental property just gave you 30 days notice, so you must find new tenants. You need to create a sign in which you can describe the house in order to attract new tenants.

a. Start Publisher if necessary, then use the For Rent template in the Signs category of the BUILT-IN templates.

b. Save the publication as **PUB B-For Rent Sign** to the location where you store your Data Files.

c. Replace the bulleted items with your descriptions of the house for rent.

d. Modify the telephone number placeholder using your number or a fictitious number.

e. Create a text box above the telephone number that says **Call *Your Name* for more information**.

f. Use a command on the PAGE DESIGN tab to change the template to a different For Rent sign.

g. Make sure you add any elements necessary so that the new design contains the same information.

h. Save the publication, submit it to your instructor, then exit Publisher.

Independent Challenge 4: Explore

You are asked to create a Web page for your school's Publisher class. (Click New in the Backstage view, type **web site** in the Search box, then make a selection from the results.) This site should discuss what topics are covered in the class.

a. Connect to the Internet and go to your school's Web site.

b. Print out the home page and the page for the department offering this Publisher course. You can use these materials as a reference throughout this project.

c. Start Publisher if necessary, then use the BUILT-IN templates to create a Web site for your Publisher class.

d. The Web page should consist of one page, using a style, color scheme, and background that complement the school's existing Web site.

e. Save your publication as **PUB B-Publisher Class Web Page** to the location where you store your Data Files.

f. Create a text box for contact information, if necessary. Add a telephone number and a fax number, and add Your Name as part of a fictitious e-mail address.

g. Replace the text placeholders with your own text, based on the topics that are covered in this class. (*Hint*: Consult your class syllabus and the materials you printed from your school's Web site.)

h. Save and print your publication, then exit Publisher.

Visual Workshop

Use the BUILT-IN Templates to create the marketing postcard (in the installed templates list) shown below. Save the publication as **PUB B-Design Diva Postcard** to the location where you store your Data Files. Use the Brocade Postcard layout, the Quarter-sheet page size, and accept other defaults. Add the Design Diva logo graphic image, apply the Mulberry color scheme, replace the placeholder text, and add new text in text boxes as necessary, using **FIGURE B-20** as a guide. Add your name to an existing text box in the publication, then save your work and submit the work to your instructor.

FIGURE B-20

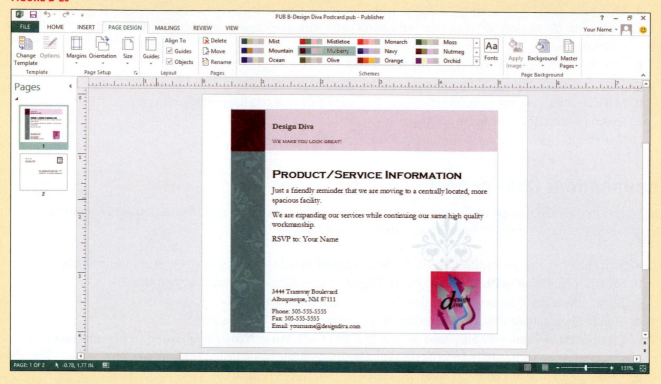

Working with Text

CASE Your current assignment is to design a flyer that will be used to promote an upcoming Design Diva Professional Design Seminar. You want the flyer to be colorful and informative, and to grab people's attention.

Unit Objectives

After completing this unit, you will be able to:

- Use layout guides
- Use ruler guides
- Format a text box
- Add bullets and numbering
- Check spelling
- Modify a Building Blocks object
- Paint formats
- Add a table
- Capstone Project: College Brochure

Files You Will Need

PUB C-1.docx
PUB C-2.docx
PUB C-3.docx

©Alena P/Shutterstock

Use Layout Guides

Learning Outcomes
• Set up margin guides
• Add a grid guide

Elements in a well-designed publication achieve a balanced and consistent look. This occurs only with careful planning and design. **Layout guides** include **margin guides** and **grid guides**, which are horizontal and vertical lines visible only on the screen. Guides help you accurately position objects on a page and across pages in a publication. Margin guides encompass the top, bottom, left and right sides of a publication, whereas grid guides appear as column and row guides. Both types of guides can be defined in the Layout Guides dialog box. For example, you can choose a number of column and row grid guides for your publication and you can define the distance for each margin guide from the four edges of the page. **CASE** ▶ *Your assignment is to create a flyer for an upcoming design seminar. You decide to use a template, then set up the layout guides to help plan for future placement of objects in the publication. You also want to experiment with a different color scheme.*

STEPS

1. **Start Publisher, click BUILT-IN in the right pane, if necessary, scroll down, then click Flyers, click All Event, then click Bars in the (More Installed Templates) Informational group**
   A preview of the selected template displays in the right pane.

2. **Click the Color scheme list arrow, scroll down, click Sunset, verify that the Secondary Business Information Set is selected, then click CREATE**

3. **Save the publication as PUB C-Design Seminar Flyer to the location where you store your Data Files**

   QUICK TIP
   In this book, ruler coordinates are given as: 5" H / 4" V referring to the intersection of 5" on the horizontal ruler and 4" on the vertical ruler as the location where you should click.

4. **Move the pointer over 5" H / 4" V, right-click the graphic placeholder (which looks like a blank area until the cursor is over it), then click Delete Object**
   The image placeholder is deleted from the flyer. When selecting an object, you can click anywhere within its borders, but coordinates are provided here to make it easy to locate each specific object.

5. **Move the pointer over 5" H / 7" V, right-click the text box, then click Delete Object**
   The text box is deleted from the flyer.

6. **Click the PAGE DESIGN tab on the Ribbon, then click Margins in the Page Setup group**
   The Margins gallery opens. You can choose from four standard margin arrangements, or customize your own settings.

   QUICK TIP
   You can type a value in each margin guide text box or use the arrows (to the right of each text box) to change the settings.

7. **Click Custom Margins (at the bottom of the list), click the Margin Guides tab if it is not already selected, then verify that the Left, Right, and Top margins are each set at 0.5", and the Bottom margin is set at 0.66", as shown in FIGURE C-1**
   The top and bottom margins are small enough to allow all the necessary information to be placed on each page. Layout guides create a grid to help you line up design elements, such as images and text boxes, on the page.

8. **Click the Grid Guides tab in the Layout Guides dialog box, click the Columns up arrow until 3 appears in the text box, click the Rows up arrow until 3 appears in the text box, click the Add center guide between columns and rows check box as shown in FIGURE C-2, then click OK**
   The pink lines represent the column guides, and the blue lines represent the column guide margins. The guides appear on the screen, as shown in FIGURE C-3, but do not print on the page.

9. **Save your work**

FIGURE C-1: Margin Guides tab of Layout Guides dialog box

Creates right- and left-hand pages

Margin settings

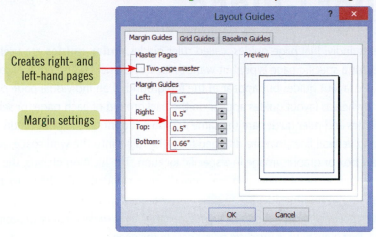

FIGURE C-2: Grid Guides tab of Layout Guides dialog box

Changes the number of columns and rows

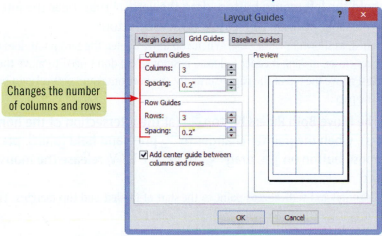

FIGURE C-3: Layout guides in publication

Your text may be different

Layout guides

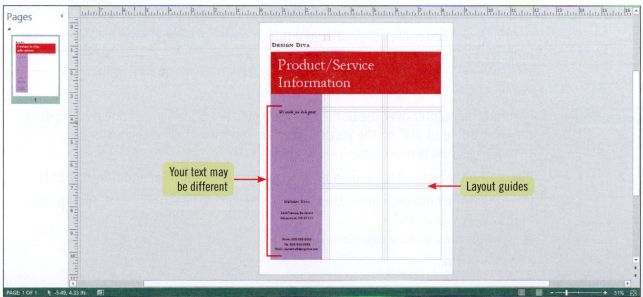

Use Ruler Guides

Publisher lets you create individual page guides, called ruler guides. **Ruler guides** are useful when you have set layout guides for a specific page type, but want to lay out elements differently on one particular page. They work just like layout guides but appear in the foreground of an individual page or selection of pages in a publication, whereas layout guides appear on the background of each page, or selected pages. Functionally, layout guides and ruler guides are the same and do not print on the publication. Ruler guides are green horizontal and vertical lines that are dragged from the rulers into the workspace, and can make it easy to position a text box or graphic image in a specific location. The location of zero, the **zero point**, on both the vertical and horizontal rulers can be moved, giving you the flexibility to make precise measurements from any point on the page. **CASE** ▸ *You want to move each ruler's zero point so you can measure distances from a specific point on a page, and add ruler guides to make it easier to position a graphic image on the first page. First, you move the vertical ruler closer to the page.*

STEPS

1. **Position** 🔖 **over the vertical ruler, press and hold [Shift], when the pointer changes to ⟷, press and hold the left mouse button, drag the vertical ruler near the left edge of the publication, release [Shift], then release left mouse button**

   The ruler is repositioned, as shown in **FIGURE C-4**. When you move a ruler, the zero point does not change; the ruler simply moves closer, making it easier to locate positions. You don't need to move the horizontal ruler because it sits just above the top of the page. Currently, the horizontal and vertical zero point is set at the top-left edge of the page.

2. **Position** 🔖 **over the Move Both Rulers button ▢ (at the intersection of the horizontal and vertical rulers), when the pointer changes to 🔖 press and hold [Shift], press and hold the right mouse button on ▢, drag 🔖, to ½" H / ½" V, release the mouse button, then release [Shift]**

   You changed the horizontal and vertical zero point to the start of the left and top margins. This makes it easy to determine exact measurements from the top-left margin.

3. **Position** 🔖 **at the top-left corner of the margin guides**

   The coordinates in the object position on the status bar are 0.00, 0.00 IN.

4. **Position the pointer anywhere over the vertical ruler, drag ◄╫► to 3" H, then release the mouse button**

   A green vertical ruler guide appears on the screen at the 3" horizontal mark.

5. **Position the pointer over the horizontal ruler, drag ╪ to 3" V, then release the mouse button**

   After looking at the new horizontal ruler guide, you realize its position is too high for the text box you plan to add.

6. **Position the pointer over the horizontal ruler guide at 3" until it changes to ╪, drag the ruler guide to 3¾" on the vertical ruler, then release the mouse button**

   The ruler guides will be helpful when a text box is added.

7. **Place** 🔖 **on the vertical ruler, then drag ◄╫► to create a vertical ruler guide at 5½" H**

8. **Place** 🔖 **on the horizontal ruler, then drag ╪ to create three horizontal ruler guides: at 6¼" V, 7" V, and 8¾" V**

   Compare your ruler guides to those shown in **FIGURE C-5**.

9. **Save your work**

FIGURE C-4: Repositioned ruler

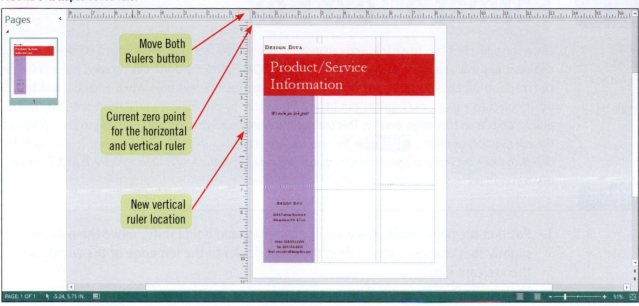

- Move Both Rulers button
- Current zero point for the horizontal and vertical ruler
- New vertical ruler location

FIGURE C-5: Horizontal and vertical ruler guides added

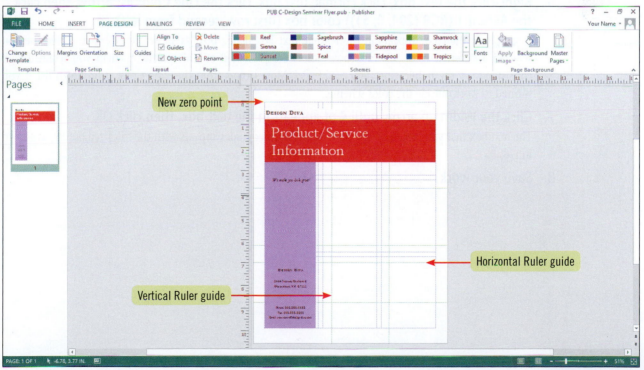

- New zero point
- Horizontal Ruler guide
- Vertical Ruler guide

Format a Text Box

Learning Outcomes
- Insert a text box
- Change line color and weight

Once you add a text box to a page, you can move or resize it. You can add and format a border using your choice of any available color or line width. The TEXT BOX TOOLS FORMAT tab contains buttons for the commands most commonly used to improve the appearance of a text box. When adding a text box or other object to a page, ruler guides can be helpful—either by providing a visual reference or by literally pulling objects so they align exactly. This magnetic feature pulls whatever you're trying to line up toward the ruler, guide, or object. **CASE** ▶ *You want to add a text box that describes how best to use logos. You decide to place the text box using the ruler guides and Snap To feature, and then enhance it with formatting attributes. To begin, you move the vertical ruler out of the way.*

STEPS

1. **Position the pointer over the vertical ruler, press and hold [Shift], move the pointer slightly so it changes to ⟺, drag the vertical ruler to the left edge of the workspace, then release [Shift]**

   The vertical ruler is now out of the way.

2. **Click the flyer heading placeholder text at 1" H / 1" V, type Professional Design Seminar, then press [Esc] two times**

   The new heading appears in the text box, and the text box is deselected.

3. **On the PAGE DESIGN tab, locate the Layout group, then verify that the Guides and Objects options each contain a check mark**

   A check mark next to an option indicates that it is selected, or activated. Clicking the option again turns it off.

4. **Click the INSERT tab on the Ribbon, then click the Draw Text Box button 🔲 in the Text group**

   The pointer changes to ╈.

5. **Drag ╈ from approximately 3" H / 3¾" V to 5" H / 6¼" V**

   The text box automatically snaps to the ruler and layout guides.

TROUBLE
A text box must be selected before you can modify it.

6. **Right-click the text box, click Format Text Box, click the Line Color list arrow, then click the Accent 1 (RGB (204, 0, 51)) color box (first row, second from left)**

   A sample of the color appears in the Format Text Box dialog box, as shown in **FIGURE C-6**. Because you selected a different color scheme, those colors are presented on this palette to help you retain design consistency in the publication. You could click More Colors from the Line Color drop down list if you wanted to work outside the color scheme.

7. **Click the Width up arrow until 4 pt appears in the text box, then click OK**

   The text box that you placed on the page using the ruler guides appears with the thick red border, as shown in **FIGURE C-7**.

8. **Save your work**

FIGURE C-6: Format Text Box dialog box

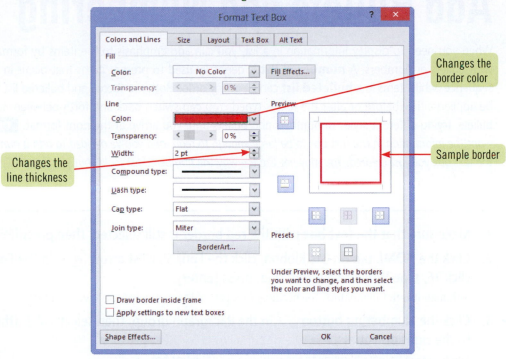

Changes the border color

Changes the line thickness

Sample border

FIGURE C-7: Text box with thick, red border

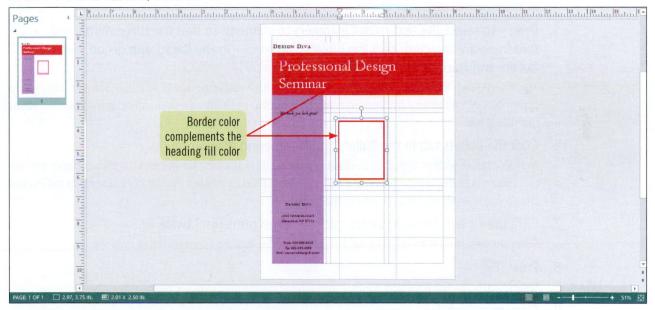

Border color complements the heading fill color

Making use of margins

When you think of **margins**, you probably think of the space surrounding the four edges of a page. The term also applies to the space that surrounds any boundary; each design object, including columns, tables, and text boxes, has its own margins. Margins are often used to create **white space**, the designer's term for space on a page that is not covered with printed or graphic material. The addition of white space is critical for clarity because without it the page looks cluttered and is difficult to read.

Add Bullets and Numbering

Learning Outcomes
• Create a numbered list
• Modify the bullets in a bulleted list

When you need to display information in a list, you can add emphasis to the items by formatting them with bullets or numbers. A **numbered list** is generally used to present items that occur in a particular sequence, while items in a **bulleted list** can be in any order. Both numbered and bulleted list formats can be applied either before or after the text is typed. You can switch back and forth between numbers and bullets, trying different styles of numbers and bullets until you arrive at the right format. **CASE** *You want the information in the text box to be large enough to read, and you've decided to add a numbered list in the text box you just created. You may not like the way the numbered list looks, but you can easily change this to a bulleted list.*

STEPS

1. **Make sure that the text box with the red border is still selected, then press [F9]**

2. **Click the HOME tab on the Ribbon, click the Font Size list arrow** `10 ▾` **in the Font group, click 16, type Why use a logo?, then press [Enter]**

   Although it is not mandatory, the heading, (not part of the numbered list) is entered first.

3. **Click the Numbering button** `▤▾` **in the Paragraph group, then select 1.2.3. (the choice to the right of None)**

   The insertion point is blinking to the right of a 1. in the text box.

4. **Type Customers look for it., press [Enter], type It distinguishes your firm from others., press [Enter], then type It is a marketing element.**

   Compare your text with **FIGURE C-8**. To apply numbers or bullets to existing text, or to change from numbers to bullets, or back again, you first must select the text you want to format.

5. **Drag** `Ⲓ` **to select the text from Customers to element. so that the three numbered sentences are selected, click the Bullets button** `▤▾` **in the Paragraph group, then click Bullets and Numbering**

   The Bullets and Numbering dialog box opens and the Numbering tab is selected. You can change the appearance of a numbered list, convert it to a bulleted list, or change the appearance of the bullets by using this dialog box.

6. **Click the Bullets tab in the Bullets and Numbering dialog box**

   Available bullet options appear in the Bullet character section, as shown in **FIGURE C-9**. To enhance any list, you can change the appearance of the bullets. Publisher lets you use a variety of characters as bullets and change the size (measured in points) of the bullets.

7. **Click the closed diamond bullet, click OK, then press [Esc] twice**

   Compare your work with **FIGURE C-10**. The numbered list has been converted to a bulleted list.

8. **Press [F9]**

   You can view the full page, and see that the bulleted list fits nicely on the page.

9. **Save your work**

Using bullets or numbers: Which is correct?

The general rule to follow for using bullets or numbers is that numbers should be used when it is necessary for steps to be followed in a specific sequence. Bullets are appropriate when the order in which steps are carried out is not important.

For example, use numbers when giving instructions for backing your car out of the garage; use bullets when describing the things you need to do before hosting a dinner party.

FIGURE C-8: Numbered list in a text box

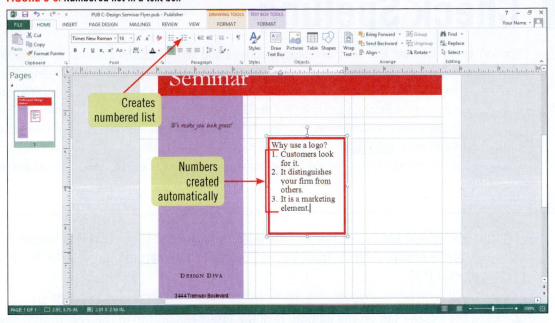

Creates numbered list

Numbers created automatically

FIGURE C-9: Bullets and Numbering dialog box

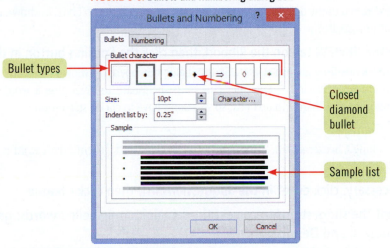

Bullet types

Closed diamond bullet

Sample list

FIGURE C-10: Numbered list changed to a bulleted list

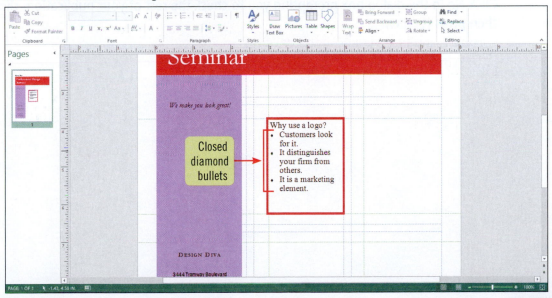

Closed diamond bullets

Check Spelling

Learning Outcomes
• Check the spelling in a document
• Accept spelling suggestions

Spelling errors can ruin the most beautifully designed and well-written publication by distracting the reader from the message. Fortunately, using the **Spelling Checker** helps you to correct misspelled words before the reader sees them. The Spelling Checker is available only if a text box is selected. You can then check spelling using the Proofing group on the REVIEW tab. Spelling errors are shown immediately as you type, indicated by a wavy red underline. You can add words that are not recognized by the Office/Publisher dictionary as you work. **CASE** *You need to add information to the flyer about the guest speaker for the seminar. Mike has provided you with a text file containing this information. Once you create a text box, you can insert the text file and check for any spelling errors.*

STEPS

1. **Click the HOME tab (if it is not already selected), click the Draw Text Box button** ⬚ **in the Objects group, drag ✛ from 5½" H / 3¾" V to the margin guide at 7½" H / 6¼" V, then press [F9]**

   The text box appears on the page. Text placed in a text box is sometimes referred to as a story.

2. **Click the INSERT tab on the Ribbon, click the Insert File button in the Text group, navigate to the location where you store your Data Files, click PUB C-1.docx, then click OK**

   The text stored in the document file PUB C-1 is inserted into the text box, as shown in **FIGURE C-11**. This text contains misspelled words that you want to correct.

3. **Click the REVIEW tab on the Ribbon, then click the Spelling button in the Proofing group**

   The Check Spelling: English (United States) dialog box opens, as shown in **FIGURE C-12**. The first incorrect word found is "prievious." Publisher checks its dictionary to determine a word's spelling and places a suggestion in the Change to text box, so you don't have to click a suggestion.

QUICK TIP
To check the spelling of an individual word, click anywhere within the word, then press [F7].

4. **Click Change**

   The Spelling Checker advances to the next misspelled word, "ebent." This word is spelled incorrectly and should be "event."

5. **If necessary, click event in the Suggestions list, then click Change**

QUICK TIP
To choose not to accept a suggested spelling, click Ignore. You can also add words Publisher identifies as misspellings, such as proper names, to the dictionary by clicking Add.

6. **Accept the suggestions to correct the remaining misspelled words: gaols, Leeder, prestigous, and Desing**

   The Spelling Checker finished checking the text box.

7. **Click No in the dialog box prompting you to check the rest of your publication, click OK, then press [Esc] twice**

   Compare your corrected text to **FIGURE C-13**.

8. **Press [F9], then save your work**

FIGURE C-11: Spelling errors in text

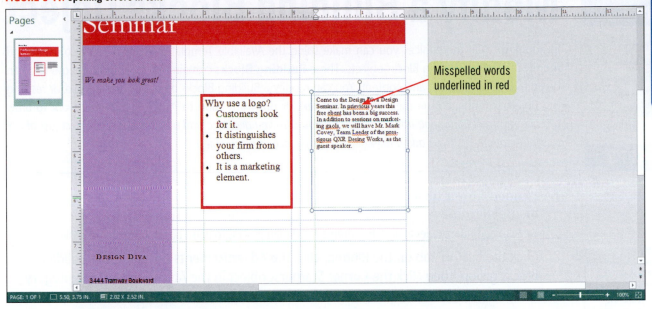

Misspelled words underlined in red

FIGURE C-12: Check Spelling dialog box

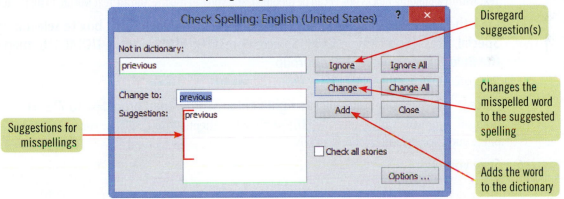

Disregard suggestion(s)

Suggestions for misspellings

Changes the misspelled word to the suggested spelling

Adds the word to the dictionary

FIGURE C-13: Corrected spelling

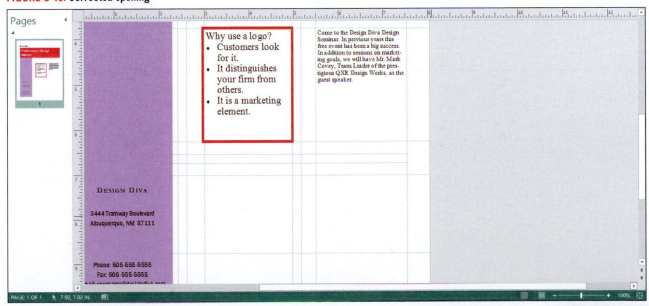

Modify a Building Blocks Object

Learning Outcomes
• Add a Building Block object to a publication

In addition to all the choices you can make using the Available Templates list, you can also insert and modify individual Building Blocks objects. These **Building Blocks** contain text or graphic images and can be edited for size, shape, and content. You can modify a Building Blocks object by adding text or resizing the object to enhance the meaning of your text or draw attention to it. **CASE** ▸ *You want to draw attention to the information about the guest speaker, so you decide to add a Building Blocks object just above this information. First, you add a ruler guide to help place this new object.*

STEPS

QUICK TIP

Once it is selected, a Building Blocks object is displayed in the Recently Used category at the top of its category palette. You can remove an object from the Recently Used list by right-clicking it, then clicking Remove from Recently Used items.

1. **Position** ▸ **over the horizontal ruler, drag** ⇕ **to 3" on the vertical ruler, then release the mouse button**

   You can add ruler guides at any time during the design process to make positioning objects easier.

2. **Click the INSERT tab on the Ribbon, click the Advertisements button in the Building Blocks group, then click the Corner Starburst object in the Attention Getters category**

   The new object is placed on the page; however, it can be moved to a location that works for your publication.

3. **Place** ▸ **over the Corner Starburst object, drag the object so its upper-left corner is at 5½" H / 3" V, then press [F9]**

   Text within a Building Blocks object can be modified, and you can use the Autofit Text feature to fill the text box.

4. **Click the Attention Grabber text in the Advertisement Object text box to select it, type Special, press [Enter], type Guest Speaker, press [Ctrl][A], click the HOME tab, then click the Bold button** **B** **in the Font group**

   Compare your work with **FIGURE C-14**.

5. **Place** ▸ **over the selected object's right-center handle, then drag** ⟺ **to 7½" H**

   Compare your work with **FIGURE C-15**. The width of the Attention Getter is now consistent with the width of the guest speaker information text box.

6. **Save your work**

FIGURE C-14: Building Blocks object positioned and new text inserted

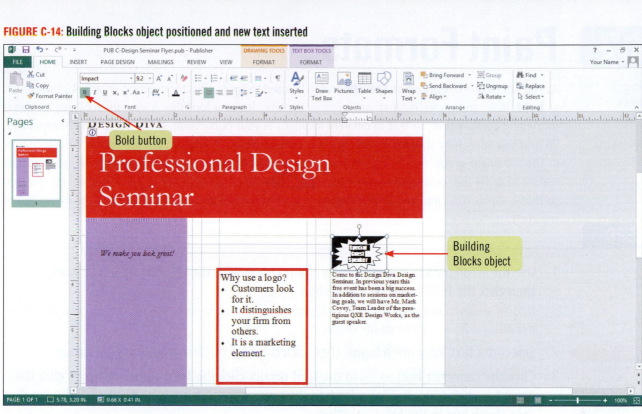

FIGURE C-15: Building Blocks object replaced and resized

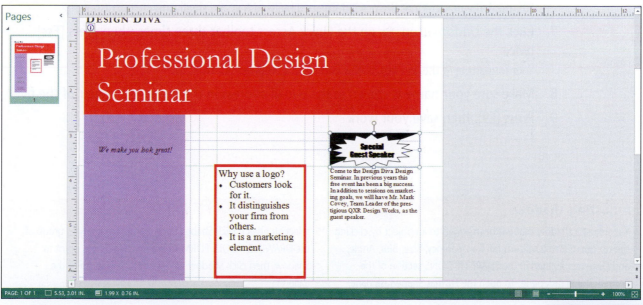

Paint Formats

As you have learned, buttons on the Ribbon can be used to apply object formatting or text attributes such as **bold**, *italic*, and <u>underlining</u> as well as to increase or decrease font size. If you are applying the same formatting combinations to text in different locations in your publication, this process can get repetitive. To help you apply formats with consistency and without difficulty, you can use the Format Painter button in the Clipboard group on the HOME tab. Once you have applied formatting attributes, you use this feature to apply the formatting to other text. **CASE** ▶ *You want to spruce up the text about using a logo so that it stands out. Once you find a formatting combination you like, you want to paint the formatting to selected text.*

STEPS

1. **Use the scroll bars to visually center the text box with the red border in the work area, then click the HOME tab on the Ribbon**

   To draw attention to certain words in each sentence, you want to apply specific formats. One method of formatting is to use buttons on the Ribbon.

2. **Select the text Why use a logo?, then click the Bold button** 🅱 **in the Font group**

3. **Click the Launcher button** ⬒ **in the Font group, click the Font color list arrow, click the Accent 1 (RGB (204, 0, 51)) color box (first row, second from left), then click the Small caps check box in the Effects section**

4. **Click More Effects, click SHADOW if necessary, click the Presets button, click Offset Diagonal Bottom Right in the Outer group, click OK, compare your dialog box to FIGURE C-16, then click OK**

   You can add as many attributes as you want by clicking the check boxes in this dialog box, but some are mutually exclusive. For example, Small caps and All caps cannot be selected at the same time.

5. **Click the HOME tab on the Ribbon if necessary, click the Format Painter button** 🖌 **in the Clipboard group, position** 🖌 **in the text box, then click and drag** 🖌 **over Customers**

   You can double-click the Format Painter to make it 'sticky' so you can apply the same formatting to more text in the publication. To turn off the feature, press [Esc].

6. **Double-click** 🖌 **, click firm, click marketing, then press [Esc]**

   You think the new color of the newly formatted bulleted text and small caps are too distracting.

7. **Click the Undo button** ↺ **on the Quick Access toolbar three times, then press [Esc] twice**

   Your formatting of the text box is now complete. Compare your work to **FIGURE C-17**.

8. **Make sure your name is shown in the e-mail address in the lower-left corner of the flyer**

9. **Press [F9], then save your work**

Adjusting shadows

You adjust a shadow that has been added to an object by clicking the up/down arrow buttons for Transparency, Size, Blur, Angle, and Distance (located in the SHAPE OPTIONS section of the Format Shape task pane. To open the Format Shape task pane, select an object, click Shape Effects in the Shape Styles group of the DRAWING TOOLS FORMAT tab on the Ribbon, point to Shadow, then click Shadow Options (at the bottom of the gallery).

FIGURE C-16: Font dialog box

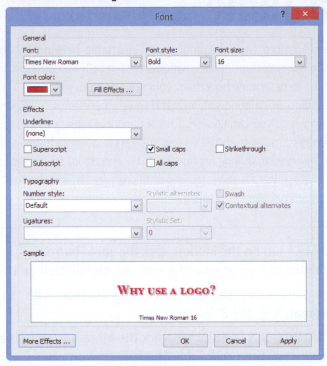

FIGURE C-17: Formatting applied

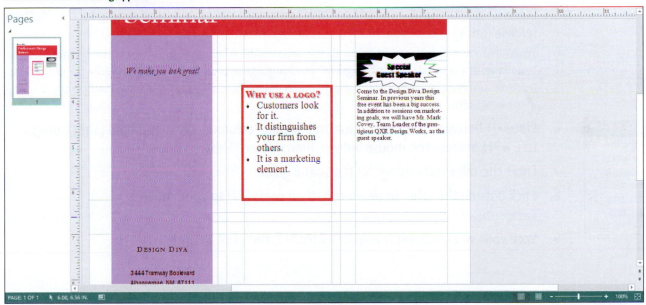

Creative deletion

Identifying poor design is an important skill, but mere recognition is not enough. Once a design flaw is identified, you have to either fix it or delete it. Not only is there nothing wrong with deleting flawed design elements, creative deletion is actually one of the most important skills a designer can learn. It is particularly important to be able to edit your own work. Look for elements that either detract from or fail to support the publication's message. If the element distracts or is unnecessary, it should be changed or deleted in favor of a constructive design element or more white space.

Add a Table

Learning Outcomes
• Insert a table in a publication
• Apply formatting to a table

Some information is more easily communicated in a table because its organization allows for quick reference. A **table** is a collection of information stored in cells in a grid of columns and rows. To create a table, you first need to determine how many columns and rows you need. You can always change the size of the table by adding or deleting columns and rows if necessary. Publisher comes with many different table formats from which you can choose. To enter text in a table, you can type directly in the cells of the table, pressing [Tab] to move from cell to cell. You can also navigate the cells in a table using the arrow keys. **CASE** *You need to include information in the flyer about the agenda for the seminar, including the title, description, and speaker for each. You decide to organize this information in a table. The table needs to contain six rows and three columns to hold all the necessary information.*

STEPS

QUICK TIP
You can also create a table using the Table button in the Objects group on the Home tab.

1. **Click the INSERT tab on the Ribbon, click the Table button ▦ in the Tables group, drag the pointer so 3 columns and 6 rows are highlighted on the grid, then click**

2. **Position the pointer over the table, then drag the table with ⟨ so the upper-left corner is at approximately 3" H / 7" V**

3. **Click the TABLE TOOLS DESIGN tab, click the More button in the Table Formats group, scroll down the list, then click Table Style 57, as shown in FIGURE C-18**
   The formatting is applied to the table.

QUICK TIP
Use ⇳ to change row height.

4. **Press [F9], type Session Title, press [Tab], type Description, press [Tab], then type Speaker**

5. **Place +‖+ on the right edge of the table, press and hold [Shift] and drag I to 7½" H, then release [Shift]**
   When first created, table columns are all the same width. When you place the pointer between column boundaries of a selected table, it changes to +‖+. Changing the boundary width changes the size of the table; however, you can change the width of a column but retain the table size by holding [Shift] while dragging to the new width.

QUICK TIP
Press [Tab] at the end of the last cell in a table to insert a new row in the table. Press [Enter] in any cell to insert lines within the row.

6. **Place +‖+ between the Description and Speaker columns, press and hold [Shift], drag I to 6½" H, release the mouse button, then release [Shift]**

7. **Enter the table data using FIGURE C-19 as a guide**

8. **Click outside the table to deselect it, then press [F9] to zoom out**
   You are pleased with the progress of the flyer.

9. **Save your work, submit it to your instructor, then exit Publisher**

Modifying the layout of a table

You can modify the layout of a Publisher table by right-clicking the table, then clicking Format Table or by clicking the TABLE TOOLS LAYOUT tab. Using the Cell Properties tab in the Format Table dialog box, you can change the margins and vertical alignment within selected cells and rotate text by 90 degrees. Use the Colors and Lines tab in the Format Table dialog box to change the fill or line color of selected cells. You can create a split cell effect for selected cells in a table by clicking the TABLE TOOLS LAYOUT tab, then clicking Diagonals. The Diagonals palette lets you divide a cell up or down, or remove a division entirely. You can also merge selected adjacent cells by clicking the TABLE TOOLS LAYOUT tab on the Ribbon, then clicking Merge Cells. Merged cells can be split up by clicking the TABLE TOOLS LAYOUT tab on the Ribbon, then clicking Split Cells.

FIGURE C-18: Table styles

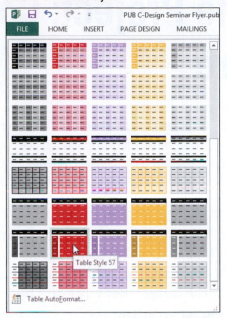

FIGURE C-19: Completed table

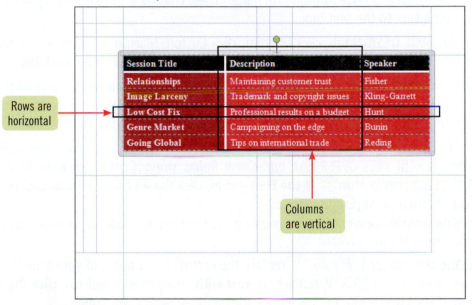

Rows are horizontal

Columns are vertical

Using AutoFormat

An existing table's design can be changed using the buttons in the Table Formats group in the TABLE TOOLS DESIGN tab. You can also choose a new Table format by clicking the More button in the Table Formats group of the TABLE TOOLS DESIGN tab, clicking Table AutoFormat at the bottom of the Table Formats gallery, selecting a new format in the Auto Format dialog box, then clicking OK, and the new table format will replace the old. **FIGURE C-20** shows the Table Style 62 format in the Auto Format dialog box. In order to use AutoFormat, you must select a table.

FIGURE C-20: Auto Format dialog box

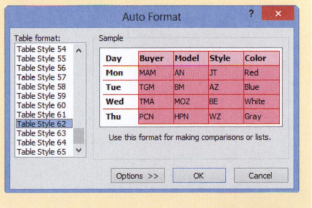

Capstone Project: College Brochure

You have learned how to change layout and margin guides and how to use ruler guides. You have also learned to format a text box, add and modify bullets and numbering, and insert Building Blocks objects. Additionally, you now know how to paint formats, add a table, and check spelling. **CASE** *You have been asked to create a flyer promoting the Camelback Community College Library Book Sale. The sale will feature the library's Great Books collection, so you want to call attention to this information in the flyer.*

STEPS

1. Start Publisher, click **Flyers** in the BUILT-IN Templates list, click **All Event**, in the More Installed Templates (Informational) section, click **Blocks**, click **CREATE**, then save the publication as **PUB C-Book Sale Flyer** to the location where you store your Data Files
   The template you selected has the right tone for the flyer.

2. Change the color scheme to **Opulent**

3. Click the **Product/Service Information placeholder**, change it to read **Library Book Sale**, then **fit the text** to the text box

4. Click the **PAGE DESIGN tab**, click **Margins**, click **Custom Margins**, change all the margin guides to **0.4"**, change the grid guides to **3 Columns** and **3 Rows**, then click **OK**

   QUICK TIP
   Draw ruler guides to help you position the object.

5. Click the **INSERT tab** on the Ribbon, click the **Advertisements button** in the Building Blocks group, click **More Advertisements**, click **Flag** in the Attention Getters section, click **Insert**, then drag the object so its **upper-left corner** is at **½" H, ½" V**

6. Press **[F9]**, resize the selected object to **2¾" H × 1½" V** by dragging the lower-right handle, click the **FREE OFFER text**, type **Great Books**, press **[Ctrl][A]**, click the **HOME tab**, click the **Launcher button** 🔲 in the Font group, click the **All caps check box**, click **OK**, press **[F9]**, then press **[Esc] two times**
   Making the Attention Getter larger and changing the text will help the reader decide immediately if he or she is interested in reading further.

7. Click the **text box at 1" H / 8¾" V**, replace the text with the name of **your school**, click the **text box at 1" H / 9.5" V**, replace the text with **your school's address**, click the **text box at 1" H / 10.5" V**, then replace the e-mail address with **your name**

8. Save your work, compare your work to **FIGURE C-21**, submit it to your instructor, then exit Publisher

FIGURE C-21: Completed publication

GREAT BOOKS

SCHOOL NAME

We make you look great!

Library Book Sale

Place text here that introduces your organization and describes your specific products or services. This text should be brief and should entice the reader to want to know more about the goods or services you offer.

SCHOOL NAME

School Address
School City State Zip

Phone: 878-555-5555
Fax: 878-555-5555
E-mail: yourname@school.edu

Practice

Concepts Review

Label each of the elements of the Publisher window shown in FIGURE C-22.

FIGURE C-22

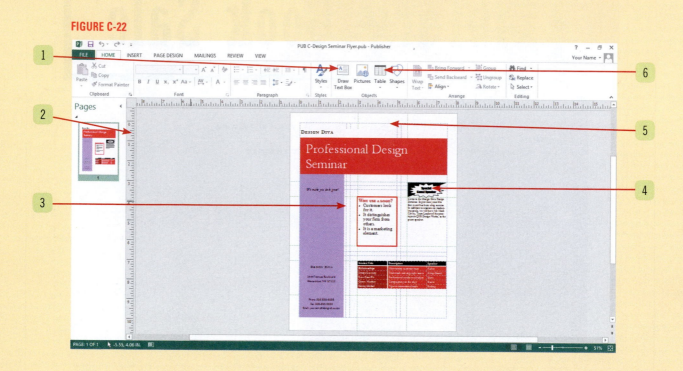

Match each of the buttons with the statement that describes its function.

7. ↔

8.

9.

10.

11. ↩

12. **B**

a. Undoes a previous action

b. Paints formatting attributes

c. Inserts a table

d. Moves rulers

e. Makes text bold

f. Changes a column's width

Select the best answer from the list of choices.

13. **On which tab is a feature that is used to create advertisements?**
    a. INSERT
    b. PAGE DESIGN
    c. LAYOUT
    d. VIEW

14. **Which of the following is *not* a font attribute?**
    a. Bold
    b. Snap
    c. Italics
    d. Shadow

15. **The Spelling feature in Publisher:**
    a. Identifies misspelled words.
    b. Finds all punctuation errors.
    c. Gets rid of the blue wavy lines.
    d. Cannot check words in a table.

16. **Each of the following buttons is used for formatting text, except _____.**
    a. *I*
    b. A
    c.
    d. **B**

17. **To maintain a table's size, resize a column while holding the _____ key.**
    a. [Shift]
    b. [Alt]
    c. [Ctrl]
    d. [Esc]

18. **In order to insert a new row in a table, position the pointer in the last cell, then press _____.**
    a. [Enter]
    b. [Tab]
    c. [Shift][Enter]
    d. [Page Down]

19. **Ruler guides are _____.**
    a. blue
    b. green
    c. pink
    d. red

20. **Each of the following is true about layout guides, except _____.**
    a. objects can snap to them
    b. they are only visible onscreen
    c. they include margin guides and grid guides
    d. they appear in the foreground

Skills Review

1. **Use layout guides.**
   a. Start Publisher, click Flyers in the BUILT-IN Templates list, then click the Company Picnic template in the All Event, Other category.
   b. Use the Secondary Business Information Set (created in a previous chapter) and the Garnet color scheme, create the publication, then save the file as **PUB C-Company Picnic Flyer** to the location where you store your Data Files.
   c. Use the PAGE DESIGN tab to open the Layout Guides dialog box.
   d. Change the margin guides if necessary to 0.5 left, 0.5 right, 0.5 top, and 0.66 bottom.
   e. Use the Layout Guides dialog box to create three columns and three rows of grid guides in this publication.
   f. Save your work.

2. **Use ruler guides.**
   a. Move the vertical ruler closer to the page.
   b. Create horizontal ruler guides at ¼" V, 1" V, 7.125" V, and 9½" V. Create vertical ruler guides at ½" H, 4" H, 5¾" H, and 7" H.
   c. Save your work.

3. **Format a text box.**
   a. Move the vertical ruler back to the left side of the screen.
   b. Click the text box at 2" H / 5" V, then zoom in to view the text box.
   c. Create a 4 pt Accent 1 (RGB (102, 0, 51)) border around the text box, zoom out so you can see the full page, then deselect the text box.
   d. Save your work.

4. **Add bullets and numbering.**
   a. Select the text box at 5" H / 5" V, then zoom in to view the text box.
   b. Replace the text under the Highlights heading with the following information, pressing [Enter] after each activity except the last one, to create a bulleted list: **Volleyball**, **Live music**, **Sack race**, **Softball**, **Pie-eating contest**.
   c. Change the bullet style to a 12 pt open right-pointing arrow, zoom out, then save the publication.

5. **Check spelling.**
   a. Select and zoom in to the text box at 2" H / 5" V, then replace the existing text in the box with the file PUB C-2.docx from the location where you store your Data Files.
   b. Correct the spelling of the selected text, then AutoFit this text using the Best Fit command. (*Hint*: You should find four spelling errors.) Do not check the spelling in the rest of the publication.
   c. Zoom out so that you can see the entire publication, deselect the highlighted text if necessary, then save the publication.

6. **Modify a Building Blocks object.**
   a. Click the INSERT tab, click the Advertisements button, click More Advertisements, scroll to the Attention Getters category, then insert the Double Slant Attention Getter.
   b. Move the object so that the upper-left edge snaps into place at the ruler guides at 5¾" H / ¼" V, then zoom in to the object.
   c. Change the default text to **Way Too Much Fun!**
   d. Zoom out, then save the publication.

7. **Paint formats.**
   a. Select the bulleted list and zoom in.
   b. Select the text Volleyball and its trailing paragraph mark and format it using the Accent 2 (RGB (255, 124, 128)) color.
   c. Use the Format Painter to paint Live music with the same formatting.
   d. With the cursor in Live music, double-click the Format Painter button.
   e. Paint the formatting to the following text, including the trailing end-of-paragraph marks: Sack race, Softball, and Pie-eating contest.
   f. Zoom out so that you can see the entire page, then save your work.

8. **Add a table.**
   a. Resize the three text boxes above the Time text box so that their right edges end at 4" H.
   b. Create a table containing six rows and three columns from 4" H / 7⅞" V to 7¾" H / 9½" V.
   c. Apply Table Style 58.
   d. Zoom in, then enter the following text for the three column headings: **Activity**, **Contact**, and **Extension**.
   e. Enter the information in **TABLE C-1**, then resize the columns so the left edge of the Extension column begins at 6¾" H.
   f. Zoom out so that you can see the full page.
   g. Deselect the table, then delete the logo placeholder, if necessary.
   h. Replace the phone number for the Contact person with your name, then save your work.
   i. Print the publication, then exit Publisher.

TABLE C-1

Activity	Contact	Extension
Volleyball	Lucy McMannus	5728
Live music	Frank Etherton	4689
Sack race	Roger Hubbard	5220
Softball	Gail Farnsworth	1096
Pie-eating contest	Greta Tolkmann	5304

© 2014 Cengage Learning

Independent Challenge 1

The firm of Top-Drawer Law Associates has hired you to design a postcard that invites people to a promotion party.

   a. Start Publisher if necessary, use the Postcards category in the BUILT-IN Templates to select the Blends Informational Postcard in the More Installed Templates section of All Marketing, use the color scheme of your choice, then save it as **PUB C-Promotion Announcement** to the location where you store your Data Files.

   b. Change all four margin guides to .25".

   c. Delete the text box containing placeholder text for a business tag line that is just under the upper margin.

   d. Move each ruler's zero point to the top-left margin, then add a vertical ruler guide at 0.5" and a horizontal ruler guide at ⅛".

   e. Move the Product/Service Information text box so that the upper-left corner is at 0.5" H / ⅛" V, create a 2 pt Accent 1 border around it, then type **TOP-DRAWER LAW ASSOCIATES ANNOUNCE**.

   f. Align all of the text boxes so their left edges snap to the vertical ruler guide.

   g. Select the text box that starts **Place text here** and insert the text found in PUB C-3.docx.

   h. Use the Spelling Checker to correct any errors in the text. Do not check the rest of the publication.

   i. Type the firm's name in the text box found at 1" H / 2⅜" V, then modify text and formatting to create a meaningful invitation.

   j. Create text that has one or more formatting effects, then use the Format Painter to copy formats for the text.

   k. Add a text box that includes your name, delete the logo placeholder if necessary, save and print the publication, then exit Publisher.

Independent Challenge 2

The seminar you are teaching in London on International Business Leadership is about to end. At the conclusion, you would like to present each attendee with a certificate of completion.

   a. Start Publisher if necessary, use the BUILT-IN Templates to select Award Certificates (in the Installed Templates category), choose Celtic Knotwork, and apply the color scheme of your choice.

   b. Save the publication as **PUB C-International Leadership Certificate** to the location where you store your Data Files.

   c. Move the zero points to the top-left margin.

   d. Replace the Name of Recipient with your name, then reformat the words "Certificate of Appreciation" to **CERTIFICATE OF COMPLETION**.

   e. Format the Certificate of Completion text box border so it is a 5 pt, solid line. Compare your publication to **FIGURE C-23**.

   f. Format the **Your Name** text using the formatting of your choice.

   g. Change "BUSINESS NAME" to **THE INTERNATIONAL SCHOOL OF BUSINESS**.

   h. Modify any other existing text to create a meaningful certificate of completion.

   i. Save and print the publication, then exit Publisher.

FIGURE C-23

CERTIFICATE OF COMPLETION

This certificate is awarded to

YOUR NAME

in recognition of valuable contributions to

THE INTERNATIONAL SCHOOL OF BUSINESS

Independent Challenge 3

The local music appreciation society asks you to design a program for its upcoming festival.

a. Start Publisher if necessary, then use the BUILT-IN Music template (under Programs, Installed Templates) to create a music program. Save the publication as **PUB C-Music Program** to the location where you store your Data Files.

b. On page 2, delete the existing table (for The Singers) and replace it with a 3-column, 8-row table with the format of your choice.

c. Make up the names of the singers, the songs they will sing, and the type of music (for example, opera, folk, or jazz) and enter this new information in the table.

d. Replace the **Conductor's Name** text with your name.

e. Format text using at least two attributes, then use the Format Painter to copy the formatting to other text.

f. Use the Spelling Checker to correct any errors in the text.

g. Save and print pages two and three of the publication, compare your publication to **FIGURE C-24**, then exit Publisher.

FIGURE C-24

Independent Challenge 4: Explore

Your keen mind, artistic tastes, and desire to make money are leading you to pursue business opportunities that involve designing publications. To become more credible, you decide to learn more about different fonts.

a. Connect to the Internet, then using your favorite search engine or Web site (such as google.com or about.com), search for information on choosing fonts and typefaces.

b. Use the BUILT-IN Templates list to create any style of flyer, then save it as **PUB C-Different Font Flyer** to the location where you store your Data Files.

c. Create a heading that uses and names your favorite font.

d. Add a text box that contains a bulleted list that uses and names five other fonts that you find easy to read.

e. Add a text box that discusses the differences between serif and sans serif fonts.

f. Format the text to illustrate both sans serif and serif fonts.

g. Add a prominently placed text box with your name in a clearly readable font and point size.

h. Use your judgment to delete any objects that do not contribute to the design of your publication.

i. Add a colorful border to the text boxes.

j. Change the appearance of the bullets in the list.

k. Use the Spelling Checker to correct any errors in the text, then save and print the publication.

l. Compare your publication to **FIGURE C-25**, then exit Publisher.

FIGURE C-25

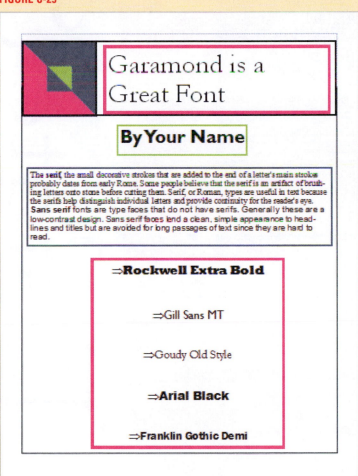

Visual Workshop

Use the BUILT-IN Templates list (using Flyers, All Event, Other, Craft Sale) to create an Estate Sale Flyer. Save this publication as **PUB-C Estate Sale Flyer** to the location where you store your Data Files. Using FIGURE C-26 as a guide, use the Orange color scheme and replace all text as shown in the figure. Include your name on the flyer. Save and print the flyer.

FIGURE C-26

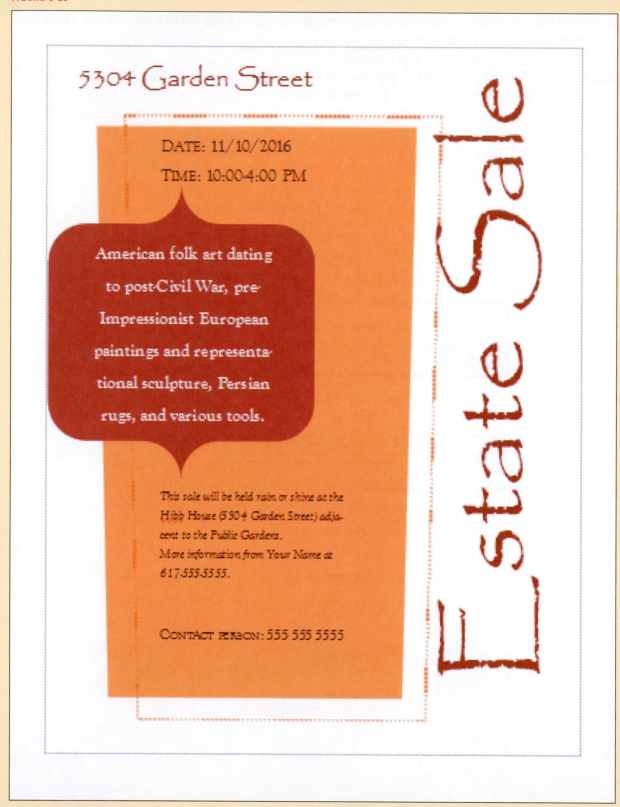

Working with Graphic Objects

CASE You have been asked to take over work on a flyer for a veterinary hospital fundraiser. The client wants the flyer to be inviting and friendly, with lots of graphics. Your first task is to choose appropriate artwork; the text will be added later.

Unit Objectives

After completing this unit, you will be able to:

- Insert and resize clip art
- Copy and move an object
- Crop an image
- Align and group objects
- Layer objects
- Rotate an object
- Use drawing tools
- Fill shapes with color and a gradient
- Capstone Project: Flower Show Project

Files You Will Need

PUB D-1.pub
PUB D-2.pub
PUB D-3.pub
PUB D-4.pub

©Alena P/Shutterstock

Insert and Resize Clip Art

Learning Outcomes
- Insert a picture
- Resize a picture

The Insert Pictures window makes it easy to dress up any publication with images. A huge variety of artwork is available both online and from commercial sources, so you can almost always find an image to represent a topic or round out a theme. With the Insert Pictures window, you can use the search feature to locate specific artwork by keyword or topic. Using this window, you can locate pictures, motion clips, and sounds, and it is not limited to the artwork that comes with Publisher. You can use commands on the INSERT tab to locate images on your computer as well as those on the Internet. **CASE** ▶ *You are ready to search for artwork for the fundraiser flyer. You want to find art representative of a veterinary hospital setting, and then resize it to fit your design for the flyer.*

STEPS

1. **Start Publisher, open PUB D-1.pub from the location where you store your Data Files, click the FILE tab, click Save As, click Browse, if necessary, then save the file as PUB D-Fundraiser Flyer**

2. **Click the INSERT tab on the Ribbon, then click the Online Pictures button in the Illustrations group**

   The Insert Pictures window opens. It contains options that allow you to limit your search to specific collections (such as Office.com, Bing, and your SkyDrive account) and to search for different types of media, such as clip art, photographs, video, and audio, arranged by content.

3. **Click the Office.com Clip Art text box, type veterinarian, then press [Enter]**

4. **Scroll down until you find the image surrounded by the green outline shown in FIGURE D-1**

5. **Position 👆 over the image shown in FIGURE D-1, click the image, then click Insert**

   The selected image is downloaded and inserted in your publication.

6. **Press [F9], position ⬚ over the clip art until the pointer changes to ⬚, drag ⬚ so that the object's upper-left corner is at 2¾" H / 3¾" V, as shown in FIGURE D-2, then release the mouse button**

7. **Place ⬚ over the lower-right corner frame handle until the pointer changes to ⬚, press and hold [Shift], drag ⬚ to the guides intersection at 5¼" H / 6⅞" V, then release [Shift]**

8. **Save your work**

Resizing an object

As you work with objects, whether they originate from your own photos or from clip art, chances are good that you'll want to resize them to fit your publication. You can resize a selected object by dragging any of its displayed handles, but often this creates altered proportions that look, well, weird. You can resize a selected object in the following ways:

- Resize an object and keep the object's center stationary by pressing and holding [Ctrl] while you drag a handle. This method keeps the object's center stationary while *maintaining the proportions* of the image.

- Maintain the object's proportions while resizing it by pressing and holding [Shift] while dragging a handle.

- Make the object a specific height and width by right-clicking it, clicking the object's Format Picture command, clicking the Size tab in the object's Format Picture dialog box, then entering measurements in the Size and rotate section.

- Specify proportions by right-clicking the object, clicking the object's Format Picture command, clicking the Size tab in the object's Format Picture dialog box, then entering the percentage of the original height or width you want in the Scale section.

FIGURE D-1: Insert Pictures window with search results

Selected image

Illustrations found in the search; your results may vary

FIGURE D-2: Clip art illustration inserted and repositioned

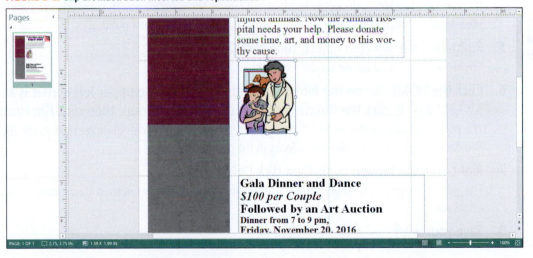

Copy and Move an Object

Learning Outcomes
- Copy an object to the Clipboard
- Paste an object from the Clipboard

You can move and copy images in a publication quickly and easily. By copying artwork, you can create interesting effects with duplicated images. You can also use copied images for experimentation in manipulating their colors, contours, cropping, dimensions, and orientations without changing the design of your original publication. For example, you can manipulate an image to create a mirror image. A mirror image shows two identical images with one flipped, so that it appears as though you are viewing the object in a mirror. When you copy an image, the copy is held temporarily in the **Clipboard**, a temporary storage area for copied or cut items. **CASE** ▶ *You want to create a mirror image using the image you just inserted. You are also considering using the image in another location in the publication. You decide to accomplish these tasks by using the Clipboard to copy and move the image.*

STEPS

1. **Right-click the selected object, then click Copy**

   Although it looks as though nothing happened, the clip art object was copied to the Clipboard. Once an image is stored in the Clipboard, you can paste it repeatedly using any pasting method.

2. **Right-click the object again, then click the Paste button 📋 (under the Paste Options mini toolbar)**

   A copy of the object appears overlapping the original object, as shown in **FIGURE D-3**. The newly copied image is selected and is offset slightly on top of the original image.

3. **Position ⬚ over the selected object copy until it changes to ⬚, then drag the object so the upper-left corner is at 5¼" H / 3¾" V**

4. **Press [F9], position the pointer over the selected object copy until it changes to ⬚, press and hold [Ctrl], press and hold [Shift], then drag ⬚ so that the upper-left corner is on the scratch area at 9" H / 3¾" V, release the mouse button, release [Shift], then release [Ctrl]**

   The second copy of the clip art is placed to the right of the original object, but off the page. You now have three images, two below the upper text box and one on the scratch area. The **scratch area** is a convenient place to store design elements while working on the overall design of a publication.

5. **Right-click the selected object, then click Cut**

   The second copy is no longer on the scratch area.

6. **Click the HOME tab on the Ribbon, click the image whose upper-left corner is at 5¼" H / 3¾" V, click the Rotate button in the Arrange group, then click Flip Horizontal**

   The copy is flipped, as shown in **FIGURE D-4**, and you can see the original image next to the flipped copy. You decide you do not like the way it looks in the publication.

7. **Right-click the flipped copy, then click Delete Object**

   The mirror image is no longer visible. Unlike objects that are cut, deleted items are *not* stored in the Clipboard.

8. **Save your work**

Using the Format Painter on clip art

The Format Painter that you can use to copy multiple formats from one selection of text to another can also be used on objects, such as lines and shapes or even clip art. Suppose, for example, that you have several pieces of clip art that you want to enhance with the same colorful line border and shadow. Apply all the formatting enhancements you want to one of the clips, double-click the Format Painter button, then click the other clip art objects. The formatting attributes will be applied to each clip art object.

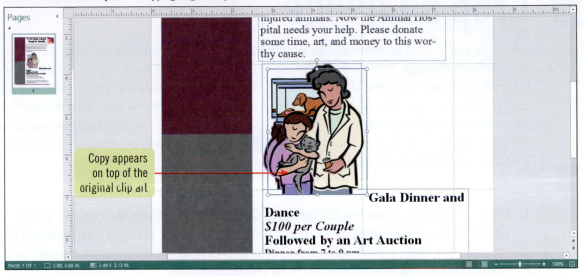

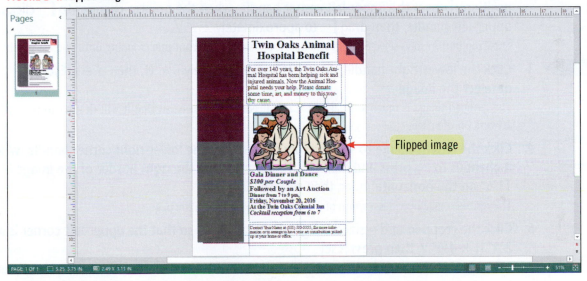

Using the Office Clipboard

The Office Clipboard appears as a pane that lets you copy and paste multiple items, such as text, images, or tables, within or between Microsoft Office applications. The Office Clipboard can hold up to 24 items copied or cut from any Office program. You choose whether to delete the first item from the Clipboard when you copy the 25th item. The collected items remain in the Office Clipboard and are available until you close all open Office programs. You can scroll through the Clipboard pane, shown in **FIGURE D-5**, to choose an item to paste; clicking the item inserts it at the current location of the cursor. You can display the Clipboard pane by clicking the Launcher ⬜ in the Clipboard group on the HOME tab, and you can specify when and where to show the Clipboard pane by clicking the Options button at the bottom of the Clipboard pane.

FIGURE D-5: Clipboard pane

Crop an Image

Learning Outcomes
- Hide part of an image
- Resize an image

Even when you find the perfect image for a publication, you may feel that it needs some modification to fit perfectly on the page. Perhaps the picture contains too much white space or part of it interferes with the publication's message. When this happens, you can trim, or **crop**, portions of the artwork to modify it to fit your needs. A graphic image can be cropped vertically, horizontally, or both. Even though they are not visible, the cropped portions of an image are still there—they are just concealed, so you can make them visible again if you change your mind. **CASE** *You want to add a photographic image to the flyer and then crop it to better suit your design.*

STEPS

1. Click the INSERT tab on the Ribbon, click Online Pictures in the Illustrations group, type **kittens** in the Office.com Clip Art search box, press [Enter], click the image shown in **FIGURE D-6** (or make a reasonable substitution), click Insert, then move the image so that the upper-left corner is at 9" H / 1" V on the scratch area

   An image of kittens is placed on the scratch area, as shown in **FIGURE D-6**.

2. Click the Crop button in the Crop group on the PICTURE TOOLS FORMAT tab, position ⊹ over the upper-left corner handle, when the pointer changes to ⌐ click the upper-left handle, then drag ⌐ to approximately 2½" V

   The Crop button stays selected until you turn it off, so you can continue cropping until you are finished.

3. Click the lower-right handle, drag ⌐ to approximately 5⅛" H, then press [Esc] to deselect the image

   The cropped image is much smaller, but it still needs to be resized so that it will fit next to the existing artwork on the page.

4. Click the kittens image to select it, position ⬈ over the lower-right corner handle, when it changes to ⬊ press and hold [Shift], drag ⬊ until the right border of the image is at 11½" on the horizontal ruler, then release [Shift]

   The resized image now has a width of 2½" and can be placed on the page.

5. Click the cropped and resized image, drag it using ⬈ so that the upper-left corner is at 2¾" H × 4½" V, then press [Esc]

   The cropped image is directly on top of the clip art for now, but you will move it later. Compare your image to **FIGURE D-7**.

6. Save your work

Cropping creatively

Cropping is used to remove portions of an image that do not support the publication's design. How do you decide what images should be cropped and how to crop them? Look for elements that either interfere with or fail to carry the publication's message. Just as with text or other objects, if a part of the image is distracting or unnecessary, it should be changed or deleted in favor of a beneficial design element. Often, white space (or unnecessary space) in a photo or in clip art should be cropped. However, if white space is needed, it can be added as a margin around the art.

FIGURE D-6: Image before cropping

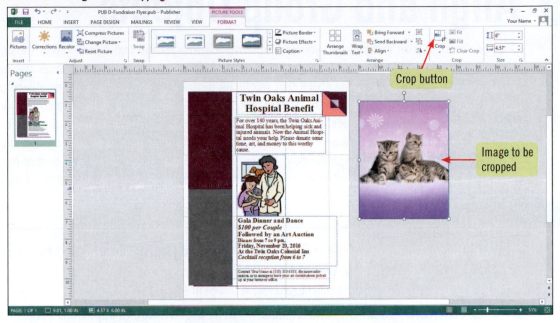

Crop button

Image to be cropped

FIGURE D-7: Image cropped, resized, and placed on page

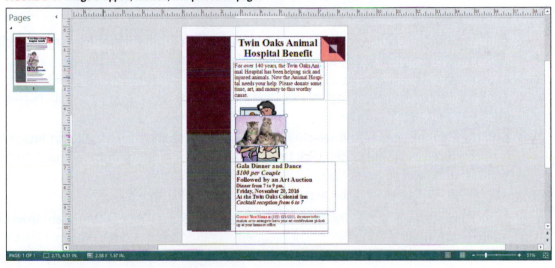

Browsing Office online clip art and media

If you have access to the Internet, you can get clip art from Office Clip art, photos, and animations. You can access this site by using your favorite browser to search for Microsoft Office images. This site offers a constantly changing selection of artwork. **FIGURE D-8** shows some of the choices offered at this Web site, although the artwork will be different when you visit the site. This site lets you update your clip art whenever you want new, exciting types of artwork to include in publications. You can download clip art, photographs, sounds, and video clips from this Web site.

FIGURE D-8: Microsoft Office Images and More Web site

Align and Group Objects

Learning Outcomes
- Group multiple objects
- Align objects
- Flip an object

Once you insert clip art and pictures, you can align multiple images and text boxes so that the layout of the publication looks clean and balanced. Alignment helps guide the reader's eye across the page by avoiding isolated patches of white space that might be distracting. Artwork and other objects can be aligned from left to right or from top to bottom. You can group images and other objects to work with them more easily. A **group** is a selection of multiple objects that you can move or resize as one unit. When you finish working with objects as a group, you can **ungroup** them to work with the objects individually again. **CASE** ▷ *You want to align the main text boxes and the two images in the flyer so that the overall appearance is neater. You also want to experiment with grouping the images and flipping them as a single object on the page to see if this would improve your design.*

STEPS

1. **With the cropped image still selected, press and hold [Shift], click the text boxes at 6" H / 3" V and 6" H / 8" V, then release [Shift]**

   Two text boxes and the image should be selected, as shown in **FIGURE D-9**.

2. **Click the HOME tab on the Ribbon, click Align in the Arrange group, then click Align Right**

   The text boxes and the photo image are lined up on the right edge, as shown in **FIGURE D-10**.

3. **Press [Esc] to deselect the objects**

TROUBLE
If you cannot drag the image to the exact coordinates given in the step, drag as close to the supplied coordinates as possible using what makes sense for the design as a guide.

4. **Press [Shift], click the cropped photo image, use ⬚ to drag the photo image until its bottom-left corner is at 5" H / 7" V, then release [Shift]**

   Pressing [Shift] while you drag an object moves it in a straight line, either vertically or horizontally. The images are aligned along their bottom edges, and the text boxes are perfectly aligned with the photo image along their right edges.

5. **With the photo image still selected, press and hold [Shift], click the clip art image to select it, release [Shift], then click the Group button ⊞ in the Arrange group on the HOME tab**

   The two selected objects can now be manipulated as a single selected object.

6. **Click Rotate ⬔ in the Arrange group on the PICTURE TOOLS FORMAT tab, then click Flip Horizontal**

   Compare your work with **FIGURE D-11**. You don't like this change. The space above the kittens' heads is unusable white space and the publication seems unbalanced with the objects reversed.

7. **Click the Undo button ↩ on the Quick Access Toolbar**

8. **Click the Ungroup button ⊞ in the Arrange group on the PICTURE TOOLS FORMAT tab, then press [Esc]**

   The objects are deselected.

9. **Save your work**

Scanning artwork

If you have a favorite photo or piece of artwork that does not exist in electronic form, you can convert it to a digital computer file with a scanner. A variety of scanners are available in either handheld, sheet fed, or flatbed format. You can scan text, line art, or full-color images with amazing accuracy, enabling you to use virtually any image in publications. Every scanner comes with its own imaging software.

FIGURE D-9: Three objects selected

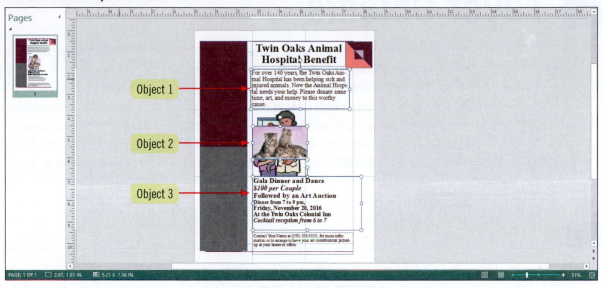

FIGURE D-10: Objects aligned right

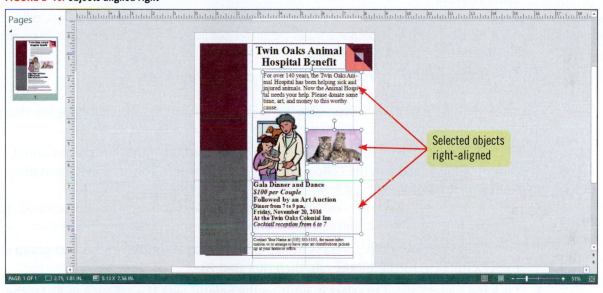

FIGURE D-11: Grouped objects flipped horizontally

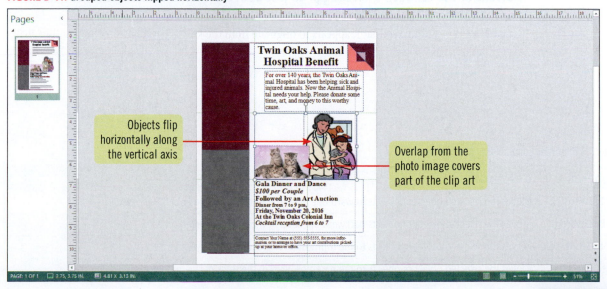

Layer Objects

When positioning objects, you might want some images to overlap, or appear as if they were in front of others. This layering effect can be used with any type of object. Sometimes you will want text to be displayed on top of a shape, or one object to overlap another object to partially conceal it. You might want to superimpose a text box in front of one object or a collection of objects. Publisher provides four options for layering objects. **TABLE D-1** outlines the four Order commands on the Arrange group. The Arrange group is conveniently available in several locations including the HOME tab, the PICTURE TOOLS FORMAT tab, and the DRAWING TOOLS FORMAT tab on the Ribbon. You can send an image to the back so that it appears to be underneath an object, or bring it to the front so it appears to be on top of an object. **CASE** *You want to experiment with layering and manipulating objects to improve the look of the flyer.*

STEPS

1. Click the **clip art image** at **4" H / 5" V**, click the **Bring Forward list arrow** in the Arrange group on the PICTURE TOOLS FORMAT tab, as shown in **FIGURE D-12**, then click **Bring to Front**

   The clip art image of the animal hospital now overlaps the photograph. You think the images look better with this amount of overlap because it makes the images look better together. You think the design might be improved by reversing the clip art image.

2. Click **Rotate** in the Arrange group, then click **Flip Horizontal**

   The overlap is maintained when the image is flipped. Flipping the clip art image lines up the subjects of the image in a strong diagonal that guides the eye from the upper-left to the lower-right. It also changes the apparent view of the veterinarian from one animal to all the animals and the little girl.

3. Click the **INSERT tab** on the Ribbon, click the **Shapes button** in the Illustrations group, click the **Cloud Callout** in the Callouts group (fourth shape in the first row), then drag $+$ from **5¼" H / 3½" V** to **8" H / 5" V**

   The image of the kittens now has a cartoon balloon to which you can add a caption. One of the effects of inserting a callout can be movement of some text in the upper text box to accommodate the object.

4. Type **They even love dogs!**, press **[Ctrl][A]**, click **the Text Fit button** in the Text group on the TEXT BOX TOOLS FORMAT tab, then click **Best Fit**

5. Click the **Cloud Callout** to select it, position the pointer over the **yellow handle** (at the bottom of the callout), then drag to just above the head of the **left-most kitten** at approximately **6" H / 5½" V**

   The callout is positioned so that it appears to originate from the kitten's head, as shown in **FIGURE D-13**.

6. **Save your work**

TABLE D-1: The Order commands

command	description
Bring Forward	Moves the selected object or objects forward one level in the stack of layered objects
Send Backward	Moves the selected object or objects backward one level in the stack of layered objects
Bring to Front	Moves the selected object or objects to the topmost level in the stack of layered objects
Send to Back	Moves the selected object or objects to the backmost level in the stack of layered objects

FIGURE D-12: Image after it is brought to front

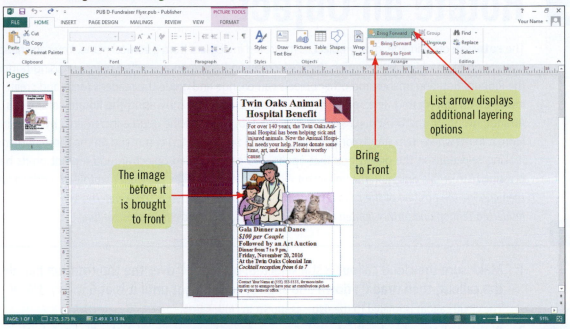

The image before it is brought to front

Bring to Front

List arrow displays additional layering options

FIGURE D-13: Clip art flipped with callout added to photo

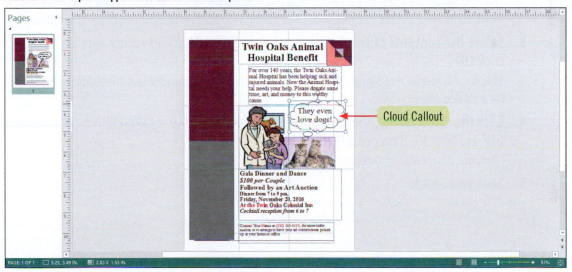

Cloud Callout

Using the Order commands

By creatively using the Order commands with text boxes and shapes, you can superimpose text boxes on all kinds of objects and shapes to make them more dramatic. You can position objects in a specific stacking order to create a complex illustration. **FIGURE D-14** shows layered text and graphics. Each object is on its own layer. This effect is achieved using the Bring Forward and Send Backward buttons in the Arrange group. Unlike Bring to Front and Send to Back, these commands move an image forward or backward only one layer at a time.

FIGURE D-14: Layered text boxes and shapes

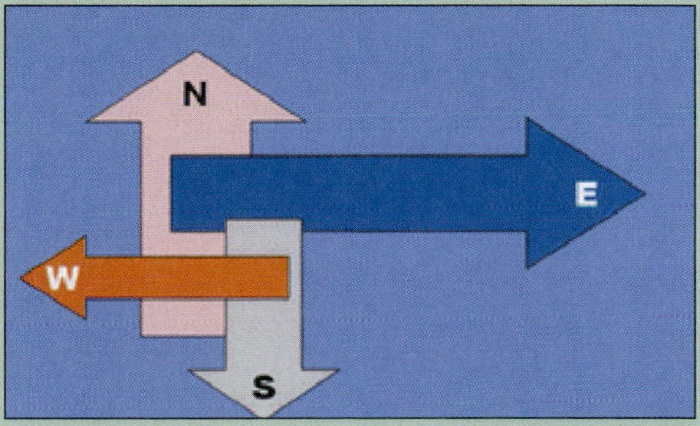

Rotate an Object

Learning Outcomes
- Manually rotate an object
- Specify the number of degrees to rotate an object

The **rotation** of an image, or any object, is measured in degrees from a vertical plane. You can change the orientation of an object by dragging the green rotation handle on a selected object or using buttons on the Ribbon. Rotating images and other objects can change and guide the reader's focus and create visual interest. You can rotate a selected object in 90-degree increments by using the Rotate commands in the Arrange group on the DRAWING TOOLS FORMAT tab, or in specific degree increments by choosing the Format item (where item stands for AutoShape, Text Box, Table, etc.) command on the shortcut menu and making selections in the dialog box that opens. You can rotate an object around a point on its base by pressing [Ctrl] while dragging the yellow rotation handle. **CASE** *You want to rotate the cartoon balloon, then change the position of the callout so it looks like a different kitten is speaking. This will help to catch the reader's attention and further lighten the tone of the publication to create a sense of fun.*

STEPS

1. **Make sure the cloud callout is still selected, position ⚓ over the top rotation handle on the callout, then drag ↻ down and slightly to the right until it is at 6¾" H / 3¼" V**
   The cloud callout is rotated to the right, as shown in **FIGURE D-15**.

QUICK TIP
You can also use the Measurement pane to adjust the rotation of the callout in addition to the spacing of the text.

2. **Right-click the cloud callout, click Format AutoShape, then click the Size tab in the Format AutoShape dialog box**
   The Size tab in the Format AutoShape dialog box is shown in **FIGURE D-16**. Using this dialog box lets you rotate an image a specific number of degrees, giving you more precise control over the rotation.

3. **Select the contents of the Rotation text box in the Size and rotate section, type 5, then click OK**
   The Shape is rotated five degrees clockwise. The object coordinates and object dimensions remain unchanged for a rotated object.

4. **Click the cloud callout, then drag the yellow handle over the tallest kitten (at approximately 6½" H / 5½" V), then press [Esc]**
   Compare your image with **FIGURE D-17**.

5. **Save your work**

FIGURE D-15: Object rotated with handle

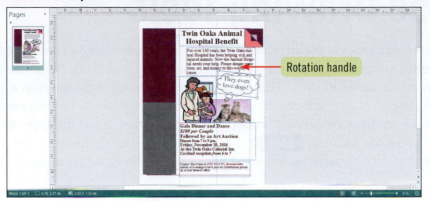

Rotation handle

FIGURE D-16: Size tab of Format AutoShape dialog box

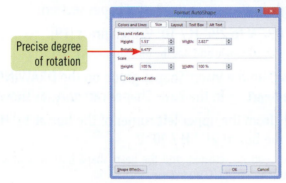

Precise degree of rotation

FIGURE D-17: Precisely rotated object

Using the Measurement pane

Publisher provides different ways to measure the dimensions and positions of objects. The Object Position coordinates and Object Size measurements on the status bar are always visible, but it can be difficult to place and size objects using them. The **Measurement pane**, shown in **FIGURE D-18**, is a direct way to precisely position and size objects to one 1/1000 of an inch accuracy. You can adjust text point size, distance between characters, and line spacing using this pane as well as an object's height, width, length, and rotation. The Measurement pane is context-sensitive, so the available options vary based on the type of object that is selected. This pane is displayed by clicking the Object Size section of the status bar, or by clicking the DRAWING TOOLS FORMAT tab on the Ribbon, then clicking the Measurement button in the Size group.

FIGURE D-18: Measurement pane

Measure... ▾ ✕	
x	5.19"
y	3.37"
⊢⊣	2.83"
⊥	1.53"
∠	5°
aaa	
↔A→	
A'W' ↔	

Use Drawing Tools

Publisher has a variety of drawing tools that you can use to create your own geometric designs. Shapes can be created using either the Shapes button in the Illustrations group on the INSERT tab or the Insert Shapes gallery on the DRAWING TOOLS FORMAT tab on the Ribbon. Any shape drawn on a page can be moved, resized, flipped, rotated, or formatted to meet your design specifications. Creating a shape is easy. You click the button for the shape you want to draw, click where you want to start the shape, and drag to create the shape in the size you need. **CASE** ▶ *You want to add a geometric design to the gray rectangle at the lower-left corner of the page. You begin by drawing a border to frame the design and make it stand out.*

STEPS

1. Click the **INSERT tab** on the Ribbon, click the **Shapes button** in the Illustrations group, then click the **Rectangle button** ▭ in the Basic Shapes section

2. Drag ┼ from ½" H / 8¼" V to 2¼" H / 10" V, then press [F9]
   The box is layered on the gray rectangle and has the dimensions 1¾" × 1¾".

3. Click the **More button** ▾ in the Insert Shapes group on the DRAWING TOOLS FORMAT tab, then point to the **heart** ♡ in the Basic Shapes category, as shown in **FIGURE D-19**

4. Click ♡, then drag ┼ from the upper-left corner of the box at ½" H / 8¼" V to the lower-right corner of the box at 2½" H / 10" V
   The heart is inside the box you just created, and the heart shape button is now displayed in the Insert Shapes group on the DRAWING TOOLS FORMAT tab.

5. Click ♡ in the **Insert Shapes gallery**, then drag ┼ to create a slightly smaller heart shape from ¾" H / 8½" V to 2¼" H / 9¾" V

QUICK TIP
If you want to repeat a designed shape with the identical dimensions, create one with all the formatting attributes you want, then copy and paste it.

6. Right-click the selected **heart**, click **Format AutoShape**, click the **Line Color list arrow**, click the **Accent 3 (RGB (224, 204, 214)) color box** (fourth from the left), then click **OK**
   The smaller heart shape is now outlined with a rose border.

7. Click the **rectangle** drawn in Step 2, then press **[Delete]**
   You like the heart shape without the framing rectangle. Compare your work to **FIGURE D-20**.

8. Save your work

Drawing perfect shapes and lines

Sometimes you want to draw an exact shape or line. To draw a square, click the Rectangle button ▭ then press and hold [Shift] as you drag. Press and hold [Shift] to create a circle using the Oval button ⬭. Press and hold [Shift] to create a horizontal, vertical, or 45-degree angle straight line using the Line button ╲

(this method draws a line at 15-degree increments). To center an object at a specific location, click the tool to create the object, place the pointer where you want the center of the object to be, then press and hold [Ctrl] as you drag the mouse. Remember to always release the mouse button before you release [Ctrl] or [Shift].

FIGURE D-19: Shapes gallery

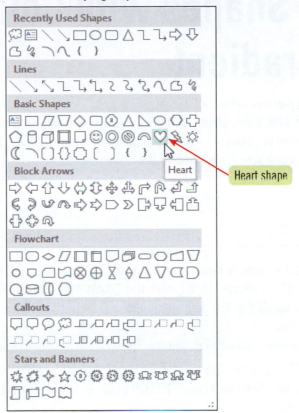

Heart shape

FIGURE D-20: Design created with drawing tools

New color appears

Learning Outcomes
- Fill a shape with color
- Apply a gradient

Fill Shapes with Color and a Gradient

Colors and patterns enhance overall design and help you create elegant original graphics. Drawn shapes can be left with their default attributes—displaying whatever background exists—or you can fill them using a variety of colors, gradients, and patterns. When choosing background colors, it's often effective to use the color scheme applied to the current publication. This includes a Main color, two or more Accent colors, and colors for hyperlinks that might be included in the publication. **CASE** *You want to add color and patterns to the shapes in your publication. You begin by adding color to the callout and one of the hearts.*

STEPS

QUICK TIP

As you drag the mouse over each color displayed by the Fill Color list arrow, its name appears in a ScreenTip that displays the numeric color values and the generic color name.

1. Select the smaller heart shape, press [F9], press [Shift], click the cloud callout shape at 7" H / 5" V, release [Shift], click the DRAWING TOOLS FORMAT tab, click the Shape Fill list arrow 🎨 ▾ in the Shape Styles group, then click the Accent 2 (RGB (255, 124, 128)) color box

   The rose color is added to the small heart shape and the cloud callout, making them stand out.

2. Press [Esc], right-click the larger heart shape, click Format AutoShape, click the Fill Color list arrow, click the Accent 1 (RGB (102, 0, 51)) color box (second from the left), then click OK

   You want to experiment with changing the appearance of the smaller heart.

3. Right-click the smaller heart shape, click Format AutoShape, click the Color list arrow in the Line section, then click Accent 3 (RGB (224, 204, 214))

4. Click the Width up button until 2.5 pt displays, then click OK to close the Format AutoShape dialog box

   A light orchid outline surrounds the small heart.

QUICK TIP

Add pattern fills to objects by clicking the desired pattern in the Format Shape dialog box.

5. Press [F9], click the Shape Fill list arrow 🎨 ▾ in the Shape Styles group on the DRAWING TOOLS FORMAT tab, click Pattern, click FILL if the list is not displayed, scroll down and click the Foreground list arrow, then click Tints

   The Fill Effects dialog box opens, and the Tint tab is active.

6. Click the Base color list arrow, click the Accent 2 (RGB (255, 124, 128)) box (the third from the left), click the 80% Shade box (second from the right in the second row) as shown in FIGURE D-21, click OK to close the Fill Effects dialog box, then click OK to close the Format Shape dialog box

   The fill color is darker and richer.

7. Right-click the rose heart shape, click Format AutoShape, then click Fill Effects

8. Click Gradient fill if it is not already selected, click the Direction list arrow, click the Linear Diagonal - Top Right to Bottom Left option, click OK to close the Format Shape dialog box, click OK to close the Format AutoShape dialog box, then press [Esc]

   Compare your work to FIGURE D-22.

9. Make sure your name appears in the text box at 4" H / 10" V, press [F9], deselect any objects, save your work and compare it with the completed flyer in FIGURE D-23, submit it to your instructor, then exit Publisher

FIGURE D-21: Fill Effects dialog box

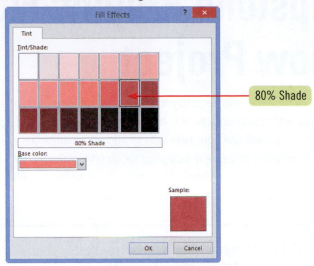

FIGURE D-22: Recolored objects with gradient

FIGURE D-23: Completed flyer

Capstone Project: Flower Show Project

You have learned the skills necessary to insert, resize, and rotate clip art. You can copy and move objects, and crop, align, and group objects. You have used drawing tools and added fill colors and gradients to drawn shapes. Now you will use your new skills to add and manipulate artwork on a Web site. **CASE** ▶ *Design Diva was contracted to create a Web page for an annual flower show. Mike is heading up this project and has some preliminary work on a design. He has asked you to improve his work by adding images. Because the Web page is advertising a flower show, you decide to start by looking for photos and clip art related to flowers.*

STEPS

1. Start Publisher, open PUB D-2.pub from the location where you store your Data Files, then save it as PUB D-Flower Show Web Page

2. Click the INSERT tab on the Ribbon, then click the Online Pictures button in the Illustrations group

3. Click the Office.com Clip Art Search text box, type daffodils, then press [Enter]

4. Insert the photograph of the basket of daffodils shown in FIGURE D-24, then close the Office.com Clip Art window, if necessary

   If you can't locate this image, make a reasonable substitution.

5. Move the picture so that the upper-left corner is at 3½" H / 7½" V, then resize the image by pressing and holding [Shift] while dragging ⤡ from the lower-right corner to 7" H / 10½" V

6. Click the HOME tab on the Ribbon, click the Rotate button in the Arrange group, then click Flip Horizontal

   Flipping the image looks nicer.

7. Create a text box at ¼" H / 3" V, type your name, modify the font and point size so that the text is readable (*Hint*: you can use the Best Fit feature), then zoom out so you can see the entire page

   Compare your work to FIGURE D-25.

8. Save your work, submit it to your instructor, then exit Publisher

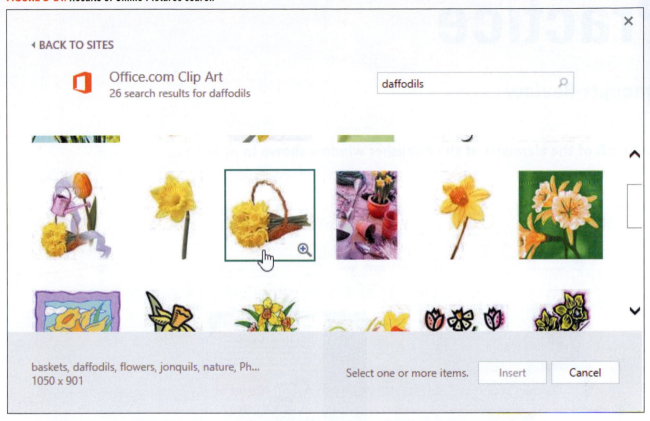

FIGURE D-24: Results of Online Pictures search

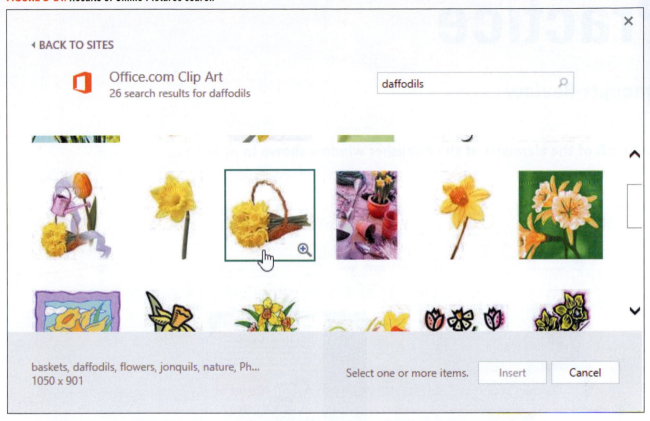

FIGURE D-25: Completed project

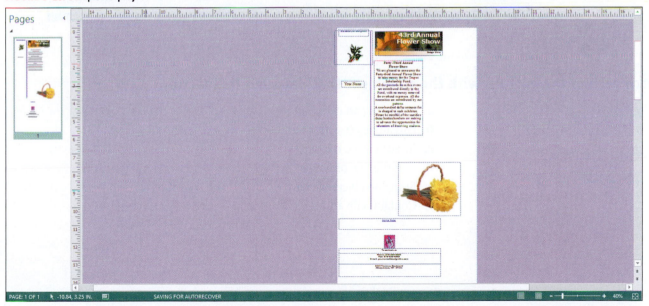

Practice

Concepts Review

Label each of the elements of the Publisher window shown in FIGURE D-26.

FIGURE D-26

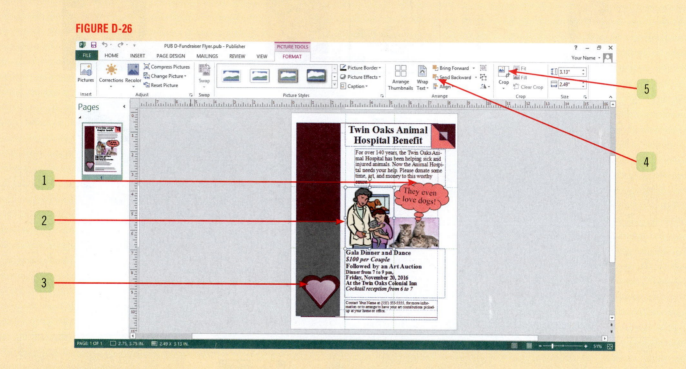

Match each of the buttons with the statement that describes its function.

6.   **a.** Conceals part of an image
7.   **b.** Fills an object with color
8.   **c.** Inserts copied content
9.   **d.** Colors a line or border
10.   **e.** Brings an object forward
11.   **f.** Contains clip art

Select the best answer from the list of choices.

12. **You can do each of the following with clip art, except _____.**
    a. crop
    b. italicize
    c. flip
    d. rotate

13. **Which button is used to add colors and patterns to objects?**
    a. [icon]
    b. [icon]
    c. [icon]
    d. [icon]

14. **Rotate an object clockwise in 90-degree increments by clicking:**
    a. Flip Horizontal.
    b. Free Rotate.
    c. Rotate Left.
    d. Rotate Right.

15. **Create a square using the Rectangle button by holding _____ while dragging.**
    a. [Ctrl]
    b. [Alt]
    c. [Shift]
    d. [Esc]

16. **Which pointer is used to insert a drawn Shape?**
    a. [icon]
    b. [icon]
    c. [icon]
    d. [icon]

17. **To resize an object, maintaining its scale while dragging, press and hold _____.**
    a. [Shift]
    b. [Alt][Shift]
    c. [Ctrl]
    d. [Alt]

18. **What key do you press and hold to create a circle?**
    a. [Ctrl]
    b. [Alt]
    c. [Shift]
    d. [Tab]

19. **Which pointer is used to copy an object without placing a copy on the Clipboard?**
    a. [icon]
    b. [icon]
    c. [icon]
    d. [icon]

20. **Which button cannot be used with clip art?**
    a. [icon]
    b. [icon]
    c. [icon]
    d. [icon]

Skills Review

Throughout this exercise, zoom in and out whenever necessary.

1. **Insert and resize clip art.**
   a. Start Publisher.
   b. Open PUB D-3.pub from the location where you store your Data Files.
   c. Save the file as **PUB D-Family Reunion Postcard**.
   d. Use the Online Pictures feature to search for clip art and photographs using the word **home**. Locate the image shown in **FIGURE D-27** or make a reasonable substitution.
   e. Press and hold [Shift], then reduce the size of the image by positioning the pointer over the lower-right handle and dragging until the dimensions are approximately 1" H × 1" V.
   f. Position the image in the lower-left corner of the publication so that the upper-left corner is at ½" H / 3" V.
   g. Save the publication.
2. **Copy and move an object.**
   a. Copy the selected image, then paste the image anywhere on the publication.
   b. Move the newly pasted copy so that the upper-left corner is at 4¼" H / 3" V.
   c. Flip the copy horizontally, then deselect it.
   d. Save the publication.

3. **Crop an image.**
   a. Move the image of the flowers from the upper-right corner of the publication so that the upper-left corner of this image is at 2" H / 2" V.
   b. Click the PICTURE TOOLS FORMAT tab, then click the Crop button. Crop the top edge of the image using the center cropping handle, hiding $\frac{1}{8}$" of the image so that the top-left corner is now at 2" H / $2\frac{1}{8}$" V, then press [Esc].
   c. Save the publication.

4. **Align and group objects.**
   a. Press and hold [Shift], select the two clip art images of the house, then add the image of the flowers to the selection.
   b. Click Align in the Arrange group on the HOME tab, then click Align Bottom.
   c. Click Align in the Arrange group on the HOME tab, then click Distribute Horizontally.
   d. Save the publication.

5. **Layer objects.**
   a. Copy the object at 1" H / $3\frac{1}{2}$" V, then paste and drag the copy so that its upper-left corner is at 1" H / $2\frac{3}{4}$" V.
   b. Send the copied object behind the original object.
   c. Copy the object at $4\frac{1}{2}$" H / $3\frac{1}{2}$" V, paste it, then drag the copy so that its upper-left corner is at $3\frac{3}{4}$" H / $2\frac{3}{4}$" V.
   d. Send the copied object behind the original object.
   e. Save the publication.

6. **Rotate an object.**
   a. Flip the image of the flowers horizontally.
   b. Right-click the image of the flowers, click Format Picture, and use the dialog box to change the rotation to 300 degrees. (*Hint*: Use the Size tab in the Format Picture dialog box.)
   c. Deselect the image, then save the publication.

7. **Use drawing tools.**
   a. Click the INSERT tab, click Shapes, then click the heart (in the Basic Shapes category).
   b. Draw the heart so that its upper-left corner is at $4\frac{1}{2}$" H / $\frac{1}{4}$" V and it has the dimensions $\frac{3}{4}$" H × $\frac{3}{4}$" V.
   c. Create a copy of this shape, paste the copy, then drag it so that the upper-left corner is at $4\frac{1}{4}$" H / $\frac{1}{4}$" V (the two hearts should overlap).
   d. Save the publication.

8. **Fill shapes with colors and gradients.**
   a. Add a red fill color to both heart shapes.
   b. Select the left heart, then change the fill transparency to 30%.
   c. Create a text box with the upper-left corner at $\frac{1}{2}$" H / $2\frac{1}{4}$" V with the dimensions 2" H × $\frac{1}{2}$" V, then insert your name, using Best Fit to adjust the point size as necessary.
   d. Save and print the publication, compare your screen to **FIGURE D-27**, submit your work to your instructor, then exit Publisher.

FIGURE D-27

Independent Challenge 1

You have decided to market yourself more effectively in the business world. Your first priority is designing a new business card. You want to create a card that reflects your interests and personality.

a. Start Publisher if necessary, use the Retro Business Card from the BUILT-IN Templates list with Landscape orientation, include a logo placeholder, then click CREATE.

b. Save the publication as **PUB D-New Business Card Design** to the location where you store your Data Files.

c. Delete any logo automatically created by the template, if necessary.

d. Enter and use any appropriate information about yourself (your name) in the Primary Business Information Set, change the company name so it reads **Design Diva**, then change the color scheme to Opulent.

e. Use at least three different drawing tools to create an interesting series of shapes in the upper-right corner of the business card. Change the fill color and fill effects of at least two shapes.

f. Use [Shift] to create a perfectly round or square shape. (If you choose, you can delete any shapes created earlier.)

g. Insert a piece of clip art downloaded from Office.com. Compare your publication to **FIGURE D-28**.

h. If desired, rotate and layer the artwork.

i. Save your work, submit it to your instructor, then exit Publisher.

FIGURE D-28

Independent Challenge 2

A local clothing store is planning a new sales promotion to increase their sale of gift certificates. The manager of the store asks you to use your design skills to create a gift certificate that is attractive and eye-catching.

a. Start Publisher, then use the Mobile Gift Certificate found in the BUILT-IN Templates list.

b. Save the publication as **PUB D-Gift Certificate** to the location where you store your Data Files.

c. Delete any logo automatically created by the template, if necessary.

d. Enter appropriate information in any Business Information Set, change the company name so it reads **Design Diva**, then change the color scheme to Plum.

Independent Challenge 2 (continued)

e. Use the Online Pictures to search for images using the word **globe**, then insert a suitable image at approximately 0" H / 2" V, resizing the image as you see fit.

f. Add a shape of your own choosing.

g. Make at least two copies of the shape, resize them, then place them according to your own sense of design.

h. Add different fill colors to the shapes.

i. Type your name next to "Authorized by" in the Authorized by text box.

j. Compare your publication to **FIGURE D-29**.

k. Save your work and submit it to your instructor, then exit Publisher.

FIGURE D-29

Independent Challenge 3

You want to spruce up your work area. A customized calendar is just what you need to help organize and add visual interest to your surroundings.

a. Start Publisher if necessary, then use the Blocks template in the Full Page section of the Calendars category of the BUILT-IN Templates list. Complete any necessary installations, if prompted.

b. Delete any logo automatically created by the template, if necessary.

c. Create a one-month calendar using the month following the current month. (*Hint*: Use the Set Calendar Dates button.)

d. Save the publication as **PUB D-Next Month's Calendar** to the location where you store your Data Files.

e. Enter appropriate information about yourself (your name) in the Primary Business Information Set.

f. Change the color scheme to one of your own choosing.

g. Add clip art of your choosing to the calendar.

h. Download and insert at least one piece of artwork from Office.com Online Clip Art which can be moved, resized, and cropped as necessary.

i. Add objects created with drawing tools, and add color and patterns, if appropriate. If necessary, resize any drawn objects.

j. Save and print the publication, submit the work to your instructor, then exit Publisher.

Independent Challenge 4: Explore

There are many sources on the Web for clip art. Some require payment to use an image, while other images are free to download. You need to find some free clip art that relates to your favorite hobby.

a. Connect to the Internet, then use your browser and favorite search engine to find free or inexpensive clip art sites.

b. Print out the home page from at least two of the sites you found. Take note of any restrictions regarding use of graphic images.

c. Right-click any of the free clip art images that appeal to you, then download them by choosing the Save Picture As or Save Image As command on the shortcut menu. Save them to the location where you store your Data Files, using the artwork's default name.

d. Start Publisher, create any design you choose using the Quick Publications category in the BUILT-IN Templates list, then save the publication as **PUB D-My Clip Art** to the location where you store your Data Files.

e. Replace a placeholder with a downloaded clip art file, add appropriate text (if necessary) to describe the artwork, then add your name somewhere on the page.

f. Format the artwork by cropping any undesirable elements, then copy or align images if necessary to enhance the publication.

g. Save and print the publication, compare your screen to **FIGURE D-30**, submit the work to your Instructor, then exit Publisher.

FIGURE D-30

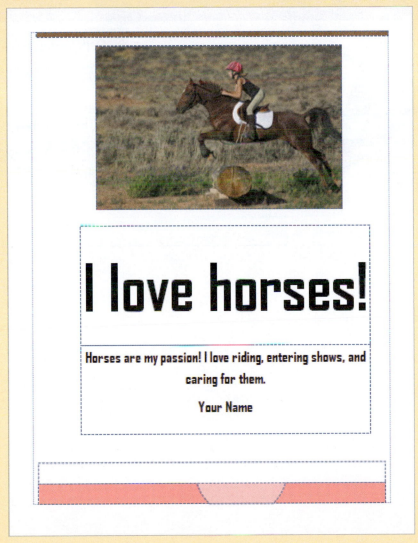

Visual Workshop

Use the elements found in PUB D-4.pub to create the party invitation shown in **FIGURE D-31**. Save this publication as **PUB D-Party Invitation** to the location where you store your Data Files. Make sure your name appears on the publication, save and print it, then submit it to your instructor.

FIGURE D-31

Enhancing a Publication

CASE Mike Mendoza has asked you to work on *Route 66 Traveler*, a quarterly newsletter for a Design Diva client. You begin by revising styles and formatting in the newsletter, so that it has a strong, consistent design, and is enjoyable to read.

Unit Objectives

After completing this unit, you will be able to:

- Define styles
- Apply and modify a style
- Change a format into a style
- Create columns
- Adjust text overflows
- Add continued on/from notices
- Add drop caps
- Create reversed text
- Capstone Project: Solar System Newsletter

Files You Will Need

PUB E-1.pub	PUB E-5.docx
PUB E-2.docx	PUB E-6.pub
PUB E-3.pub	PUB E-7.pub
PUB E-4.docx	

Define Styles

You can maintain consistent formatting, even in multipage publications, by using styles. A **style** is a defined set of text and formatting attributes, such as font, size, and paragraph alignment. As a reader moves from page to page, consistent styles make it easy to recognize what is an article headline, what is pull-quote text, and so on. All of the styles specific to a particular publication are displayed in the Styles list and are shown in the list exactly as each style will look. You can create your own styles and modify those that already exist. These new styles apply only to the publication for which they are created, but they can also be imported into other publications. By naming a style, you can make it available for further use. It is important to assign a descriptive name to a style in order to distinguish it from other styles that exist. **CASE** ▶ *You want to define a new style for the body text in the newsletter. You want the body text to be easy to read and to complement other text in the publication.*

STEPS

1. **Start Publisher, open** PUB E-1.pub **from the location where you store your Data Files, then save it as** PUB E-Route 66 Traveler

2. **Click the** HOME tab **on the Ribbon if necessary, click the** Styles button 🅰 **in the Styles group, then click** New Style

   The New Style dialog box opens, as shown in **FIGURE E-1**. In this dialog box, you can change the font and font size, modify the alignment of indents and lists, change the line and character spacing, adjust the tabs, and even modify the appearance of the horizontal rules.

3. **Type** 66 Body Text **in the Enter new style name text box, then click the** Font button **in the Click to change section**

4. **Click the** Font list arrow, **scroll the** font list, **click** Times New Roman, **click the** Font size list arrow, **click** 14, **then click** OK **to close the Font dialog box**

   The 66 Body Text style consists of the Times New Roman font, which is a very common type style for the body text of documents because it is easy to read, with a point size of 14.

5. **Click** Paragraph, **click the** Alignment list arrow, **click** Right, **then click** OK **to close the Paragraph dialog box**

   The sample in the New Style dialog box indicates how the new style will look, as shown in **FIGURE E-2**.

6. **Click** OK **to close the** New Style dialog box, **click anywhere in the** Route 66 Traveler text box, **click** 🅰, **scroll down to the** Font Scheme Styles area **of the Styles list, compare your list to** **FIGURE E-3**, **then press [Esc]**

   The New Style dialog box closes and the 66 Body Text style has been created.

7. **Save your work**

Choosing fonts

Font types generally fall into one of two categories: serif fonts and sans serif fonts. **Serifs** are small decorative strokes added to the end of a letter's main strokes. Serif, or Roman, types are useful for long passages of text because the serifs help distinguish individual letters and provide continuity for the reader's eye. Times New Roman and Courier are two popular serif fonts. **Sans serif** fonts are typefaces that do not have serifs. Examples include Arial or Helvetica. Sans serif faces lend a clean, simple appearance to headlines and titles but are avoided for long passages of unbroken text because they are more difficult to read than serif fonts.

FIGURE E-1: New Style dialog box

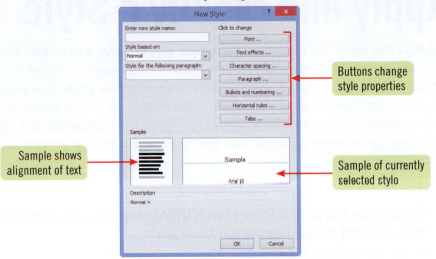

Buttons change style properties

Sample shows alignment of text

Sample of currently selected style

FIGURE E-2: Style changes appear in New Style dialog box

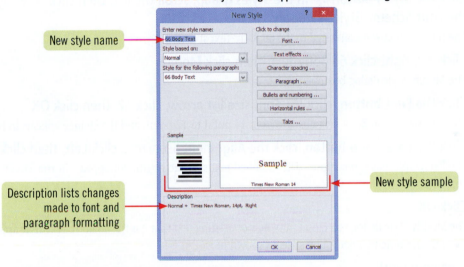

New style name

New style sample

Description lists changes made to font and paragraph formatting

FIGURE E-3: Styles list displaying new style

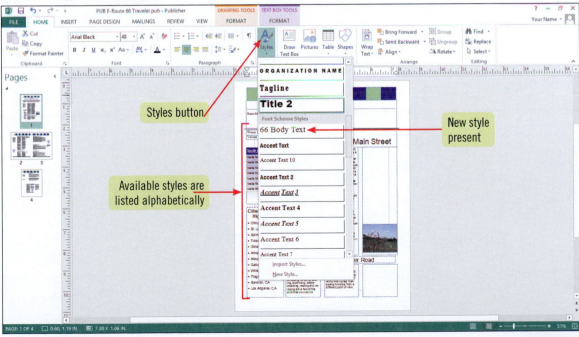

Styles button

New style present

Available styles are listed alphabetically

Image courtesy of Elizabeth Eisner Reding

Apply and Modify a Style

Applying a style is easy. You simply select the text you want to format, then click the style in the Styles list on the HOME tab. Because any style can be modified, you have the freedom to change the appearance of all the text assigned to a specific style within a publication. Once you define a style, you can apply it to text so that your publication develops a consistent look with similar attributes, or you can change the style, and the newly modified style will be applied automatically to all text that has been assigned that style. **CASE** *You decide that the font size for the style you created is too large, so you want to modify it. Then you will be ready to apply the modified style to a story.*

STEPS

1. **Click the text box at 3" H / 5" V, press [Ctrl][A], then click the Zoom In button ➕ on the status bar until 80% appears as the Zoom level**

   You can see the top and bottom of the text box.

2. **Click the Styles button 🔤 in the Styles group, scroll the list, then click 66 Body Text in the Font Scheme Styles category**

   The selected text was converted to the 66 Body Text style.

3. **Click 🔤, right-click 66 Body Text, then click Modify**

   The Modify Style dialog box opens.

4. **Click the Font button, click the Font size list arrow, click 12, then click OK**

   The font size for 66 Body Text changes from 14 point to 12 point, and the change appears in the sample.

5. **Click the Paragraph button, click the Alignment list arrow, click Left, then click OK**

   The Paragraph dialog box closes. The modified text size and alignment appears in the Modify Style dialog box, as shown in **FIGURE E-4**.

QUICK TIP
You can determine the attributes of any existing style by placing the pointer over the style name in the Styles in use palette.

6. **Click OK**

   The Modify Style dialog box closes. Any new or existing text that has the 66 Body Text style applied to it will show the modified 66 Body Text style, as shown in **FIGURE E-5**.

7. **Save your work**

FIGURE E-4: Modify Style dialog box

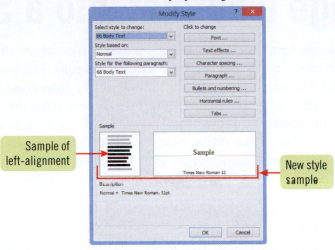

Sample of left-alignment

New style sample

FIGURE E-5: Modified style applied

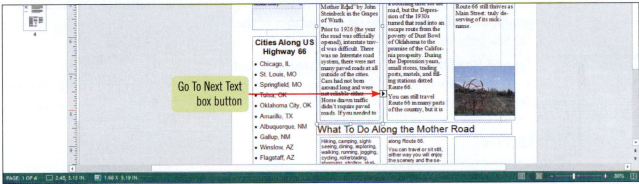

Go To Next Text box button

Image courtesy of Elizabeth Eisner Reding

Adjusting spaces between characters

Sometimes words on the page don't look quite right: They may seem packed too close together or spread too far apart. This is particularly true of typefaces at 14 points and larger. Adjusting the spacing between specific character pairs, or **kerning**, can make large text look better and be easier to read. Publisher automatically kerns characters with point sizes of 14 and larger, but you can kern any characters you choose by selecting the character pair(s) to be adjusted, right-clicking the selection, pointing to Change Text, then clicking Character Spacing. You can use the Character Spacing dialog box shown in **FIGURE E-6** to change scaling (the width of the text characters) and tracking (the distance between text characters), in addition to kerning, and the point size where automatic kerning begins. Kerning can also be controlled using the Measurement pane. The Measurement pane can be opened by clicking the Measurement button on the DRAWING TOOLS FORMAT tab in the Size group, clicking the Object Size or Object Position sections of the status bar, or clicking Show Toolbar in the Character Spacing dialog box.

FIGURE E-6: Character Spacing dialog box

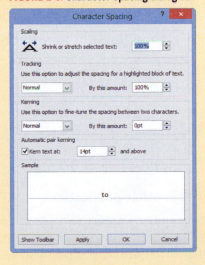

Change a Format into a Style

You can create a style from formatted text even if you don't know all the attributes that make up the appearance of the text. To do so, you create a **style by example**. First, you select the text that has the format you want to use, click New Style at the bottom of the Styles in use palette, then type a name in the Enter new style name text box. Creating a style by example makes the style available for use over and over again in the publication. This may sound similar to using the Format Painter, but there is an important difference. The Format Painter reformats selected characters according to the formatting attributes of currently selected characters, but does not store or name the set of attributes or update similarly formatted text automatically. **CASE** ▶ *You like the look of the story title and want to create a style from this format that you can use throughout the publication.*

STEPS

1. **Click anywhere in the headline Traveling America's Main Street in the text box at 3" H / 2¾" V**
   The text box containing the headline is selected.

2. **Click the HOME tab on the Ribbon if necessary, click the Styles button [A] in the Styles group, then click New Style (at the bottom of the list)**
   The New Style dialog box opens.

3. **Type 66 Heading in the Enter new style name text box**
   You entered a new name for the Style that was created from the selected text in the lead story headline. The Sample box shows you the current style's font and size as well as its alignment setting and new style name. Compare your settings to those in **FIGURE E-7**.

4. **Click OK**
   The New Style dialog box closes.

5. **Click anywhere in the Route 66 Traveler text box at 5" H / 1½" V, click [A], click New Style, type 66 Masthead in the Enter new style name text box, then click OK in the New Style dialog box**
   The new style is shown in the Styles list, and can be applied to any text in the publication.

6. **Click [A], then scroll down to the Font Scheme Styles category and verify that there are three new styles added to the list**
   Compare your Styles list to **FIGURE E-8**.

7. **Press [Esc], then save your work**

Using styles in other publications

Suppose you've created styles in one publication that you want to use in other publications. Do you have to re-create them in the new publication? No, you only need to import them. You can export styles from any Publisher or Word document (source file) and import them into the current, open publication (destination file).

To do this, display the Styles list in the destination publication, then click Import Styles. Select the source publication (or Word document) that contains the styles you want to import, then click OK. All the styles from the selected publication or document will be imported.

FIGURE E-7: New Style dialog box

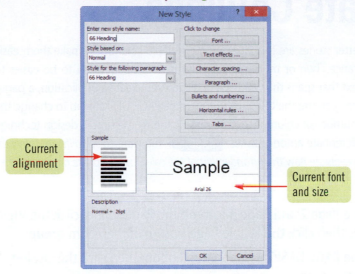

Current alignment

Current font and size

FIGURE E-8: New style names appear in Styles list

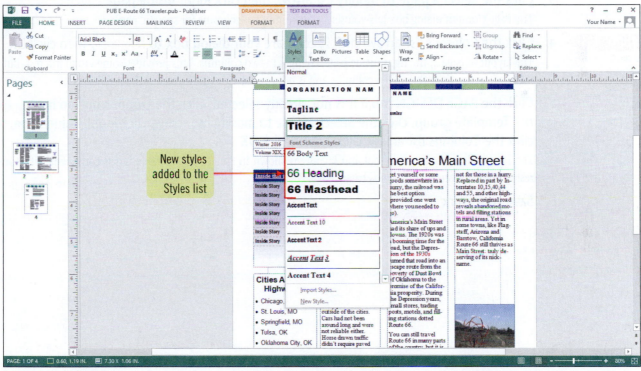

New styles added to the Styles list

Image courtesy of Elizabeth Eisner Reding

Horizontal text alignment

Text can be horizontally aligned in four ways: left-aligned so that text lines up at the left margin; right-aligned so that text lines up at the right margin; centered so that each line is equally spaced between the margins; and justified so that lines of text are balanced evenly between the right and left margins. Justified and left-aligned text are the most common settings for ordinary text. In most publications, text is left-aligned because the ragged right edge adds an element of white space, making it easier for the reader to move between lines. Some people are attracted to the neatness of text that lines up perfectly on the left and right when justified. While justified text may lend an air of formality to a publication, it requires extra attention to hyphenation and careful proofing to avoid awkward-looking gaps of white space. It does offer the advantage of letting you fit more text in the same amount of space than using left-aligned text.

Create Columns

Most newsletter stories are formatted using multiple columns to make them easier to read and to improve their appearance. Two or more narrow columns on a page tend to be easier to scan than a single wide column of text that spans the whole page. When you create a publication, a page may have a three-column layout, but you can use the Options button in the PAGE DESIGN tab to change the layout to fewer columns, or a mixed number of columns, on the same page. These simple design techniques can add visual interest and help differentiate among stories. **CASE** ▶ *You want to see different ways the columns can be arranged on page 3 to evaluate how the arrangement of the columns affects the overall design of the publication.*

STEPS

1. Click the **Page 2 and Page 3 icon** on the Pages pane, click the **VIEW tab** on the Ribbon, then click the **Whole Page button** in the Zoom group

2. Click the **PAGE DESIGN tab** on the Ribbon, then click the **Options button** in the Template group

    The Page Content dialog box opens.

3. Click the **Select a page to modify list arrow**, then click **Right inside page**

    The Page Content dialog box lets you select the number of columns for specific pages.

TROUBLE
If you get an error message that Publisher cannot complete this operation, please try Steps 2–4 again.

4. Click the **Columns list arrow**, click **2**, compare your dialog box to **FIGURE E-9**, then click **OK**

    The layout of page 3, the right inside page, changes to two columns. This provides some visual interest, but is less attractive than the mixed columns and is not consistent with the rest of the publication.

5. Click the **PAGE DESIGN tab** if it is not already selected, click the **Options button** in the Template group, click the **Select a page to modify list arrow**, click **Right inside page**, click the **Columns list arrow**, click **3**, then click **OK**

    The layout changes to a three-column layout, as shown in **FIGURE E-10**. The design is consistent with the rest of the publication and seems balanced.

6. Save your work

Using baseline guides to align columns

If you are working on a multicolumn publication and want to align multiple columns of text so they are evenly spaced, you can use baseline guides. **Baseline guides** help align text to the baseline so the text appears balanced along columns, and belong to the set of layout guides along with margin guides, column guides, and row guides. You can adjust baseline guides by clicking the PAGE DESIGN tab on the Ribbon, then clicking the Guides button in the Layout group. Click Grid and Baseline Guides on the palette to open the Layout Guides dialog box. Click the Baseline Guides tab, adjust the settings, then click OK. You can turn the baseline guides on and off by clicking the VIEW tab on the Ribbon, then clicking the Baselines check box in the Show group.

FIGURE E-9: Page Content dialog box

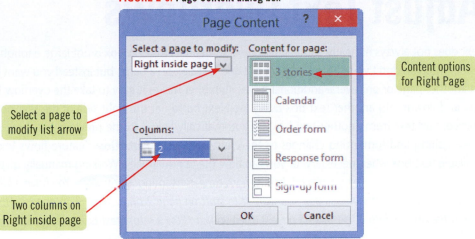

Select a page to modify list arrow

Two columns on Right inside page

Content options for Right Page

FIGURE E-10: Layout of pages with three columns

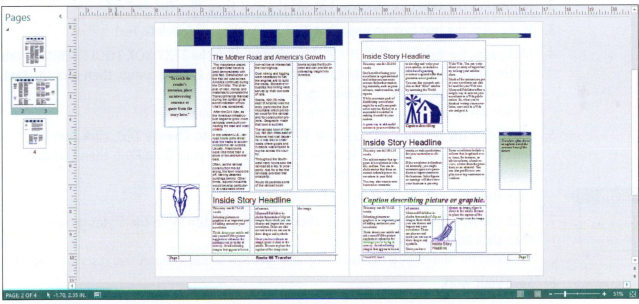

Manually creating multiple columns

The Draw Text Box button, which is available from either the HOME or INSERT tabs, creates a text box with a single column. You can add multiple columns to a text box by clicking the Columns button in the Paragraph group on the HOME tab or the Alignment group of the TEXT BOX TOOLS FORMAT tab, and then selecting the number of columns you want. The text box is then divided into multiple columns of equal width with equal space between them. The number of columns and the spacing between them can be changed using the Columns dialog box. To access the Columns dialog box, first right-click a text box, click Format Text Box, select the Text Box tab, then click the Columns button or click the Columns button in the Alignment group on the TEXT BOX TOOLS tab, then click More Columns. The Columns dialog box opens, as shown in **FIGURE E-11**.

FIGURE E-11: Columns dialog box

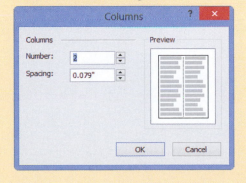

Adjust Text Overflows

Learning Outcomes
• Link text boxes
• Flow text in linked text boxes

Text does not always fit neatly within a text box. Sometimes the text box is not large enough to contain it. Sometimes you don't want a story to fit in just one text box on a page, but instead you want it to continue on another page or on several additional pages. Publisher makes it easy to take the overflow from one text box and flow it into another text box using the Next button at the right side of the text box. Text boxes that contain text from another text box are automatically linked to the previous text box, so it's easy to make editing and formatting changes to the entire story. The **Autoflow** feature flows text to the next available text box when necessary, or you can flow the text manually. Working manually gives you greater control over where the text is placed, but is more time consuming. **CASE** ▶ *You have a long story about Route 66 to insert in the newsletter. You want it to start on page 2 and continue on page 3. First you need to import the text file into a text box on page 2, then you can flow it into a text box on page 3.*

STEPS

1. Click the VIEW tab on the Ribbon, then click the Whole Page button in the Zoom group

2. Right-click the text box on page 3 at 10" H / 3" V, then click Delete Text

3. Right-click the text box on page 2 at 7" H / 9" V, then click Delete Text

4. Make sure the text box at 7" H / 9" V is selected, click the TEXT BOX TOOLS FORMAT tab on the Ribbon, click the Create Link button 🔗 in the Linking group, then click the text box on page 3 at 10" H / 2" V with 🖈

   The text box on page 3 is now linked to the text boxes at the bottom of page 2.

5. Right-click the text box on page 2 at 3" H / 9" V, point to Change Text, click Text File, select PUB E-2.docx from the location where you store your Data Files, then click OK

   Publisher automatically flows text to the next available text box.

QUICK TIP
To break a link between connected frames, click 🔗.

6. Click the text at 3" H / 9" V, then press [Ctrl][A]

7. Click the HOME tab on the Ribbon, click the Styles button 𝐴 in the Styles group, then click 66 Body Text

   The text in the entire story is changed to 12-point Times New Roman. Compare your pages to **FIGURE E-12**.

8. Save your work

FIGURE E-12: Text flowed into multiple text boxes

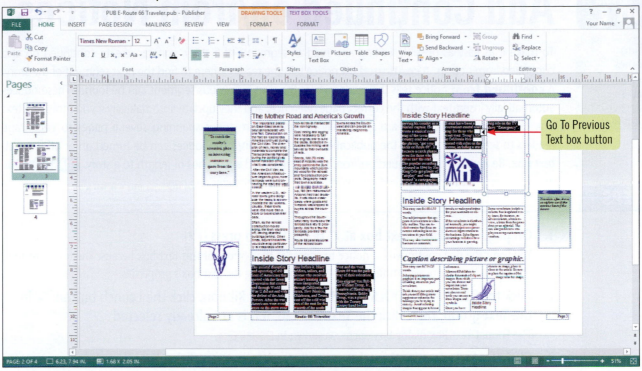

Go To Previous Text box button

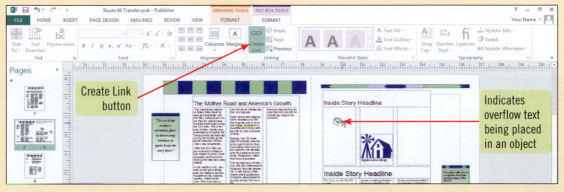

Manually linking text boxes

You can manually create links between text boxes, enabling you to continue stories in boxes that are not adjacent. To do this, you have to break the existing link between one text box and another. A link is broken by clicking one of the linked text boxes, then clicking the Break button in the Linking group on the TEXT BOX TOOLS FORMAT tab. You can create a link between text boxes by clicking the Create Link button in the Linking group. When a link is created, the pointer changes to. Position in the text box where you want the text to flow, as shown in **FIGURE E-13**, then click.

FIGURE E-13: Preparing to pour manually linked text

Create Link button

Indicates overflow text being placed in an object

Add Continued on/from Notices

To make it as easy as possible to find and read all segments of a story, you can create continued on and continued from notices. A **continued on** notice tells the reader where to find the next segment of the story. A **continued from** notice tells the reader where the story's previous segment can be found. These notices automatically insert text with the correct page reference, and they update automatically if you move the text box. Sometimes publications are specifically designed with stories spanning several pages to encourage readers to see all the pages in the publication. Continued on/from notices can be turned on or off for each text box. Be aware that continued on/from notices may add a few lines of length to a story. **CASE** *You insert continued on and continued from notices in the story that spans two pages.*

STEPS

1. **On page 2, click the text box at 7" H / 9" V, then press [F9]**

   You want the first continued on notice to appear at the bottom of this text box because the text continues on page 3. You create a continued on notice by modifying the text box's properties.

2. **Click the TEXT BOX TOOLS FORMAT tab on the Ribbon, click the Launch button ⌐ in the Text group, then click the Text Box tab, if it is not already selected**

   The Format Text Box dialog box opens, as shown in **FIGURE E-14**.

3. **Click the Include "Continued on page" check box, then click OK**

   Compare your page to **FIGURE E-15**. You want to insert a continued from notice in the text box on page 3. If a single text box is connected to both continued from and continued on text boxes, you can insert the continued on and continued from notices at the same time.

4. **Click the Go to Next Text Box button ▶ at the bottom-right edge of the text box on page 2**

   The insertion point is on page 3 at the continuation of the story. The story needs a continued from notice on page 3.

5. **Press [F9] to center the selected text box on the screen, click the Launch button ⌐ in the Text group, click the Text Box tab if necessary, click the Include "Continued from page" check box, then click OK**

   The continued from notice appears at the beginning of the text box, as shown in **FIGURE E-16**.

6. **Press [Esc] twice, then press [F9]**

7. **Save your work**

Changing the style of continued notices

If you don't like the format of a continued on or continued from notice, you can change it. Each type of continued notice has a defined style. Change the style of a continued notice by selecting the notice you want to change, making formatting modifications, clicking the Styles button in the Styles group on the HOME tab, clicking New Style on the Styles palette, entering a new name, then clicking OK in the New Style dialog box.

FIGURE E-14: Format Text Box dialog box

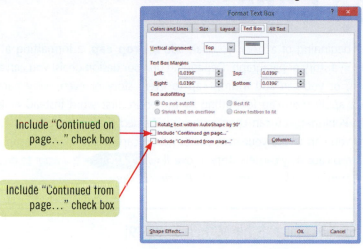

Include "Continued on page…" check box

Include "Continued from page…" check box

FIGURE E-15: Continued on notice

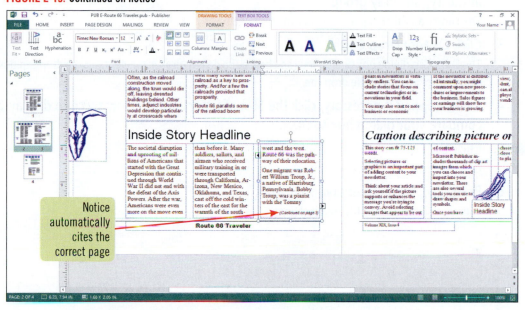

Notice automatically cites the correct page

FIGURE E-16: Continued from notice

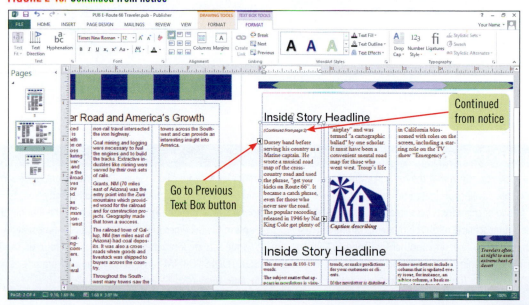

Continued from notice

Go to Previous Text Box button

Add Drop Caps

To draw attention to the beginning of a story, you can add a **drop cap**, a formatting attribute that enlarges the first character in a story or paragraph. Depending on your design goals, you can add just one drop cap to a publication, or you can add a drop cap to every story or even every paragraph in a publication. You can even apply drop cap formatting to the entire first word instead of just the first character, if you prefer. In Publisher, you can choose from predefined character types that use different fonts and line heights, or you can create your own custom drop cap. Because a drop cap adds to the length of a story, adding drop caps may cause a story to overflow. **CASE** ▶ *You want to dress up several stories using drop caps. You start by applying a drop cap to the current story.*

STEPS

1. **Click the text box on page 2 at 3" H / 9" V, then press [F9]**

> **QUICK TIP**
> The default font for the drop cap is the same as the font in the selected story.

2. **Click the TEXT BOX TOOLS FORMAT tab on the Ribbon, then click the Drop Cap button in the Typography group**

    The Drop Cap gallery appears, as shown in **FIGURE E-17**.

3. **Click Custom Drop Cap**

    The Drop Cap dialog box opens. You can change the default drop cap height, set the drop cap position, and adjust other aspects of the drop cap.

4. **Click Dropped if necessary, click the Size of letters down arrow twice to display 2, then compare your dialog box to FIGURE E-18**

> **QUICK TIP**
> Don't overuse the drop cap feature or it will seem tired and gimmicky.

5. **Click OK**

    Compare your work to **FIGURE E-19**.

6. **Press [Esc] twice, then save your work**

    Your work is saved with the modifications.

Working with font schemes and Stylistic Sets

Using a font scheme ensures that the fonts in a publication work together to create a well-coordinated result. A font scheme is a defined set of two or more fonts associated with a publication. For example, a font scheme might be made up of one font for headings, one for body text, and another for captions. Font schemes facilitate changing all the fonts in a publication to give it a new look. Within each font scheme, both a major font and a minor font are specified. Generally, a major font is used for titles and headings, and a minor font is used for body text. To use a font scheme, click the PAGE DESIGN tab on the Ribbon, then click Fonts in the Schemes group, or create a new font scheme. Stylistic Sets are located in the Typography group on the TEXT BOX TOOLS FORMAT tab and may contain from one to twenty Stylistic Sets.

FIGURE E-17: Drop Cap gallery

Indicates plain text

Click to customize drop cap

Custom Drop Cap...

FIGURE E-18: Custom Drop Cap tab in Drop Cap dialog box

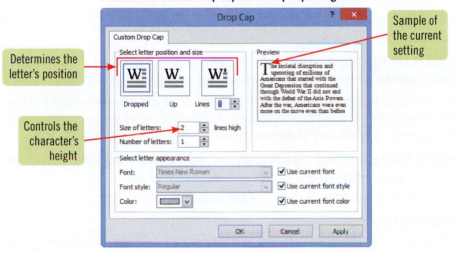

Sample of the current setting

Determines the letter's position

Controls the character's height

FIGURE E-19: Drop cap added

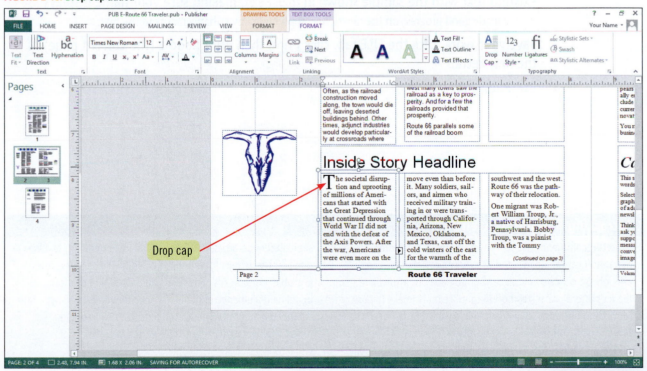

Drop cap

Create Reversed Text

A great way to emphasize selected text on a page is to create reversed text. **Reversed text** is a formatting effect that changes text from the standard look of dark characters on a light background to the more dramatic look of light characters on a dark background. Although any color combination can be used, using contrasting colors is recommended to ensure readability. In print publications, reversed text is often used in titles and headings because it is eye catching and readable in larger text sizes. In smaller text sizes, reversed text can be more difficult to read, unless you are printing at high resolutions on good-quality paper. To create this effect, you change the font color and the background fill for the text you want to reverse. **CASE** ▶ *You want to format the inside story headline at the bottom of page 2 as reversed text.*

STEPS

1. Click the Inside Story Headline text at 3" H / 7½" V

2. Type The Musical Map of Route 66
   The headline text is replaced.

3. Press [Ctrl][A], click the Font Color list arrow [A▾] in the Font group on the HOME tab, then click the Accent 5 (White) option (top row, last color)
   The text in the text box seems to disappear. When creating reverse text, the order in which you change the font color or fill color doesn't matter. Regardless of the order, when you create black and white reverse text, at some point, they will both be the same color.

4. Right-click the text box, click Format Text Box, click the Fill Color list arrow, click the Main (Black) option (top row, first color), then click OK
   The background changes to black and the text reappears.

5. Press [Esc] twice
   You can see the reversed text effect of white text on a black background. Compare your work to **FIGURE E-20**.

6. Press [F9], click the pull quote placeholder at 1" H / 3" V, press [F9], then replace the existing text with the sample shown in **FIGURE E-21**, making sure your name displays
   You've made good progress on the newsletter, applying many enhancements to the text.

7. Save your work, click the FILE tab, click Print, then print page 2 (the current page) of the newsletter

8. Exit Publisher

Attracting a reader's attention

Experts recommend that you never use more than three different fonts on a page, and usually suggest that two are enough. So how do you make your publications attract a reader's attention? Instead of using more fonts, make full use of formatting options. Use bold and italic versions of your fonts for prominence, and reverse text for a stylized headline. Use colored text for added style. Never underline type, and don't use full capitalization in ordinary text. In the past, underlining text was done on typewriters for emphasis when no alternatives were available, but now it's considered outdated and poor form. In online documents, underlined text often indicates a hyperlink in a document. With a desktop publishing program, you have the ability to attract readers with a wide variety of visual tools.

FIGURE E-20: Reversed text

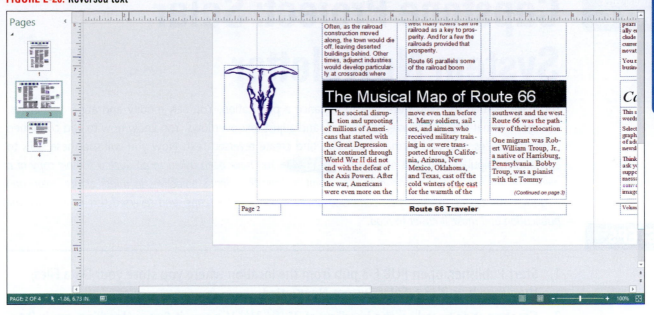

FIGURE E-21: Pull quote text

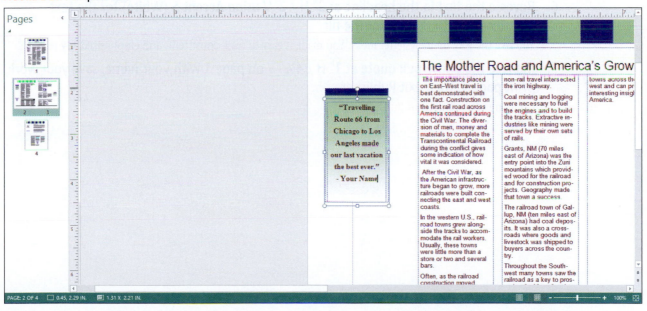

Capstone Project: Solar System Newsletter

You have learned the skills necessary to enhance a publication. You can modify and apply text styles, change a format into a style, create columns, and adjust text overflows. You know how to add continued on/from notices, add and format drop caps, and create reversed text. Now you will use these skills to add and manipulate text in a newsletter. **CASE** ▶ *You have been asked to produce a sample copy of a newsletter for a group of astronomers. You want to keep the client's objectives in mind: clarity, color, and elegance. You decide to use styles, continued on/from notices, drop caps, and reversed text to enhance the publication and make it easier to read.*

STEPS

1. Start Publisher, open **PUB E-3.pub** from the location where you store your Data Files, then save it as **PUB E-Solar System Newsletter**

2. Create a style based on the headline at **3" H / 3½" V**, name it **Space Headline**, apply it to the headline at **3" H / 8½" V**, then press **[Esc]**

3. Click the text box at **3" H / 9" V**, then insert the text file **PUB E-4.docx** and click **Yes** if asked to Autoflow text

4. Add **continued on** and **continued from** text to the inserted story

5. Add **custom drop caps** with two-line high letters to the first paragraphs of both stories on page 1

6. Reverse the **text** in the headline at **3" H / 2" V** using Accent 5 (White) for the text and Accent 1 (Dark Red) for the fill

   You like the way the newsletter looks. You made it easy to read, consistent, and emphasized key text.

7. Replace the **entire pull quote** at **1" H / 4½" V** on page 1 with your name, save your work, print page 1, then exit Publisher

   Compare your work to **FIGURE E-22**.

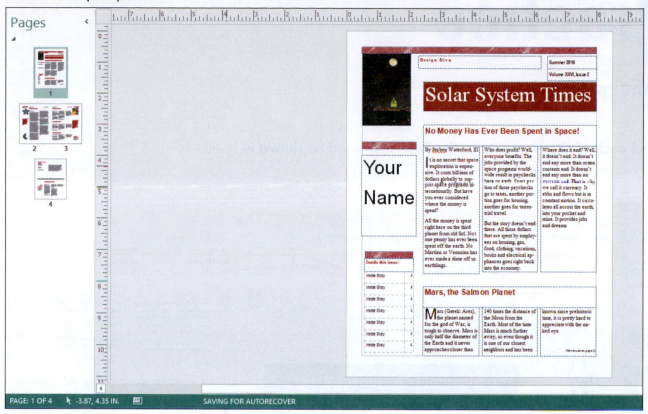

Publisher 2013

Practice

Concepts Review

Label each of the elements in the Publisher window shown in FIGURE E-23.

FIGURE E-23

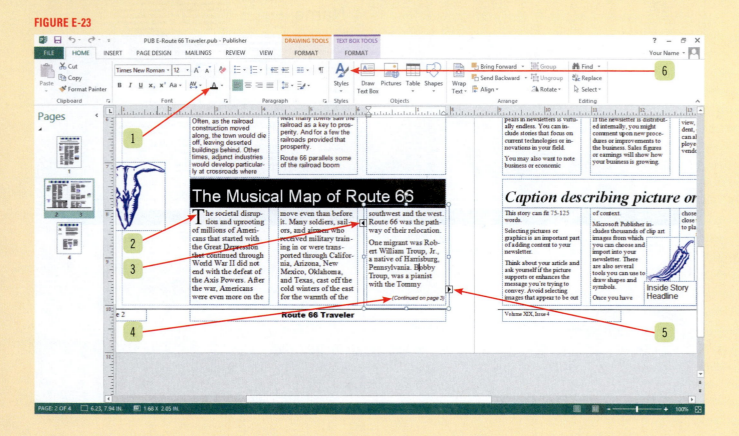

Match each of the buttons or pointers with the statement that describes its function.

7.   **a.** Go to Previous Text Box button

8.   **b.** Breaks a text box link

9.   **c.** Text in Overflow button

10.   **d.** Go to Next Text Box button

11.   **e.** Use to flow text

12.   **f.** Create Link button

Select the best answer from the list of choices.

13. Adjusting the spacing between a pair of characters is called _____.
    a. spacing
    b. kerning
    c. fonting
    d. adjusting

14. Which button indicates the existence of overflow text?
    a. ▦
    b. ∞
    c. ↺
    d. ▣

15. Which dialog box is used to create continued on/from notices?
    a. Continued Notices
    b. Notices
    c. Frame Formatting
    d. Format Text Box

16. In which dialog box can you change the spacing of columns in a text box?
    a. Text Box Characteristics
    b. Columns in Text box
    c. Columns
    d. Text Box Formatting

17. After you click the Create Link button, the pointer looks like _____.
    a. ⬇
    b. ⬆
    c. ▣
    d. ▦

18. Select the entire contents of a text box by pressing _____.
    a. [Shift][A]
    b. [Alt][A]
    c. [Ctrl][A]
    d. [Esc][A]

19. In which dialog box can you add, modify, or remove a drop cap?
    a. Drop Cap
    b. Format Text Box
    c. Fancy First Letter
    d. Spacing Between Characters

20. Changing a format into a style is called _____.
    a. Format stylization.
    b. Creating a style by example.
    c. Styling a format.
    d. Creating a format master.

21. Which button takes you to the next text box?
    a. ▣
    b. ∞
    c. ▶
    d. ⊞

22. Which pointer do you use to flow overflow text into a different text box?
    a. ⬇
    b. ⬆
    c. ⬧
    d. ↖

Skills Review

1. **Define styles.**
    a. Start Publisher.
    b. Use the BUILT-IN Templates list to create a newsletter. Select the Southwest Newsletter (in More Installed Templates), then use the Secondary Business Information Set and the Trout color scheme.
    c. Save the file as **PUB E-Guanajuato Newsletter** to the location where you store your Data Files.
    d. Create a new text style that is 18-point Franklin Gothic Demi, left-aligned.
    e. Name the new style **Southwest Headline**.
    f. Save your work.

2. **Apply and modify a style.**
    a. Click the Page 2 and Page 3 icon, then apply the Southwest Headline style to the inside story headline at 3" H / 7¾" V.
    b. Return to page 1 of the newsletter.
    c. Change the font size of the Southwest Headline style to 20 point.
    d. Change the effect of the Southwest Headline style to Offset Diagonal Bottom Right.
    e. Apply the Southwest Headline style to the Secondary Story Headline on page one.
    f. Save your work.

3. Change a format into a style.

a. Click the Lead Story Headline on page 1. Use the New Style dialog box to create a style called **Amigos Headline** that uses the same formatting.

b. Apply the Amigos Headline style to the Inside Story Headline on page 3 at 10" H / 7¾" V.

c. Save your work.

4. Create columns.

a. Open the Page Content dialog box.

b. Change the number of columns on the left inside page to a mixed-column layout, then close the dialog box.

c. Create a new style called **Amigos body text** that is left-aligned, 12-point Times New Roman.

d. Save the publication.

5. Adjust text overflows.

a. Select the text box on page 2 at 3" H / 2" V, then delete the text.

b. Above the empty text box, select the Inside Story Headline on page 2 and change it to **Guanajuato Rocks**.

c. Select the text box on page 3 at 10" H / 6" V, then delete the text.

d. Select the Inside Story Headline on page 3 at 10" H / 5" V, then change it to **Guanajuato Rocks**.

e. Select the Lead Story Headline text on page 1 at 2½" H / 3" V, then change it to **Guanajuato Rocks**.

f. Delete the text from the text box on page 1 at 3" H / 4" V, and insert the text file **PUB E-5.docx**.

g. Select the entire new story, then apply the Amigos body text style.

h. Click the Create Link button, then flow the text into the empty text box on page 2.

i. Click the Create Link button, then flow the remaining text into the empty text box on page 3.

j. Save the publication.

6. Add Continued on/from notices.

a. Add a continued on notice in the third column text box in the **Guanajuato Rocks** story on page 1.

b. Click the Go to Next Text Box button, then add a continued from notice and a continued on notice in the single column of the Guanajuato Rocks story on page 2.

c. Click the Go to Next Text Box button, then add a continued from notice in the first column of the Guanajuato Rocks story on page 3.

d. Save the publication.

7. Add drop caps.

a. Click anywhere in the first paragraph of the Guanajuato Rocks story on page 1.

b. Create a custom first letter drop cap three lines high, using the default font.

c. Save your work.

8. Create reversed text.

a. Select the contents of the Newsletter Title on page 1 at 1" H / 1½" V, and replace it with the name **Guanajuato**.

b. Change the font color to Accent 3 (RGB (153, 0, 0)) (first row, fourth color from the left).

c. Change the fill color to Main (Black).

d. Replace the text "Special Points of Interest" on page 1 at 1" H / 6¾" V with your name.

e. Save your work.

f. Submit the publication to your instructor.

g. Exit Publisher.

Independent Challenge 1

A local investment company, Finance Wizardry, wants to hold monthly seminars to help people feel more comfortable with financial instruments. They have hired you to create a brochure that announces these free seminars. You decide to use the BUILT-IN templates list to create the brochure and start planning some of the brochure style elements.

a. Start Publisher, if necessary, then create a new publication using the Slant Event Brochure from the BUILT-IN templates list. Use the Business Information set of your choosing to enter placeholder information.

b. Change the color scheme to Orchid.

c. Save the publication as **PUB E-Finance Wizardry Brochure** to the location where you store your Data Files.

d. Create a style called **Main Heading** that uses a 14-point Arial italic font and is center-aligned.

e. Apply the Main Heading style to the Main Inside Heading at 1" H / ¾" V on page 2.

f. Select the story on page 2 at 1" H / 4½" V and add a two-line custom drop cap.

g. On page 1, replace the text in the text box at 9" H / 4" V with the name **Finance Wizardry**.

h. Create a reversed text effect in the text box at 9" H / 1¾" V. Change the text to the Accent 5 (White) color. Change the fill to the Main (Black) color.

i. Substitute your name for the business name at 5" H / 6½" V. Check the spelling for all the stories.

j. Save your work and submit it to your instructor.

k. Exit Publisher.

Independent Challenge 2

To attract new homebuyers and businesses, the Chamber of Commerce hires you to create an informational Web page about your community. You use Publisher to create a document that will be used to model the Web page.

a. Start Publisher, if necessary, then open PUB E-6.pub from the location where you store your Data Files.

b. Change the color scheme to Tropics.

c. Save the publication as **PUB E-Community Promotion** to the location where you store your Data Files.

d. Create a style by example called **Homepage Headline** based on the Our Home Town Home Page headline.

e. Apply the new style to the "A Great Place To Live" headline.

f. Use your word processor to write a three- to four-paragraph story describing what you like about your community. Save this story as **PUB E-A Great Place**.

g. Delete the text in the text boxes at 2" H / 5½" V and 2" H / 2" V.

h. Insert the "PUB E-A Great Place" text file into the text box at 2" H / 2" V. Center-align the text and do not use autoflow if asked.

i. Manually pour the overflow text from the first text box into the second text box at 2" H / 5½" V.

j. Add a two-line-high custom drop cap to the first paragraph of your story.

k. Insert your name in the e-mail address at the bottom of the page.

l. Replace the text in the text box at 2½" H / 1¼" V with your city and state.

m. Check the spelling in the publication. Save and print the publication.

n. Exit Publisher.

Independent Challenge 3

Your school wants to hold a fundraiser for the local homeless shelter. You volunteer to create a flyer promoting the fundraiser.

a. Start Publisher, if necessary, and use the Mobile Flyer template (in the All Event section) from the More Installed Templates - Informational category to create a new publication. Use the Business Information set of your choice to enter your own placeholder information.

b. Choose your own color scheme.

c. Save the publication as **PUB E-Homeless Shelter Flyer** to the location where you store your Data Files.

d. Decide on a title for your fundraiser, then enter it in the text box at 2" H / 2" V.

e. Make up your own text describing the event for the text box at 5" H / 8" V.

f. Create a new style called **Fundraiser Text** using 14-point Comic Sans MS, right-aligned.

g. Apply this style to the text box at 5" H / 8" V.

h. Insert your name in the e-mail address at 1" H / 10" V.

i. Insert an appropriate piece of clip art in the blank area in the center of the flyer, then resize it if necessary. (*Hint*: If you have Internet access, you can use clip art from Online Pictures.)

j. Enter the time and date of the fundraiser in a new text box at 1½" H / 7½" V. Compare your publication to **FIGURE E-24**.

k. Apply the Cherry color scheme.

l. Adjust the spacing between two letters in the flyer title by 80%.

m. Adjust the stories to fit in their text boxes on the first page.

n. Check the spelling in the publication. Save your work and submit it to your instructor.

o. Exit Publisher.

FIGURE E-24

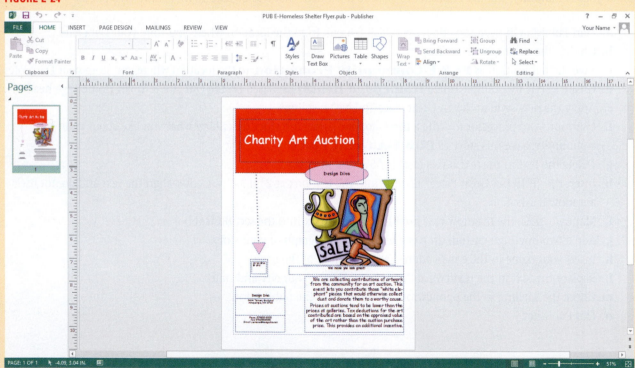

Independent Challenge 4: Explore

This Independent Challenge requires an Internet connection. BBB Road Club is organizing a bus trip to see the leaves change in New England during late September and October. They have asked you to design a promotional brochure for this event. Before you design the brochure, you want to use the Internet to find out more about the New England countryside and its foliage.

a. Connect to the Internet, then use your browser and favorite search engine to find information about the New England countryside and its foliage. You can search on the term "**leaf peepers**". Find out what towns and attractions might be of interest when the leaves are changing.

b. Start Publisher, if necessary, and use the Profile Informational Brochure (in the More Installed Templates section) from the BUILT-IN Templates list. Use the Business Information set of your choice.

c. Change to the color scheme of your choice.

d. Save the publication as **PUB E-New England Foliage Brochure** to the location where you store your Data Files.

e. Use the information you obtained from the Internet to write a four- to six-paragraph document about what to see and do in New England using a word-processing program such as Word. Save this document as **PUB E-New England Attractions** to the location where you store your Data files.

f. Replace any default text with text about New England. (You do not have to replace the placeholder images or the caption placeholders.)

g. Choose two locations on different pages for the New England Attractions document. Create additional text boxes if necessary.

h. Delete any placeholder text from the text boxes, then flow the story into the text boxes.

i. Add drop caps to the beginning of each paragraph, and add continued on/from notices where appropriate.

j. Insert your name in the e-mail address on page 2 of the publication.

k. Remove the drop caps from all but the initial paragraph on page 2.

l. Change the style of the continued on/from notices using the style-by-example method. (Use a Bold Arial 7-point font. Name the new style "New Continued-On Text." You can also create a new continued from style called "New Continued-From Text.") Compare your publication to FIGURE E-25.

m. Check the spelling in the publication.

n. Save the publication.

o. Submit your work to your instructor.

p. Exit Publisher.

FIGURE E-25

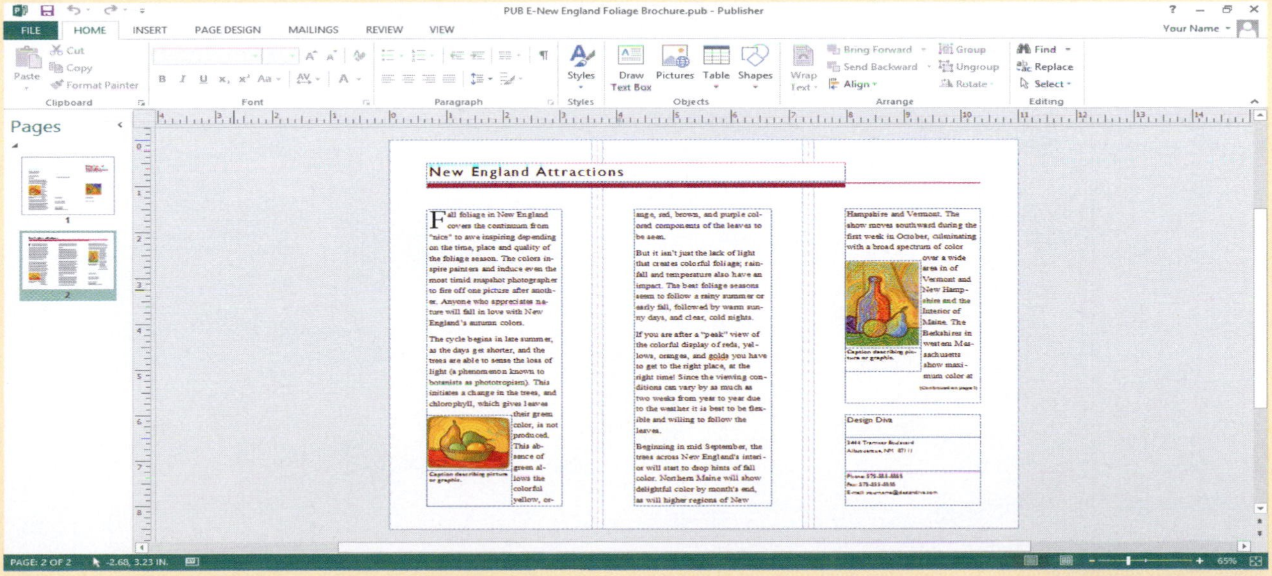

Visual Workshop

Open PUB E-7.pub from the location where you store your Data Files. Save this publication as **PUB E-SW Brochure**. Using **FIGURE E-26** as a guide, modify the styles and add additional formatting as necessary so your publication matches the one shown. Save the publication, then print it.

Images courtesy of Elizabeth Eisner Reding

FIGURE E-26

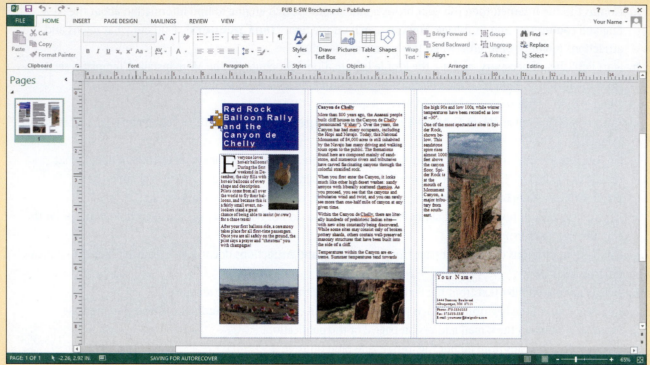

Improving a Design

CASE ▶ The nonprofit organization Global Parenting is a Design Diva client. You have been assigned the task of reviewing their in-house monthly newsletter and improving its design.

Unit Objectives

After completing this unit, you will be able to:

- Critique a publication
- Strengthen publication text
- Rearrange elements
- Modify objects

- Refine a page
- Experiment with design elements
- Capstone Project: Flower Shop Flyer

Files You Will Need

PUB F-1.pub	PUB F-4.pub
PUB F-2.pub	PUB F-5.pub
PUB F-3.pub	PUB F-6.pub

©Alena P/Shutterstock

Critique a Publication

Casting a critical eye toward someone's work can be challenging for both the reviewer and the designer. Some of us feel uncomfortable criticizing someone else's work and even more uncomfortable when that criticism is directed at our own work. But when done constructively, critiquing can be a positive learning experience for everyone involved. Many of us learn best by having our mistakes pointed out, and then making corrections. The way we respond to design is a highly subjective process, but some fundamental principles can be applied to any critiquing process. Examining the strengths and weaknesses of another person's work can be a helpful method of refining a publication so that it looks professional and achieves its goals. It can also help you develop a more constructive eye toward your own designs. As you learn to critique designs, you may find that the most effective designs are the simplest. **CASE** ▶ *You are ready to review the client's in-house monthly newsletter,* Creative Parent. *You review a previous version of the newsletter shown in* **FIGURE F-1** *and think about the critiquing process.*

DETAILS

• **Take in all the elements**

To get started, ask yourself a series of questions that determines the purpose of a particular page and whether the arrangement of elements helps achieve that goal. These questions include: To what elements are your eyes drawn? Where is the text? Is the text legible? Are any/all of the elements on the page necessary? Are any elements distracting? Are any of the elements lacking in impact? In **FIGURE F-1**, your eyes may be drawn to the central graphic and the blue text box because of their size, position, and color. Unfortunately, the contrast between the text and the dark blue in the box makes the text difficult to read. The caption is split into two parts by the central graphic, making it difficult to comprehend the safety message. While the masthead is attractive, the lack of color makes it appear lost. Also, the elongated table of contents distracts the eye from the image of the children and the crossing guard.

• **Decide what is important**

Every publication has a goal to achieve or a message to communicate. Each page should support the publication's overall goal. While the message of this issue of *Creative Parent* is children and safety, the goal of a particular page may be getting readers to read the executive director's article on the topic. During the critiquing process, you should continually ask yourself whether the design achieves the goal—and if not, why not. What's getting in the way? What needs to be changed, removed, or strengthened to reach your audience and guide them toward important information?

• **Share the message with the reader**

As the designer, your focus is on assembling various visual elements—graphic images, text, or tables—that share the message with the reader. **FIGURE F-2** shows a preliminary rearrangement of the cover elements. In this design, the central element is the children and the crossing guard. This graphic has been cropped to eliminate unnecessary imagery. By rearranging the elements on the page, the message of children and safety is featured more prominently. Using white space and eliminating or refining distracting elements, such as the blue text box and the table of contents, guide the reader's eye to focus on the central image.

• **Keep it simple**

Microsoft Publisher offers so many exciting and interesting design elements that it's often tempting to use as many objects from the Building Blocks library and the Design Gallery as possible. Such overindulgence can lead to a cluttered, ineffective design that will not help readers see the whole message, and they may miss the point entirely. The best approach is to choose a few key elements that convey the message, then feature those items prominently. In the redesigned cover, there is only one central design object. The reader is free to read the text beneath the image, but it is not necessary to understanding the safety message.

FIGURE F-1: Initial cover art

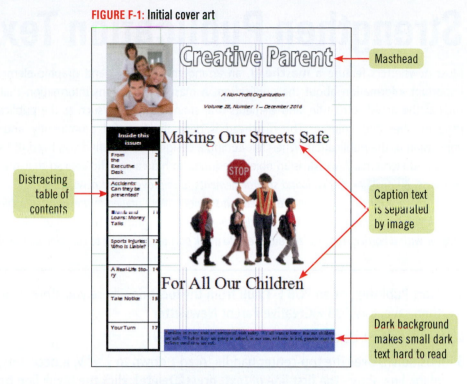

Masthead

Distracting table of contents

Caption text is separated by image

Dark background makes small dark text hard to read

FIGURE F-2: Revised cover art

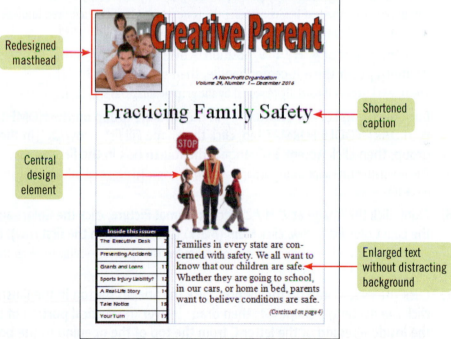

Redesigned masthead

Shortened caption

Central design element

Enlarged text without distracting background

Images of family and school children © Photodisc/Getty Images

Using diplomacy

How do you tell people that their work could use some improvement? People's designs are a reflection of their own opinions about what makes an effective and attractive publication. Therefore, it isn't easy to tell people why and how their publications could be improved, and you must be sensitive to their feelings when delivering feedback. You may be able to minimize hurting someone's feelings by involving the person whose work you're critiquing in the solution phase. If you make the changes yourself, or instruct someone else to, not only will you create friction in the workplace, but the original author may be offended and will have learned nothing in the process. By working with people to help them revise their work, they will benefit from maintaining control over it and will learn some important design concepts in the process.

Strengthen Publication Text

Learning Outcomes
- Reposition and arrange objects to improve design
- Hide unwanted imagery with a mask

Most newsletters feature a **masthead**, an arrangement of text and graphic elements that provide important information about the publication. A masthead contains information that rarely changes, such as the newsletter's title, and elements that change regularly, such as the publication date or the issue number and volume. The masthead is generally featured prominently and provides a first impression of the publication. When fine-tuning a design, you may find you need to use a mask to hide unwanted elements. A **mask** is an object designed to hide a specific area so that the final result looks seamless. **CASE** ▶ *You've found several elements to improve in the newsletter. First, you want to modify the masthead so the graphic and text create a stronger, more unified impression. To achieve this, you want the title to be more prominent and to overlap slightly with the graphic. You want to call more attention to the graphic with a border, and realize you'll need to mask part of the border to combine all the elements smoothly.*

STEPS

1. Start Publisher, open **PUB F-1.pub** from the location where you store your Data Files, then save it as **PUB F-Creative Parent Newsletter**

QUICK TIP
Use the horizontal and vertical scroll bars to center the masthead on the screen, if necessary.

2. Click the text box at **4" H / 2½" V**, then press **[F9]**

3. Position ⌖ over the **top-center handle**, drag ↕ down to **2½" V**, if necessary, click the **blank line above the first line of text**, press **[Delete]**, click the **blank line beneath the text A Non-Profit Organization**, press **[Delete]**, then press **[Esc]** twice

    You have resized the text box containing the issue information and removed unnecessary blank lines; the text box is now in better proportion to the elements around it. See **FIGURE F-3**.

4. Click the **object** at **4" H / 1" V**, position ⌖ over the **bottom-center handle**, drag ↕ to **1¾" V**, position ⌖ over the **left-center handle**, then drag ⟺ to **2¼" H**

    The title is larger and partially obscured by the graphic image, as shown in **FIGURE F-4**.

QUICK TIP
WordArt is a feature that lets you create stylized text. It will be covered in more detail in Unit H.

5. Click the **Bring Forward button** 🔳 in the Arrange group on the HOME tab, click the **WORDART TOOLS FORMAT tab**, click the **Shape Fill list arrow** in the WordArt Styles group, then click **Accent 3 (Orange)** (the fourth box in the first row)

    The newsletter title appears to overlap part of the image. The colorful title has more impact than using the black text.

6. Right-click the **image** at **2" H / 2" V**, click **Format Picture**, click the **Colors and Lines tab**, click the **Line Color list arrow**, click **Main (Black)** (the first box in the first row), then click **OK**

    The masthead image is surrounded by a black border. The black line visible between the "C" and the "r" in the title can be hidden using a mask.

QUICK TIP
You can more accurately reposition a selected object by pressing the arrow keys (◄, ▲, ►, or ▼).

7. Click the **INSERT tab** on the Ribbon, click the **Shapes button** in the Illustrations group, click the **Rectangle shape** ▢, then drag ╋ over the vertical portion of the black line at the inside opening of the letter C from the top of the opening to the bottom of the opening to create a narrow rectangle that surrounds the segment of the line

8. Right-click the **rectangle**, click **Format AutoShape**, click the **Line Color list arrow**, click **No Outline**, click the **Fill Color list arrow**, click **Accent 5 (White)** (the eighth box in the first row), then click **OK**

    The rectangle acts like a patch: It was formatted to blend into the background and is positioned between the text and the graphic image.

9. Press **[Esc]** to deselect the rectangle, then save your work

    Compare your masthead to **FIGURE F-5**.

FIGURE F-3: Resized text box

Smaller text box reflects decreased importance

FIGURE F-4: Enlarged title

Masthead text partially hidden

FIGURE F-5: Redesigned masthead

Mask hides line from object box

Images of family and school children © Photodisc/Getty Images

Examining the components

Because critiquing an entire publication can be overwhelming, you may find it helpful to examine its individual components. In the case of a newsletter cover, the components include the masthead, the artwork and text, and the table of contents. Within the masthead, you can consider the size, appearance, and placement of the newsletter title and artwork, and the size and placement of other text boxes. On inside pages, the elements to consider can include the number of stories, related artwork, and the surrounding white space. When a page is viewed in its entirety, it can be difficult to spot specific strengths and weaknesses. Looking at individual elements on a page, however, can make it easier to locate and refine problem areas, so that the end result is a cohesive, powerful publication.

Rearrange Elements

The appearance of elements on a page is important, but of equal importance is the way in which the elements are arranged. The components of any page should form a cohesive unit so that the reader is unaware of all the different parts, yet influenced by the way they work together to emphasize a message or reveal information. For example, if a large image is used, it should be easy for the reader to connect the image with any descriptive text. Design should offer an easily understood connection between the text and the artwork, and the reader should be able to seamlessly connect them. **CASE** ▶ *You want to rearrange the elements so that the table of contents is smaller and the title for the story on page 1 is more concise and eye-catching.*

STEPS

1. **Press [F9], click the table at 1" H / 3½" V, then drag the top-center sizing handle ↕ down to 7⅜" V**

   The table is reduced in size, which opens up the left side of the page. (The text in the table of contents will be revised at a later date.)

2. **Right-click For All Our Children at 4" H / 8½" V, then click Delete Object**

   Compare your screen to **FIGURE F-6**.

3. **Click Making Our Streets Safe at 3" H / 3½" V, place ⟺ on the left-center handle, then drag ⟺ left to ½" H**

4. **Right-click anywhere in the Making Our Streets Safe text box, then click Best Fit**

   The text is selected and enlarged. The location of this text is now at the optical center of the page. The **optical center** occurs approximately three-eighths from the top of the page and is the point around which objects on the page are balanced.

5. **Press [Ctrl][A], type Practicing Family Safety, then press [Esc] twice**

   The new title has been automatically resized to fit the text box and better expresses the message of the cover. Compare your work to **FIGURE F-7**.

6. **Save your work**

FIGURE F-6: Text box deleted

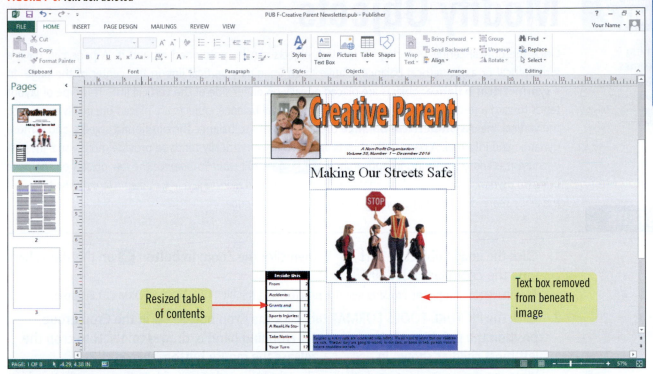

Resized table of contents

Text box removed from beneath image

FIGURE F-7: Title text completed

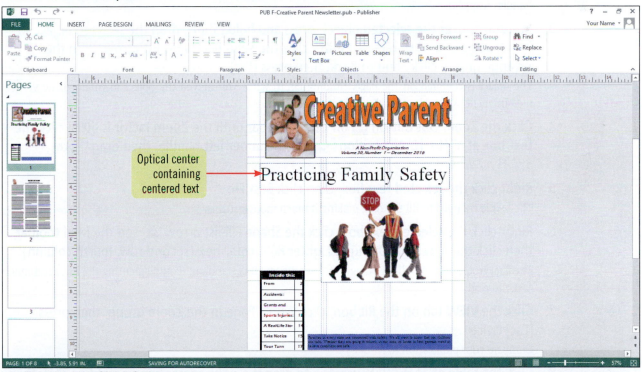

Optical center containing centered text

Images of family and school children © Photodisc/Getty Images

Overcoming the fear of white space

What is the most important difference between the file open now and the one opened at the beginning of this unit? White space. The best example of the use of white space is margins surrounding a page. This white space acts as a visual barrier—a resting place for the eyes. Without white space, the words on a page would crowd into each other, and the effect would be a cluttered, ugly page.

Using white space makes it possible for you to guide the reader's eye from one location on the page to another. One of the first design hurdles that must be overcome is the irresistible urge to put too much *stuff* on a page. When you are new to design, you may want to fill each page completely. Remember, less is more. Think of white space as a beautiful frame setting off an equally beautiful image.

Modify Objects

Learning Outcomes
- Crop an image
- Enhance page design with object placement

Once the optical center of a page is located, objects can be positioned around it. A page can have a symmetrical or asymmetrical balance relative to an imaginary vertical line in the center of the page. In a **symmetrical balance**, objects are placed equally on either side of the vertical line. This type of layout tends toward a restful, formal design. In an asymmetrical balance, objects are placed unequally relative to the vertical line. **Asymmetrical balance** uses white space to balance the positioned objects, and is more dynamic and informal. A page with objects arranged asymmetrically tends to provide more visual interest because it is more surprising in appearance. **CASE** *You want to balance the few objects on the page using an asymmetrical layout. You want to crop the image and rearrange a few elements to make better use of the white space. You begin by zooming into the image on the page.*

STEPS

1. **Click the image object at 5" H / 5" V, then click the Zoom In button on the status bar until the Zoom factor is 100%**
   The image containing the crossing guard is selected, and the PICTURE TOOLS FORMAT tab appears.
2. **Click the PICTURE TOOLS FORMAT tab, click the Crop button in the Crop group, position the pointer over the left-center cropping handle, drag to 4⅛" H to crop the left-most child as shown in FIGURE F-8, release the mouse button, then click**
   When the cropping tool is turned off, the girl on the left is no longer visible in the image and the object handles reappear.
3. **Position over the selected object, press and hold [Shift], drag the selected object so its left edge is at 3" H, release [Shift], click the Send Backward list arrow in the Arrange group, click Send to Back, then press [Esc]**
   The object is centered on the page. Holding [Shift] while you moved the object maintained the vertical measurement as you changed the horizontal position.
4. **Click the Zoom Out button on the status bar until the Zoom factor is 60%, click the text box at 5" H / 10" V, position over the upper-left handle, then drag to 3⅛" H / 7¾" V**
5. **Right-click the selected text box, then click Best Fit**
   The text is enlarged to fill the box, making it much more readable.
6. **Right-click the selected text box, click the Shape Fill list arrow on the Mini toolbar, then click the Accent 3 (Orange), Lighter 80% color box (second row, fourth column)**
   The background is now a light orange, making the text box stand out (complementing the title) and much easier to read.
7. **Click the VIEW tab on the Ribbon, click Whole Page in the Zoom group, then press [Esc] twice**
   Compare your publication to FIGURE F-9.
8. **Click the table at 1" H / 9" V, use to drag the right-center handle right to 3" H, then press [Esc]**
   The table width is increased, making it easier to read. Your screen should look like FIGURE F-10.
9. **Save your work**

FIGURE F-8: Image cropped

Cropped image outline

FIGURE F-9: Text box improved

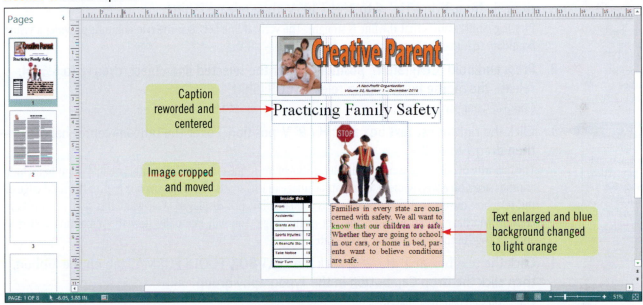

Caption reworded and centered

Image cropped and moved

Text enlarged and blue background changed to light orange

FIGURE F-10: Objects moved and resized

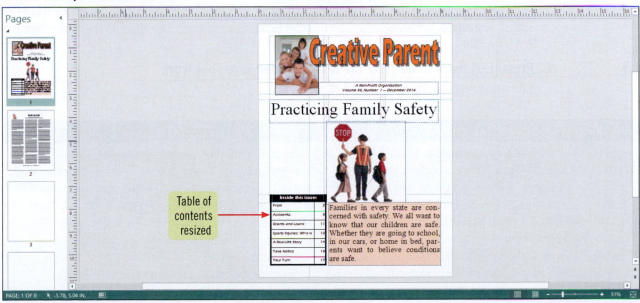

Table of contents resized

Images of family and school children © Photodisc/Getty Images

Refine a Page

The goal of page design is getting readers to read each story. Pages that contain nothing but text can be mind-numbing and overwhelming, causing readers to quit before finishing the story. To encourage readers to continue, you can break up the monotony of a large story with graphics, photographs, and other design elements. You can also split a story into multiple text boxes on two or more pages. The executive director of *Creative Parent* wrote an important article that will be featured in this issue. The current layout has this story occupying the entire second page. **CASE** ▶ *You decide to refine this page by adding vertical lines between the columns, splitting the story onto multiple pages, and formatting the story with a drop cap. You start by drawing the column lines on the page.*

STEPS

1. **Click the Page 2 icon on the Pages pane, click the INSERT tab on the Ribbon, click the Shapes button in the Illustrations group, click the Line shape** ◻, **press and hold [Shift], drag** ┼ **from 3" H / 1½" V to 3" H / 10" V, then release [Shift]**

   Pressing [Shift] assures that the line is straight. The vertical line between the two columns provides a visual boundary that makes the column text easier to read.

2. **Press and hold [Ctrl] [Shift], position** ▷ **over the selected line object, drag** ▷ **to 5½" H, release the mouse button, then release [Ctrl] [Shift]**

   Compare your page to **FIGURE F-11**.

3. **Click the right-most text box at 7" H / 9" V, position** ↕ **over the bottom-center handle, then drag** ↕ **to 3" V**

   The majority of column 3 is now available, as shown in **FIGURE F-12**. At a later date, you may want to include another story, an advertisement, or a graphic image in this space. The overflow box ▣ on the right edge of the text box means that additional text is available but not displayed. You want this text to stop here because you have other plans for the rest of this page. You will manually flow the remaining text into another page of the newsletter at a later date.

4. **Click the text box at 2" H / 2" V, click the TEXT BOX TOOLS FORMAT tab on the Ribbon, then click the Drop Cap button in the Typography group**

   The Drop Cap palette displays.

5. **Click Drop Cap Style 1 (first row, second column)**

   The drop cap appears in the first paragraph of the story. The addition of this feature caused the text to be slightly rearranged, but because there are no other elements on this page, the effect on the current layout is not important.

6. **Press [Esc] twice to deselect the text box, then save your work**

   Compare your publication to **FIGURE F-13**.

Working with advertisements

Publications often depend on advertising dollars to defray costs and increase profits. So it's in a publisher's interest to display ads in a manner that will gain the greatest exposure. That's one reason stories usually are not laid out in one continuous text box, with ads lumped together in another section. If a reader turns through several pages to finish reading a story, he or she is more likely to see the ads that are interspersed with editorial content. This means that advertising artwork can become an integral part of page layout.

Your advertisers and your readers want clever, attractive ads that consumers will remember. In many cases, your advertisers will give you camera-ready artwork. This artwork is complete and only needs to be included in the layout. The good news is that you don't have to do the work of designing the advertisement. The bad news is that you often have no say in terms of the ad's appearance or design values. In most publications, the cost of running an advertisement is determined by size, color, and placement on the page.

FIGURE F-11: Vertical lines between columns

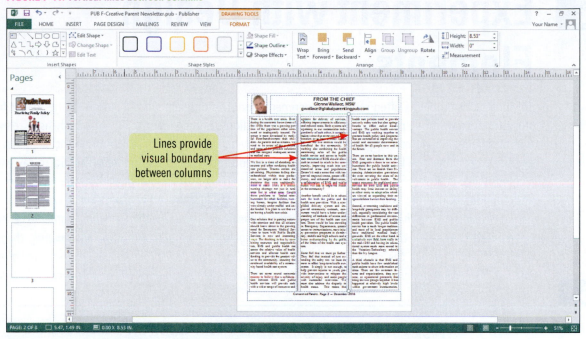

Lines provide visual boundary between columns

FIGURE F-12: Text box shortened

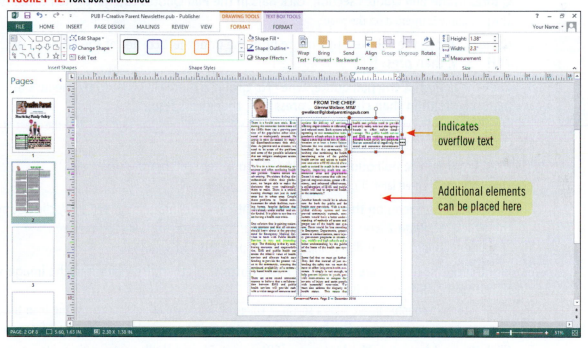

Indicates overflow text

Additional elements can be placed here

FIGURE F-13: Drop cap added

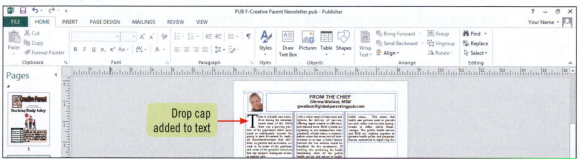

Drop cap added to text

Images of family, school children, and manager © Photodisc/Getty Images

Improving a Design

Experiment with Design Elements

Learning Outcomes
- Create and relocate a pull quote
- Move an object to the scratch area

Solving layout problems often requires experimentation. Design elements should guide the reader from story to story, without providing unnecessary distractions. Some design elements, such as a relevant graphic image or an interesting advertisement, can provide a nice mental break. Among the elements you can use to enhance the layout of a page are pictures, drop caps, and pull quotes. It's hard to say which element will best improve a particular page; sometimes you must experiment with a variety of elements and configurations until you find the layout that works. **CASE** *You want to experiment with several design elements to see which ones look most effective in the new space in the third column. In order to generate the reader's interest, you'd also like to extract a compelling sentence from the story, modify it slightly, then use it as a pull quote. Finally, this page seems to need some color so you decide to include a health-related graphic image. The previous designer placed a piece of clip art on page 5 that you think will complement this article.*

STEPS

1. **Verify that page 2 is the active page, click the INSERT tab on the Ribbon, click the Page Parts button in the Building Blocks group, click More Page Parts, click All Pull Quotes in the Pull Quotes section, click Bars in the Pull Quotes category, then click Insert**
   The pull quote is inserted on the page.

2. **Using ⬚, move the selected pull quote until the upper-left corner of the object is at 2" H / 3" V, then press [F9]**

3. **Click the center of the pull quote, type "No group is more devastated by the lack of medical attention than children.", press [F9], then press [Esc]**
   Compare your page to **FIGURE F-14**. The text box is still selected, but you're not sure you like the effect of this element because the page still looks busy.

4. **Use ⬚ to drag the pull quote to 10" H / 3" V on the scratch area**
   The object can be used later, if necessary.

5. **Click the Page 5 icon on the Pages pane, right-click the image at 7" H / 9" V, click Copy, then click the Page 2 icon on the Pages pane**
   The clip art is on the Clipboard and can be pasted on page two.

6. **Right-click the scratch area, click the Paste button 🗋, then use ⬚ to drag the image so that its upper-left corner is at 2" H / 4" V**
   You feel that the graphic image adds a splash of color to the page and looks more inviting than the pull quote, as shown in **FIGURE F-15**. This page is far from finished, but you are done working on it for now.

7. **Click the text box at 4" H / 1" V, press [F9], select Glenna Wallace, type Your Name, press [Esc] twice, then press [F9]**

8. **Save your work, submit your work to your instructor, then exit Publisher**

FIGURE F-14: Pull quote in story

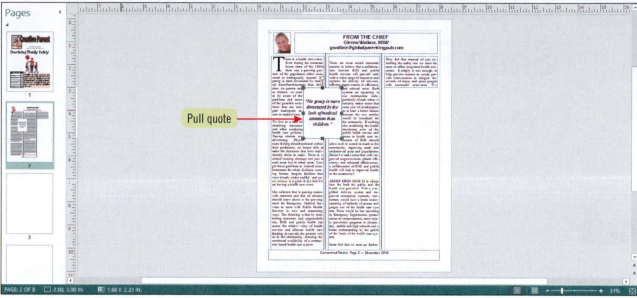

Pull quote

Images of family, school children, and manager © Photodisc/Getty Images

FIGURE F-15: Image in story

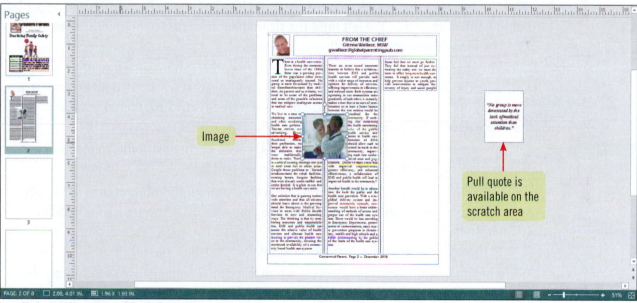

Image

Pull quote is available on the scratch area

Images of family, school children, and manager © Photodisc/Getty Images
Image of doctor © Digital Vision/Getty Images

Using contrast to add emphasis

Contrast is an important design principle that provides variety in the physical layout of a page and publication. Just as you can use a font attribute to make some text stand out from the rest, you can use contrasting elements to make certain graphic objects stand out. You can create contrast in many ways, like

- changing the sizes of objects
- varying object weights, such as making a line heavier surrounding an image

- altering the position of an object, such as changing the location on the page, or rotating the image so it is positioned on an angle
- drawing attention-getting shapes or a colorful box behind an object that makes it stand out (called a **matte**), or
- adding carefully selected colors that emphasize an object.

Capstone Project: Flower Shop Flyer

You have learned how to critique a publication, strengthen publication text to grab your reader's attention, rearrange elements so they work together effectively, and work with objects and page layouts to create a professional publication. **CASE** *You are asked by the owner of a flower shop to critique a problematic flyer. The flyer is for a newly opened flower shop, and the owner wants to offer a 30 percent discount on annuals during the grand-opening celebration. The initial publication is colorful, but it is disorganized and fails to promote the discount. In critiquing the flyer, you find that the border of roses distracts from the text and central object in the flyer. You start improving this design by removing the border of roses.*

STEPS

1. Start Publisher, open PUB F-2.pub from the location where you store your Data Files, then save it as PUB F-Flower Shop Flyer

    Compare your flyer to FIGURE F-16.

2. Click the graphic object at 7" H / 4" V, press [Delete], then delete the objects at 2" H / 3½" V, 2" H / 8½" V, and 6½" H / 8½" V

3. Click the bouquet at 5" H / 5" V, press and hold [Ctrl], then use ⬃ to drag the upper-left sizing handle up and to the left until the sizing handle snaps to the ruler guides at 1½" H / 2½" V, then release [Ctrl]

4. Click the text box at 4" H / 7" V, use ⬚ to drag the object so that its upper-left corner is at the guides at 1½" H / 8" V, select the date and time text, click the Bold button **B** on the Mini toolbar, change the font size of the selected text to 20, then press [Esc]

    The repositioned text box and the contrasting text are more attractive.

    > **QUICK TIP**
    > You can resize the text box or use a smaller point size if all the text doesn't fit.

5. Click the text box at 2" H / 2" V, press [Ctrl][A] to select the text, type Your Name's Flowers, press [Enter], then type Grand Opening and Sale

6. Press [Ctrl][A], click the Center button ≡ in the Paragraph group on the HOME tab, select the text Your Name's Flowers, click the Font Size list arrow 10 ⌄ on the Mini toolbar, then click 48

    The text now looks balanced, and the name of the shop is more prominent.

7. Click the Shapes button in the Objects group, click the Rectangle shape ▢, drag + from 1" H / 1" V to 7½" H / 8" V, right-click the object, click the Shape Outline list arrow on the Mini toolbar, scroll down in the color palette, click No Outline, click the Shape Fill list arrow on the Mini toolbar, click the Accent 3 (RGB(204, 204, 235)) color box (first row, fourth column), click the Send Backward list arrow in the Arrange group on the DRAWING TOOLS FORMAT tab, click Send to Back, then press [Esc]

8. Click the INSERT tab on the Ribbon, click Advertisements in the Building Blocks group, click More Advertisements, scroll down to Coupons, click Open Background, click Insert, modify the text to advertise Featured Annuals at 30% OFF with the flower shop name and address shown in the flyer, then delete the expiration date and modify the size and placement of the object as shown in FIGURE F-17

    Your design changes have resulted in a stronger flyer that is sure to capture the attention of potential customers.

9. Save your work, submit your work to your instructor, then exit Publisher

FIGURE F-16: Existing flyer

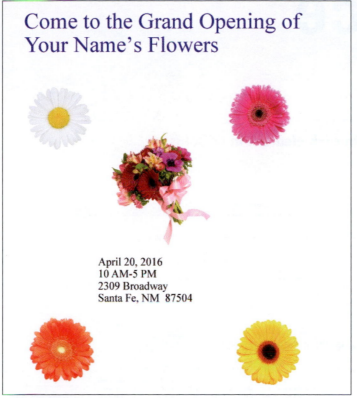

Come to the Grand Opening of
Your Name's Flowers

April 20, 2016
10 AM-5 PM
2309 Broadway
Santa Fe, NM 87504

Image of bouquet © Photodisc/Getty Images
Images of flowers © E+/Getty Images

FIGURE F-17: Modified flyer

Your Name's Flowers
Grand Opening and Sale

April 20, 2016
10 AM-5 PM
2309 Broadway
Santa Fe, NM 87504

Featured Annuals
30% OFF
Your Name's Flowers
2309 Broadway, Santa Fe, NM 87504
Tel: 555 555 5555

Image of bouquet © Photodisc/Getty Images

Practice

Concepts Review

Identify the design flaw in each element in FIGURE F-18.

FIGURE F-18

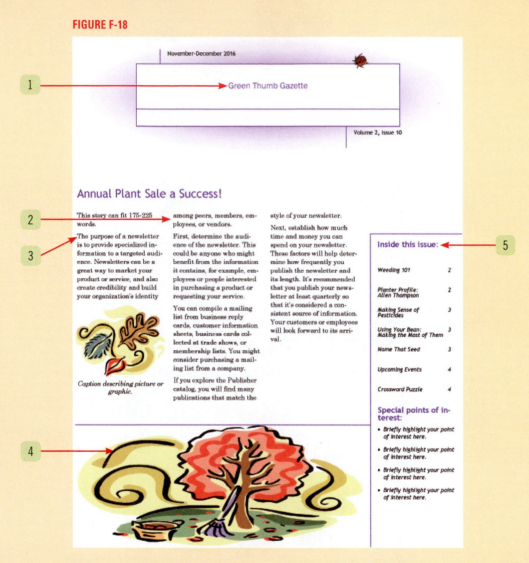

Match each of the design flaws noted below with a solution.

6. The publication looks monotonous and boring

7. Stories that span several pages have no reference to where the next part of the story is located

8. Columns of text run together

9. Too many design elements on the page

a. Add a visual boundary

b. Insert continued on/continued from notices

c. Increase the amount of white space

d. Add contrast, such as a matte, to the publication

Select the best answer from the list of choices.

10. In asymmetrical balance, the elements on a page are _____.
    a. placed equally on either side of the vertical line
    b. grouped near the center of the page
    c. placed unequally on either side of the vertical line
    d. placed in the white space

11. _____ is an important design principle that provides variety in a physical layout.
    a. Contrast
    b. Symmetrical balance
    c. White space
    d. Diplomacy

12. Which of the following is *not* an example of white space?
    a. Margins
    b. Space between lines of text
    c. Space around a graphic
    d. Lines separating columns of text

13. A consistent arrangement of text and graphic elements that appears at the top of each issue of a publication is called a _____.
    a. mask
    b. matte
    c. masthead
    d. mark

14. Which of the following is *not* true about working with advertisers?
    a. They may give you camera-ready artwork to place.
    b. They help support your publication financially.
    c. The cost of running an advertisement is determined by its size, amount of colors, and placement in the publication.
    d. Ads are most likely to be read when grouped together on a single page.

15. Placing objects equally on either side of an imaginary vertical line in the center of the page is called _____.
    a. asymmetrical objectivity
    b. asymmetrical balance
    c. symmetrical balance
    d. symmetrical positioning

16. The optical center occurs where on the page?
    a. Three-eighths from the top
    b. In the center of the publication
    c. Three-eighths from the bottom
    d. Upper-right corner

Skills Review

1. **Critique a publication.**
   a. Start Publisher, open **PUB F-3.pub** from the location where you store your Data Files, then save it as **PUB F-Daily Specials Menu**. Throughout this exercise, zoom in and out as necessary.
   b. Take a look at each visual element on the page. Determine where the focal points are and whether there are any unnecessary or distracting elements on the page. Find three things you would change to improve the publication.
   c. Create a text box on page 2 that includes your thoughts on what the goals of the publication are and how well you think the publication meets the goals.
   d. Create a second text box on page 2, type **Critiquing the publication**, then write your three improvements and how you would implement them.

2. **Strengthen publication text.**
   a. Think about how you can use what you've learned about effective design to strengthen text in the menu.
   b. Move the text boxes for the name of the restaurant, the text **Daily Specials**, and the text box that includes the date (in this order) up near the top of the page. Leave a 2" margin between the top of the page and the restaurant name text box. Leave a 3½" margin between the left edge of the page and the three text boxes.
   c. Delete the graphic in the upper-right corner of page 1, then increase the size of the graphic in the upper-left corner of the page to approximately 2¾" H × 2¾" V.
   d. BestFit the text containing the restaurant name, left-align the text in the text box, then change the font color from black to a livelier color.
   e. Adjust the size of the text box to a narrower width as necessary.

f. Increase the font size of the **Daily Specials** menu item text to 14 point, if necessary, left-align the text in the text box, then make it the same font and font color as the restaurant name.

g. Increase the font size of the date text to 12 point, and make it the same font but a different font color than the restaurant name. Adjust the size of the text box if necessary.

h. Save your work.

3. Rearrange elements.

a. Move the table so that its upper-left corner is 1" H / 4¼" V.

b. Delete the graphics in the lower-left and right corners.

c. Move the text box containing the information about accepted credit cards to the bottom of the page at ¾" H / 8¼" V.

d. Move the text box containing the address, phone number, and Web site so that its upper-left corner is ¾" H / 9½" V.

e. Save your work.

4. Modify objects.

a. Click the table.

b. Press [Ctrl][A] twice, then increase the font size by pressing [Ctrl] [ ]] (right bracket) five times.

c. Resize the table so that its dimensions are 6½" H × 3½" V. Adjust any rows as necessary so that the text fits.

d. Use the fill color of your choice on the table to provide contrast between the background and the table. Make sure that the fill color complements the font colors you used in the restaurant name text.

e. Save your work.

5. Refine a page.

a. Select all the cells in the table on page 1.

b. Format the table so that black lines surround each cell. (*Hint*: Use the TABLE TOOLS DESIGN tab, then click the Borders list arrow in the Borders group.)

c. Save your work.

6. Experiment with design elements.

a. Click the INSERT tab, use the Advertisements button in the Building Blocks group, scroll to the Coupons section, then click the Top Oval Coupon.

b. Drag the coupon to the scratch area.

c. Click the "2 for 1" text box, then type **Dessert Special**.

d. Click the "Name of Item or Service" text box, then type **Free dessert with lunch entrée**.

e. Click the "Describe your location by landmark or area of town" text box, then type **12 Kimball Street**.

f. Delete the expiration date on the right side of the coupon, and then enter an expiration date of **September 1, 2016** in the telephone number text box. Type **Your Name's Kitchen** in the Organization Name text box.

g. Move the coupon to 4¼" H / 8¼" V, then compare your publication to **FIGURE F-19**.

h. Save the publication, print it, then exit Publisher.

FIGURE F-19

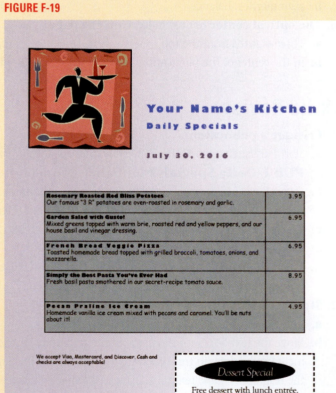

Independent Challenge 1

Patricia Martinez is an attorney who has hired you to redesign her business card. She is concerned that the layout of her current card makes it too hard to read and does not convey an elegant, organized image.

a. Start Publisher, open PUB F-4.pub from the location where you store your Data Files, then save it as **PUB F-Corporate Business Card**.

b. Use your design knowledge to make corrections, then replace the existing name in the business card with your name.

c. Save the changes, print the publication, then exit Publisher.

Independent Challenge 2

Your design services consulting firm is really taking off. A local business has asked you to redesign a certificate they use to recognize excellence among their staff. The firm wants to convey a professional, cutting-edge image, although they are not averse to having fun.

a. Start Publisher, open **PUB F-5.pub**, then save it as **PUB F-Certificate of Appreciation** to the location where you store your Data Files.

b. Change the name in the existing publication to your name.

c. Print the publication before any other changes are made, then mark at least five areas that need improvement.

d. Make the changes you noted in the previous step.

e. Draw a straight line under the title, then modify it so it is a thicker, dashed line.

f. Find and insert appropriate clip art, then compare your publication to **FIGURE F-20**.

g. Save and print the publication, then exit Publisher.

FIGURE F-20

Independent Challenge 3

As the Design Coordinator at Super Design and Layout, you want to find convincing examples of good and bad design in print and on Web sites. Seeing both types of examples will be helpful to your employees. You can use the Web to find examples of good and bad design.

a. Connect to the Internet, then open your browser and favorite search engine.

b. Find one Web site that offers design tips, then print the home page.

c. Find one example of a Web site you consider to have bad design, then print the home page. Mark on the printed page the elements you think exhibit bad design, and note how you would fix these elements.

d. Find one example of a Web site you consider to have good design, then print the home page. Note what elements work well on the Web site.

e. Create a document describing your findings using your favorite word processor, and save it as **PUB F-Good and Bad Design Critique** in the folder where you store your Data Files.

f. Make sure your name appears somewhere on each printed page.

g. Illustrate the document with examples of the Web pages by navigating to the page in your browser, pressing the Print Screen button, then switching to the document and pressing [Ctrl][V].

h. Save and print the document, then exit the program.

Independent Challenge 4: Explore

You are asked to be the guest speaker at an upcoming class on Microsoft Publisher, and the topic is design techniques. As part of the class, you want to show a publication that has elements of poor design. During the class, you plan an active discussion to address the flaws in this problematic publication.

a. Start Publisher, create a newsletter using your choice of design, then save it as **PUB F-Design Techniques** to the location where you store your Data Files.

b. Using the first page in the publication, incorporate improper techniques, such as a page that has too little white space, text that is too small, or a story that has no visual boundaries. Use as many incorrect elements as possible. (*Hint:* You can use any graphic elements and text stories available on your computer.)

c. Add your name to the masthead at the top of the first page.

d. Save this publication as **PUB F-Design Techniques-Good** to the location where you store your Data Files.

e. Fix all the areas you consciously created using poor design techniques. See **FIGURE F-21** as an example.

f. Save the publication, print the first page, then exit Publisher.

FIGURE F-21

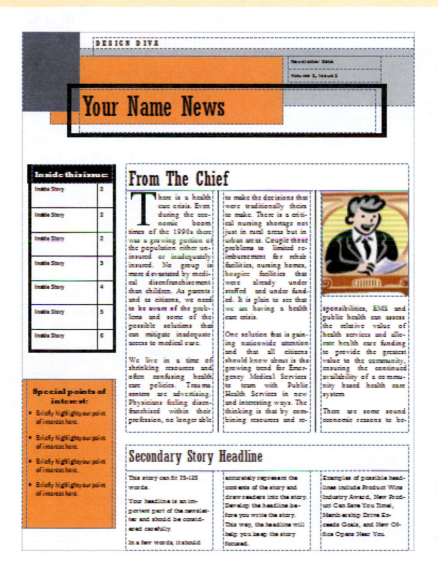

Visual Workshop

Open **PUB F-6.pub** and save it as **PUB F-Tour Guide Flyer** to the location where you store your Data Files. Use your knowledge of design techniques and your Publisher skills to make the document look like the flyer in **FIGURE F-22**. Print the publication.

FIGURE F-22

Your Name's Vacation Nation Hospitality Services – Invites YOU

Apply for Tour Guide Training. The hospitality industry is booming and you can capitalize on its growth. You can become a Certified Tour Guide.

- Retirement benefits
- 401 K plans
- Interesting people
- Exotic locales
- Unlimited growth
- Subsidized shelter
- Good pay
- Rapid promotions

Call 555 555-5555 today for an application packet and complete information

Images courtesy of Elizabeth Eisner Reding

Working with Multiple Pages

CASE > You have been asked to design a catalog of Navajo rugs for a Native-American trading company. The client wants a tasteful catalog that educates potential customers, but lets the colorful rug designs speak for themselves. When finished, this catalog will be over 60 pages long. For now, you'll focus on getting the major design elements in place.

Unit Objectives

After completing this unit, you will be able to:

- Add pages
- Delete pages
- Work with a master page
- Create a header and footer
- Add page numbers
- Edit a story
- Modify a table of contents
- Create labels
- Capstone Project: Jewelry Tools Catalog

Files You Will Need

PUB G-1.pub	PUB G-5.pub
PUB G-2.docx	PUB G-6.docx
PUB G-3.tif	PUB G-7.pub
PUB G-4.tif	PUB G-8.tif

©Alena P/Shutterstock

Add Pages

Learning Outcomes
- Insert pages in a publication
- Change catalog page configuration

You can add pages to a publication one at a time or in batches. Depending on the type of publication you are creating and how it is laid out for printing, you may want to add pages in multiples of two or four. A catalog, for example, prints pages in sets of four, so adding pages in multiples other than four can make printing difficult. You can add background items (such as layout guides) and objects (such as headers and footers) to new pages using the Master Page feature. A **master page** is the background of a publication page, where repeated information such as a pattern, header, or footer can be viewed and edited. You also have the option to copy text or graphic objects from any page to a newly inserted page. **CASE** *You have created a new publication for the catalog, and are ready to add pages to it.*

STEPS

1. **Start Publisher, open PUB G-1.pub from the location where you store your Data Files, then save it as PUB G-Rug Catalog**

   The publication that is the start of the catalog opens with eight pages. You can add pages either before or after the current page. To retain a consistent design, you can insert pages and place text boxes and picture frames in the same locations on each page.

2. **Click the Page 2 and Page 3 icon on the Pages pane (expanding the Pages pane if necessary), click the INSERT tab on the Ribbon, click the Page button list arrow in the Pages group, then click Insert Page**

   The Insert Catalog Pages dialog box opens, where you can choose from many layouts for the new page or pages.

3. **Click the Left-hand page list arrow, scroll down, click 4 items, offset pictures, click the Right-hand page list arrow, scroll down, then click 4 items, squared pictures**

   Compare your Insert Catalog Pages dialog box to **FIGURE G-1**. The samples show the selected layouts.

4. **Click More in the Insert Catalog Pages dialog box**

   The Insert Page dialog box opens, as shown in **FIGURE G-2**. You can use this dialog box to control the number of new pages to add as well as options, such as inserting blank pages and duplicating all of the objects on a specific page. To move a page, begin by inserting a new page containing duplicate objects from the page you want moved, then delete the original page.

5. **Click Cancel in the Insert Page dialog box, click OK in the Insert Catalog Pages dialog box, then click Yes to automatically insert four pages**

   By clicking Cancel in the Insert Page dialog box, the page types in the Insert Catalog Pages dialog box were reset to the default, and the newly inserted pages (4–7) have the default layout (One column, all text) on both pairs of pages. Compare your work to **FIGURE G-3**. The page 4–5 icon button is selected on the Pages pane, and the additional icon buttons indicate that the publication now has 12 pages.

6. **Save your work**

Using multiple master pages

A master page gives you the freedom to create a consistent background for pages. In Publisher, you can also create multiple master pages. This means, for example, that in a newsletter publication you can have a specific master page for classified ads and another master page for daily news stories. You can view a master page by clicking the VIEW tab on the Ribbon, then clicking the Master Page button. This automatically displays the MASTER PAGE tab. When the Pages pane is visible, click the Add Master Page button in the Master Page group of the MASTER PAGE tab to create a new master page. You can also edit an existing master page by clicking the Master Pages button in the Page Background group on the PAGE DESIGN tab on the Ribbon.

FIGURE G-1: Insert Catalog Pages dialog box

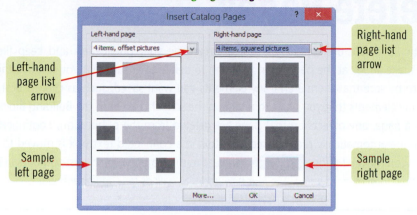

Left-hand page list arrow

Right-hand page list arrow

Sample left page

Sample right page

FIGURE G-2: Insert Page dialog box

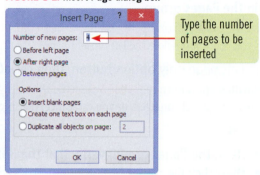

Type the number of pages to be inserted

FIGURE G-3: Publication with added pages

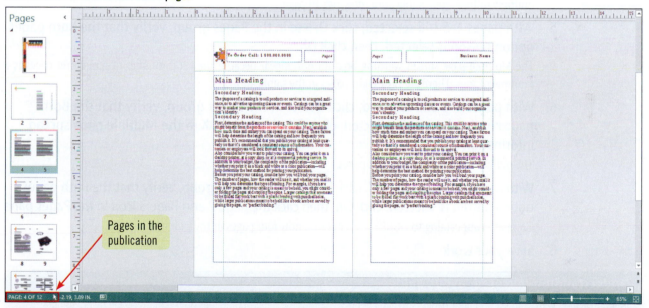

Pages in the publication

Printing multipage documents

When you think of a page, you probably think of one 8½" × 11" sheet of paper; but from a printer's point of view, several pages may actually fit on one sheet of paper. A four-page brochure can be printed front and back on one sheet of paper and folded in half so that there are four pages. Commercial printers of publications larger than four pages print pages this way and then the folded pages are bound together. This is why catalogs print in multiples of four, because they are printed on the front and back of a single piece of paper. When printing books or other large publications, paper is printed in multiples of eight, called **signatures**. Blank pages at the end of a book indicate there was not enough text to fill the last signature.

Delete Pages

Learning
Outcomes
• Select pages for
  deletion
• Delete pages in a
  publication

You should delete unnecessary pages to streamline your publication and keep file sizes manageable. Always take a look at the pages that you plan to delete to ensure that you remove the correct pages. You want to be sure that there aren't any elements you want saved, such as clip art or a pull quote. You can store any elements that you want to retain on the scratch area or in the Building Blocks Library. When you delete a page, any objects on that page are deleted from the publication, continued on/continued from notices are automatically recalculated, and text in a connected text box is moved to the closest available text box on the next page. **CASE** ▶ *You need to eliminate some unnecessary pages in the catalog. You want to delete a total of eight pages: the four new pages as well as four additional pages.*

STEPS

QUICK TIP
You can also delete pages by right-clicking a page icon in the Pages pane, then clicking Delete.

1. **Verify that pages 4–5 are selected, click the PAGE DESIGN tab on the Ribbon, then click Delete in the Pages group**

   The Delete Page dialog box opens, as shown in **FIGURE G-4**. The Both pages option button is selected, although you could just delete the left or right page.

2. **Click the Left page only option button, then click OK**

   The information box shown in **FIGURE G-5** opens. This tells you that you can delete a single page, but your layout may be negatively affected, or you can cancel the single page deletion.

QUICK TIP
If you delete a page in error, immediately click the Undo button on the Quick Access Toolbar.

3. **Click Cancel**

4. **Click Delete in the Pages group, verify that the Both pages option button is selected, click OK, then click OK in the Multiple page spread warning box**

   The Multiple page spread information box appeared because you were deleting only two pages, not a multiple of four. Your publication now has 10 pages.

5. **With pages 4–5 still selected, click Delete in the Pages group, verify that the Both pages option button is selected, then click OK**

   The Multiple page spread warning box did not appear because the total number of remaining pages is a multiple of four. There are now eight pages in the publication.

6. **With pages 4–5 still selected, click Delete in the Pages group, verify that the Both pages option button is selected, click OK, then click OK in the Multiple page spread information box**

   The publication now contains six pages.

7. **With pages 4–5 still selected, click Delete in the Pages group, verify that the Both pages option button is selected, click OK, then click the Page 2 and Page 3 icon in the Pages pane**

   Compare your catalog to **FIGURE G-6**. There are now four pages in the publication.

8. **Save your work**

Understanding mirrored layout guides

In a publication with both left and right pages (such as a bound book or magazine), you can use **mirrored guides** so that facing pages have opposite margins and layout guides. This can make your material easier to read and more consistent in appearance. When you click the Two-page master check box in the New Master Page dialog box, the names of the Left and Right margin guides become Inside and Outside margin guides. A bound publication should have larger inside margins to allow for the space taken up by the binding. You can switch the layout guides for the publication pages on the master page by dragging a layout guide. The pointer changes to a resize pointer. Drag the guide to any location, using the vertical and horizontal rulers for exact measurements. You can also return layout guides to their original locations by clicking the Undo button on the Quick Access Toolbar before performing any other action. While you have Master Pages open, you can open the Layout Guides dialog box by clicking the Guides button in the Layout group on the PAGE DESIGN tab of the Ribbon.

FIGURE G-4: Delete Page dialog box

FIGURE G-5: Multiple pages information dialog box

FIGURE G-6: Two-page spread

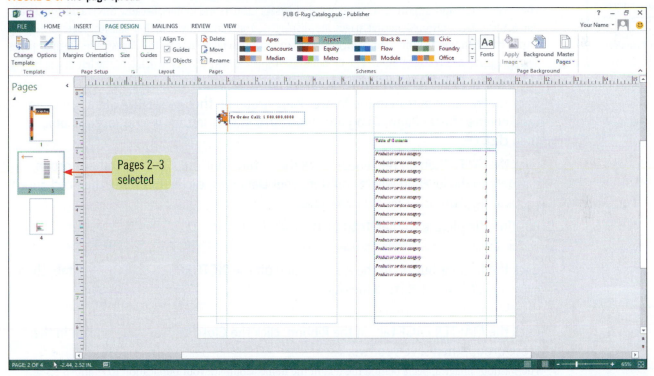

Pages 2–3 selected

Saving objects on a page

When a page is deleted, all the objects on that page are also deleted. But what if you want to save some of those objects for later use? Simply drag the object onto the scratch area. Objects in the scratch area are saved along with the publication and can be viewed and accessed from all pages in the publication. When you decide where you want an object from the scratch area to be used, move it to its new location using any copying or pasting technique. Alternately, you can cut an object before deleting the page so it will automatically be stored on the Office Clipboard, where you can easily retrieve it until you close the publication. You can also store an object in the Building Blocks Library by right-clicking the object, then clicking Save as Building Block. The object will be visible in the area of the Building Blocks where it was saved and can be inserted whenever you need it.

Work with a Master Page

Learning Outcomes
• Add an image as a watermark
• Rename a Master Page
• Recolor an image

Every publication has at least one master page that can be used to add text or objects that you want on every page. A publication with **mirrored guides** has both left and right master pages; a publication without mirrored guides has a single master page. You can use a master page to add an object, such as a logo, to each page. A **washout**, also known as a **watermark**, is another element you can add to the master page. It's a faded or washed-out looking image that appears behind text and objects on a page. **CASE** *You have prepared descriptive text about Navajo rugs that you want to insert in a text box on page 2. Once you insert this text, you will add a watermark of a rug image to the background page.*

STEPS

1. **Click the INSERT tab on the Ribbon, click the Draw Text Box button** ⬛ **in the Text group, then drag ╋ from 1" H / 1½" V to 4⅞" H / 7¾" V**

   The text box appears on page 2.

2. **Right-click the text box, point to Change Text, click Text File, locate and select the file PUB G-2.docx from the location where you store your Data Files, then click OK**

   All of the text fits within the text box, as shown in **FIGURE G-7**.

   QUICK TIP
   You can modify an existing master page by switching to Master Page view and editing objects.

3. **Click the VIEW tab on the Ribbon, then click Master Page in the Views group**

   The master pages appear, with guides and placeholders for headers and footers. Because this is a mirrored-page publication, two mirrored master pages are displayed. You can easily tell that master pages are being displayed when you see the light-orange background in the scratch area in the Pages pane. Regular pages display against a gray background. The Ribbon now displays the MASTER PAGE tab to the left of the HOME tab. Master pages can accommodate both text and graphics.

4. **Click the Rename button in the Master Page group on the MASTER PAGE tab to open the Rename Master Page dialog box, type Intro Master in the Description text box, then click OK**

5. **Click the INSERT tab on the Ribbon, click the Pictures button in the Illustrations group, navigate to the location where you store your Data Files, click PUB G-3.tif, then click Insert**

   The picture is placed across the two master pages.

6. **Position the picture so that its top-left corner is at 1" H / 1½" V**

   The picture is positioned within the master page.

7. **Click the Recolor button in the Adjust group on the PICTURE TOOLS FORMAT tab, then click Sepia (row 1, 3rd from the right)**

   Compare your screen to **FIGURE G-8**.

   QUICK TIP
   You can toggle between regular and Master Page views by pressing [Ctrl][M].

8. **Click the MASTER PAGE tab on the Ribbon, click the Close Master Page button in the Close group, then save your work**

   The washout image appears behind the text in the frame. Compare your publication to **FIGURE G-9**.

Using left and right master pages

If you have mirrored layout guides, you also have left and right master pages. Having both a left and right master page increases your design options. For example, you might want to have an image appear in the bottom-left corner on the left master page, and the bottom-right corner on the right master page. To change from double to single master pages, open the Master Page by pressing [Ctrl][M], or clicking the VIEW tab on the Ribbon, then clicking the Master Page button in the Views group. Click the Two Page Master button on the MASTER PAGE tab. This button acts as a toggle, letting you switch between a one- and two-page master page. If you change from a two-page master to a one-page master, the right master page is now used as the publication's background page and is applied to all the pages.

FIGURE G-7: Text file added to publication

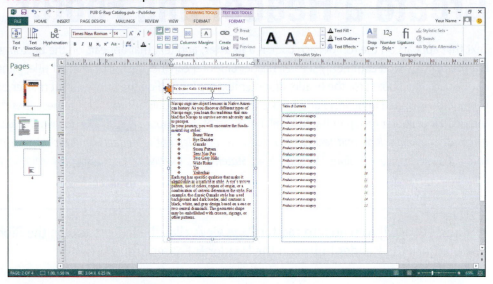

FIGURE G-8: Sepia image added to master page

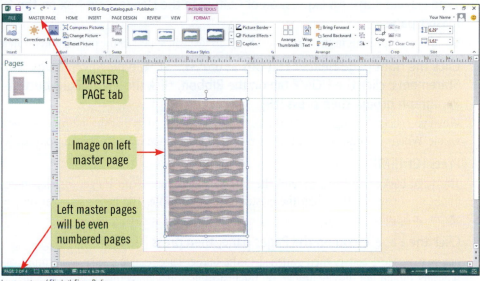

MASTER PAGE tab

Image on left master page

Left master pages will be even numbered pages

Image courtesy of Elizabeth Eisner Reding

FIGURE G-9: Text in foreground, image on master page background

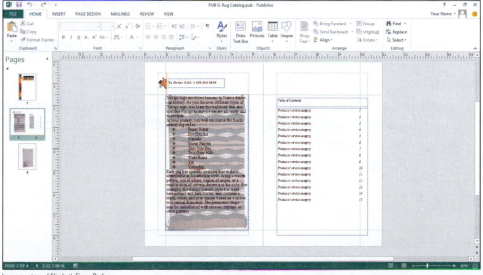

Image courtesy of Elizabeth Eisner Reding

Create a Header and Footer

Text that appears on the top of each page is a **header**, and text that appears on the bottom of each page is a **footer**. Text you commonly see in a header or footer can include the document title, page number, or date. Special text boxes for the header or footer text are located on the right and left master pages. Images can also be included in headers and footers to enhance the publication. **TABLE G-1** describes the buttons in the Header & Footer group in the MASTER PAGE tab of the Ribbon. **CASE** *You want to give the catalog a more professional look and feel, so you decide to add descriptive headers. You include the theme for this catalog, which is Navajo Rugs: Strong Visual Statements, as well as the descriptive phrase: Navajo Rugs: An Expression of Culture.*

STEPS

1. **Press [Ctrl][M] to switch to Master Page view, click the INSERT tab on the Ribbon, then click the Header button in the Header & Footer group**

   The view changes to the master page. The INSERT tab is active, and the background page Header text box at the top of the left page is selected.

2. **Type Navajo Rugs: An Expression of Culture in the Header text box on the left master page**

   Because you typed this in the Header text box, this text will appear in the publication on all left-hand pages.

3. **Click the right page Header text box at 6¼" H / ¼" V, type Navajo Rugs: Strong Visual Statements, click the HOME tab on the Ribbon, click the Align Right button ≡ in the Paragraph group, then press [F9]**

   When you clicked the right-page text box, the display changed so that the left-page text box was no longer visible. When you pressed [F9], the headers on both pages were visible. Compare your pages to **FIGURE G-10**.

4. **Press [Ctrl][M]**

   The page background is gray and the MASTER PAGE tab is no longer visible, indicating that the publication pages, rather than the master pages, are visible. The headers appear on pages 2 and 3, as shown in **FIGURE G-11**.

5. **Click the Page 1 icon on the Pages pane, then press [Ctrl][M]**

   You made page 1 active, then switched to the Master Page. Catalogs, like other multipage publications, typically should not display headers on the first page. You address this by creating a new master that will not include headers or footers.

6. **Click the Add Master Page button 📄 in the Master Page group on the Ribbon**

   The New Master Page dialog box opens.

7. **Type First Page in the Description text box, click the Two-page master check box to deselect it, then click OK**

   You created a new single-page master page.

8. **Verify that the Master Page (A) is selected, click the Apply To button in the Master Page group, click Apply to Current Page, then press [Ctrl][M] to close the master page**

   You applied the new master page which contains no headers or footers to Page 1.

9. **Save your work**

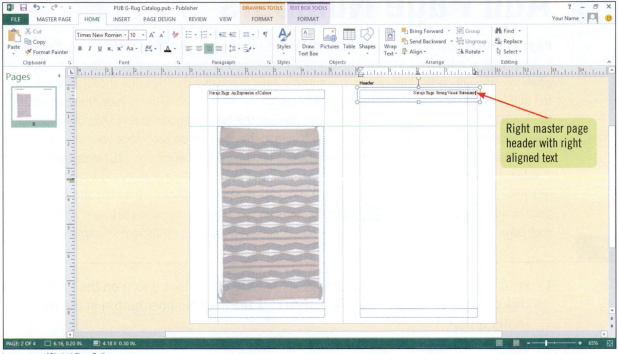

Right master page header with right aligned text

Image courtesy of Elizabeth Eisner Reding

FIGURE G-11: Headers visible on left and right pages

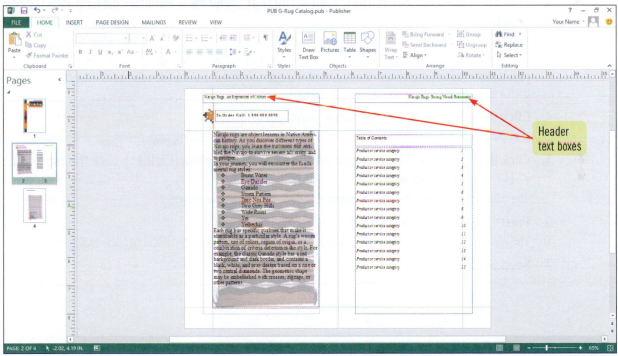

Header text boxes

Image courtesy of Elizabeth Eisner Reding

TABLE G-1: Header & Footer group buttons

button name	description
Insert Page Number	Inserts a page number automatically into a header or footer
Insert Date	Inserts current date into a header or footer
Insert Time	Inserts current time into a header or footer
Show Header/Footer	Used to toggle between the header and footer

Add Page Numbers

Page numbers help readers know where they are in a publication and find specific stories. Notices that include page numbers make it possible to find the continued parts of stories that appear in multiple text boxes on different pages. You can insert automatic page numbers either by using the Page Number button in the Header & Footer group of the INSERT tab on the Ribbon, or the Insert Page Number button on the MASTER PAGE tab on the Ribbon. You can also use the Page Numbers dialog box. Using Publisher's page numbering tools is easier than manually typing in the numbers on each page yourself—and ensures the numbers are always correct. With automatic page numbering, a pound sign (#), rather than an actual number, is inserted on the master page as a placeholder. Publisher then automatically substitutes the correct page number for the placeholder in the publication pages. As pages are added and deleted, your page numbers remain accurate. **CASE** ▶ *You want page numbers to appear in the footers at the bottom of each page, except the first page. You want the page numbers to appear in the bottom-left corner of each page.*

STEPS

1. **Press [F9] to zoom out if necessary, click the Page 2 and Page 3 icon on the Pages pane, click the INSERT tab on the Ribbon, then click the Page Number button in the Header & Footer group**

   The Page Number gallery opens, as shown in **FIGURE G-12**.

2. **Click Bottom Left**

3. **Click the Page Number button, then verify that Show Page Number on First Page is *not* selected**

   The page numbering feature will count the first page, but the number will not appear on that page because the applied master does not include the header and footer on that page. In most cases, displaying the page number on the first page of a publication is not necessary, so if you do not change the master this is a useful feature.

4. **Click the page 1 icon on the Pages pane**

   Compare page 1 of your publication with **FIGURE G-13**. Note the missing page number and no header.

5. **Click the Page 2 and Page 3 icon on the Pages pane, press [Ctrl][M], click the footer at 7" H / 8" V, then press [F9]**

   The master page shows the page number feature as "#" inside the footer.

6. **Press [F9], then press [Ctrl][M]**

   The publication is displayed in Two-Page Spread view. You like the look of the headers and footers.

7. **Save your work**

FIGURE G-12: Page Number gallery

FIGURE G-13: Header does not appear on page 1

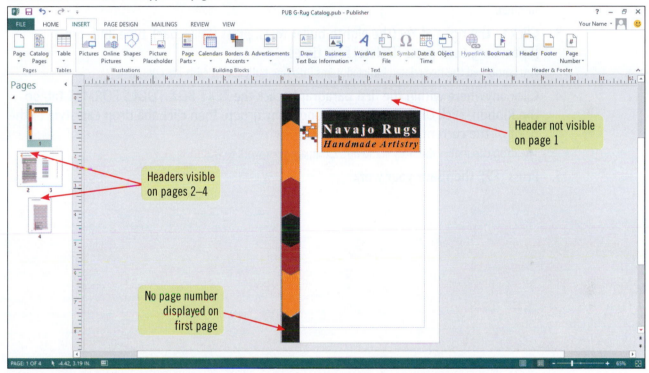

Renaming a master page

You can rename a master page to give it a more meaningful name (one that defines a specific use, for example). To rename a master page, right-click the master page you want to rename, click Rename, then type a new name. You can also rename a master page by clicking the Rename button in the Master Page group on the MASTER PAGE tab on the Ribbon. You can tell that a master page has been renamed by positioning the cursor over the Master Page thumbnail and reading its ScreenTip, as shown in FIGURE G-14.

FIGURE G-14: Renamed master page in Pages pane

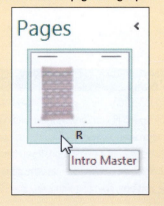

Edit a Story

As you have learned, you can type a story directly into a text box or prepare it in another program and insert it as a text file. Once you have placed a story in a publication, text editing is done right in Publisher. If you are not dealing with a lot of text, you will find it easy to edit the story using Publisher's editing features. When text is edited, the changes are saved in the publication. **CASE** ▶ *After reading the publication, you realize you need to edit the descriptive text on page 2 to tighten up some of the wording.*

STEPS

1. **Click the text box at 3" H / 3" V, then press [F9]**

   The text is magnified, as shown in **FIGURE G-15**. Any edits you make to this text are automatically reflected in the Publisher text box.

2. **Select the text discover different types of, then type explore**

   You changed the phrase "discover different types of" to "explore" in the first paragraph to make it more succinct.

3. **Click to the right of Yei (the eighth bullet text), press [Spacebar], type and, press [Spacebar], then press [Delete] four times**

   You combined the two related bulleted items into one bullet. Your edits are complete.

4. **Click anywhere within the first paragraph, click the TEXT BOX TOOLS FORMAT tab on the Ribbon, click Drop Cap in the Typography group, then click the drop cap style to the right of the current selection**

   The drop cap makes the story stand out. Compare your work to **FIGURE G-16**.

5. **Press [F9], then save your work**

Copyfitting text

As you create a publication, you may find that you have either too much or too little text to fit comfortably in a column or page. **Copyfitting** is a term used to describe the process of making the text fit the available space within a publication. If you have too much text, you can narrow the margins, decrease the point size of the font, enlarge the text box, flow text into a text box on another page, or delete some text by editing. You can solve the problem of too little text by inserting a graphic image or pull quote, making margins wider, increasing the point size of the font, or adding some text. To use the Best Fit command, click the Text Fit button on the TEXT BOX TOOLS FORMAT tab in the Text group. The Best Fit command works by increasing or decreasing the point size of the fonts.

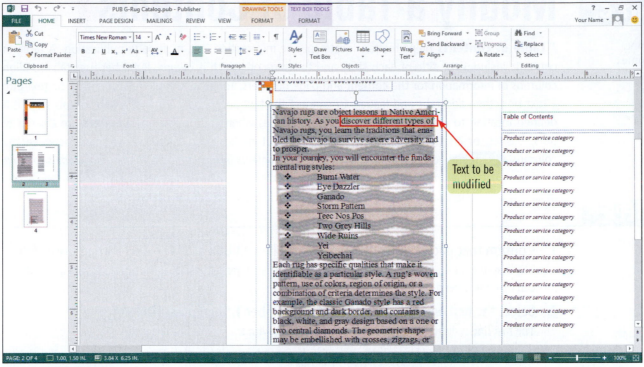

FIGURE G-16: Edited story

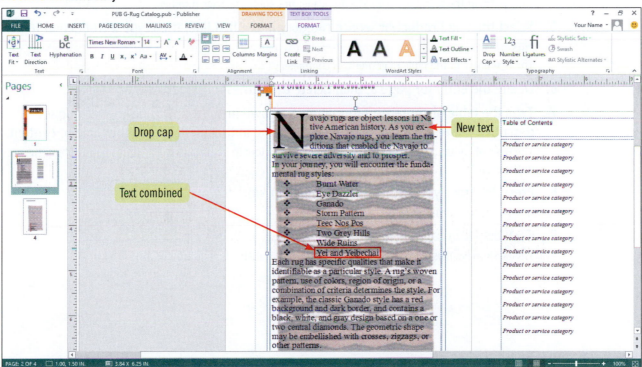

Modify a Table of Contents

Learning Outcomes
- Modify table of contents text
- Apply dot leaders to a table of contents

A **table of contents** helps readers locate specific information in a multipage publication. A table of contents includes the title of each story and the page on which it begins. Publisher uses tabs to align columns of information for the content and page numbers. To create a table of contents, type text into a text box, then add tabs and leaders to connect the text and page numbers. A **tab**, or tab stop, is a defined location to which the insertion point advances when you press [Tab]. **Leaders** are a series of dots, dashes, or lines that lead up to a tab, and automatically adjust to fit the space between the columns. **CASE** *You want to modify the table of contents in the catalog by adding dot leaders to make reading easier. Although you still have several pages of content to add to this publication, you'll also make entries to approximate where information will be located.*

STEPS

1. **Confirm that pages 2–3 are selected, click the text box at 7" H / 2½" V, then press [F9]**
   The first item in the table of contents is for page 1. The reference to this page is not necessary, as the reader can easily see everything that's on page 1.

2. **Select the first line of text as well as the number 1, then press [Delete]**
   The first line is deleted, and the first line now begins with the reference to page 2.

3. **Press [Ctrl][A] to select all the text in the text box, right-click the selected text, point to Change Text, then click Tabs**
   The Paragraph dialog box opens and the Tabs tab is selected, as shown in **FIGURE G-17**.

4. **In the Leader section of the Paragraph dialog box, click the Dot option button, click OK, then click outside of the text box to deselect the text**
   Each entry in the text box now has a dot leader preceding the page number.

5. **Select the text Product or service category in the first line, then type Introduction to Navajo Rugs**
   The first entry in the table of contents is complete.

6. **Delete the entry for page 3, then delete the entries for pages 13–15**

7. **Type the table of contents information as shown in FIGURE G-18 using the techniques described in Step 5, then substitute your name in the final entry to the table of contents**
   The table of contents looks good. It will work well as a tool to help clients locate information about the rugs in the catalog.

8. **Press [F9], save your work, then submit your work to your instructor**
   Review the four printed pages of the catalog.

9. **Click the FILE tab, then click Close**
   The publication closes. Publisher remains open and available for additional work.

FIGURE G-17: Paragraph dialog box with Tabs tab selected

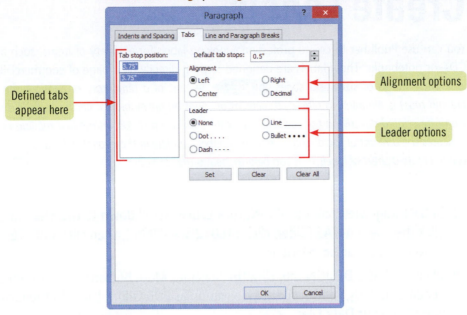

Defined tabs appear here

Alignment options

Leader options

FIGURE G-18: Completed table of contents

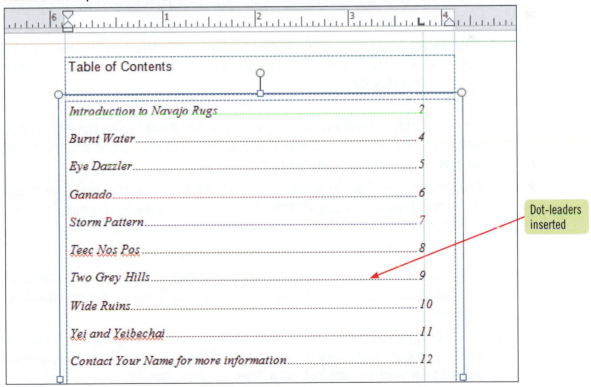

Dot-leaders inserted

Inserting a new table of contents

You can insert a ready-made table of contents into a publication using the Page Parts feature on the INSERT tab. Activate the page where you want the table, click the Page Parts button in the Building Blocks group on the INSERT tab, then click More Page Parts. Scroll down to the Tables of Contents category, click the style you want to add, then click Insert.

Create Labels

Learning Outcomes
• Create labels using a template

You can use Publisher to create professional-looking labels for a variety of items, such as retail products, CDs, or notebooks. These labels are designed to print directly on a page of commercially available labels in a wide range of sizes and styles. **CASE** ▶ *As part of a temporary promotion, the client (a seller of Navajo rugs) is planning to offer a 20 percent discount on online orders. Because this is a short-term offer, it won't be printed directly on the catalog. You plan to include a sticker on the first mailing of the catalogs that indicates the amount of the discount. You find a label template in the Available Templates list that you want to use to create a sheet of labels that can be attached to the catalogs.*

STEPS

QUICK TIP
The label brand and model number required for printing varies based on the label design you use. You may need your Microsoft Publisher Installation DVD to complete this step.

1. In Backstage view, click **BUILT-IN**, click **Labels**, scroll down to the Manufacturers group, click the **Avery A4/A5 folder**, click **5160 (2.5 × 0.906")**, then click **CREATE**
   A blank label appears on the screen.

2. Click the **PAGE DESIGN tab**, click the **Schemes More button** 🔽, click **Mulberry** in the Schemes gallery, then save the publication as **PUB G-Rug Label** to the location where you store your Data Files

3. Click the **VIEW tab** on the Ribbon, then click **Master Page** in the Views group

4. Click the **INSERT tab** on the Ribbon, click **Pictures** in the Illustrations group, click **PUB G-4.tif** from the location where you store your Data Files, then click **Insert**
   Compare your label to **FIGURE G-19**.

5. If necessary, use 🔀 to drag the picture so that it is centered on the label, right-click the **object**, click **Format Picture**, drag the **Brightness slider** to **75%**, drag the **Contrast slider** to **25%**, then click **OK**
   The image is now a much lighter shade than before.

6. Press **[Ctrl][M]** to close the master page, click the **HOME tab** on the Ribbon if necessary, click the **Draw Text Box button** in the Objects group, draw a **text box** from **½" H / ¼" V** to **2" H / ½" V**, then type **Authentic Navajo Rug**

7. Press **[Ctrl][A]**, click the **Italic button** 𝐼 in the Font group, click the **Align Center button** 🔳 in the Alignment group, click the **Font list arrow** in the Font group, then click **Times New Roman**

8. Right-click the **text box**, click **Best Fit**, then press **[Esc]** twice

9. Click the **HOME tab** on the Ribbon if necessary, click the **Draw Text Box button** 🅰 in the Objects group, draw a **text box** from **½" H / ⅝" V** to **2" H / ¾" V**, then type **20% Online Discount**

10. Press **[Ctrl][A]**, click 🔳, click the **Font list arrow** in the Font group, click **Times New Roman**, click 𝐼, right-click the **text box**, click **Best Fit**, press **[Esc]** twice, save your work, submit your work to your instructor, then exit Publisher
    Compare your label to **FIGURE G-20**.

FIGURE G-19: Label master page with image inserted

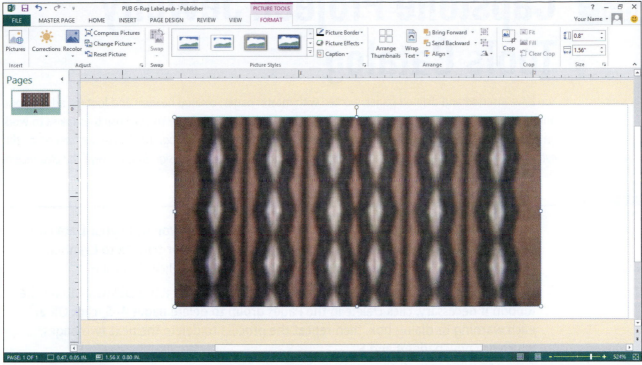

Image courtesy of Elizabeth Eisner Reding

FIGURE G-20: Completed label with adjusted image

Image courtesy of Elizabeth Eisner Reding

Creating CD/DVD labels

If you like creating CDs of your original music and photographs or DVDs from your video collection, you may want to create jewel case labels for them. To do so, click BUILT-IN, then click the Labels category. When you scroll down to and open the All Media category, you'll see a variety of case inserts and jewel case labels you can use.

Capstone Project: Jewelry Tools Catalog

You have inserted and deleted pages, worked with master pages, created headers and footers, added page numbers, modified a table of contents, created a label, and edited a story. You will use these skills to work on a new catalog. **CASE** ▶ *You are designing a metal workers' catalog. The target customers for this catalog are jewelers. You think they will appreciate a simple, uncluttered design that conveys the elegance of their craft. The client will add pictures and text later.*

STEPS

1. Start Publisher, open PUB G-5.pub from the location where you store your Data Files, save it as PUB G-Jewelry Tools Catalog, then change the color scheme to Cranberry
   Most of the design elements in the first three pages will be carried throughout the catalog.

2. Click the Page 4 and Page 5 icon in the Pages pane, click the PAGE DESIGN tab on the Ribbon if necessary, click Delete in the Pages group to delete pages 4–5, click OK at each warning or dialog box, then repeat the process to delete the next two pages, which are now pages 4 and 5
   The publication now has four pages.

3. Click the Page 2 and Page 3 icon in the Pages pane, view the master page, click the INSERT tab on the Ribbon, click Online Pictures, type jewelry in the Office.com Clip Art text box, select a suitable image (such as the sample used in FIGURE G-21), then click Insert

4. Position the image so that its top-left corner is at 1¼" H / 3" V, resize it so the bottom-right corner is at 4¼" H / 6" V, click the Corrections button in the Adjust group on the PICTURE TOOLS FORMAT tab, click the Brightness: 50%, Contrast: 50% box (3rd row, 3rd from the left)
   The image is now centered and lighter, and will look elegant with black text imposed over the gold color.

5. Click the INSERT tab on the Ribbon, click the Header button in the Header & Footer group, then type Artisan Tools for the Jewelry Arts in the Header text box on the left master page

6. Click the Footer button in the Header & Footer group on the INSERT tab, type Page, press [Spacebar], click the Page Number button in the Header & Footer group, click Insert in Current Text Box, copy the entries in the left footer to the right footer, click the HOME tab on the Ribbon, click the Align Right button ▤ in the Paragraph group to right-align the right footer, then close the master page
   Page numbers will help customers navigate to specific items.

7. Press [F9], right-click the text box at 6½" H / 2" V, point to Change Text, click Tabs, click the Line option button, then click OK
   The entry for page 1 still must be deleted.

8. Click the text box, press the [➡] key to deselect the selected text, then press [Delete] until the entry for page 1 is removed, click the text box at 2" H / ¾" V on page 2, substitute your name for the phone number, press [Esc] twice, then compare your work to FIGURE G-21

9. Save your work, submit your work to your instructor, then exit Publisher

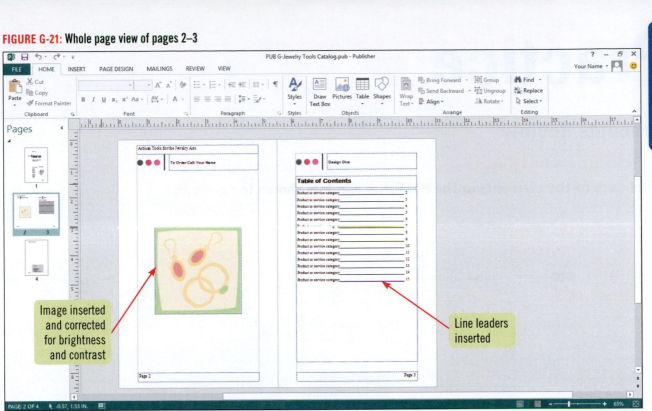

Image inserted
and corrected
for brightness
and contrast

Line leaders
inserted

Practice

Concepts Review

Label each of the elements in the Publisher window shown in FIGURE G-22.

FIGURE G-22

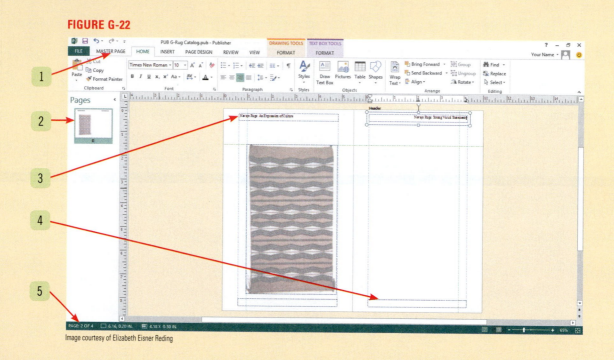

Image courtesy of Elizabeth Eisner Reding

Match each of the features with the correct term, menu, dialog box, or command.

6. Footer
7. TEXT BOX TOOLS FORMAT tab
8. Header
9. [Ctrl][M]
10. Paragraph dialog box
11. PAGE DESIGN tab

a. Contains the command that adds a drop cap
b. Switches in and out of Master Page view
c. Text that repeats at the top of each page
d. Contains the command that deletes a page
e. Text that repeats on the bottom of each page
f. Contains the command that adds dot leaders

Select the best answer from the list of choices.

12. **Where in a publication are headers and footers usually placed?**
    a. In AutoShapes
    b. In picture frames
    c. On the Clipboard
    d. On the master page(s)

13. **Each of the following is true about adding a page, except _____.**
    a. Pages can be added before or after the current page.
    b. You can only add one page at a time.
    c. Existing layout guides are added to the new page(s).
    d. You can duplicate objects found on other pages in the publication.

14. **The Delete button, which can be used to remove pages from a publication, is on the _____ tab.**
    a. HOME
    b. INSERT
    c. PAGE DESIGN
    d. VIEW

15. **Which character symbolizes automatic page numbers?**
    a. @
    b. #
    c. !
    d. &

Skills Review

1. **Add pages.**
   a. Start Publisher, open the Catalogs category in the BUILT-IN section, then select the Marquee template. Use the Secondary Business Information set, then change the color scheme to Opulent.
   b. Save the file as **PUB G-DVD Store Catalog** to the location where you store your Data Files.
   c. Display pages 2–3.
   d. Insert four pages after page 3 (with the default settings). You now have 12 pages.
   e. Save your work.

2. **Delete pages.**
   a. Display pages 8 and 9, delete them, then display and delete the new pages 8 and 9.
   b. Display pages 6 and 7, delete them, then delete pages 4 and 5. You now have four pages.
   c. Display pages 2 and 3, then save your work.

3. **Work with a master page.**
   a. Change to Master Page view.
   b. Open the Insert Pictures window, search Office.com Clip Art using the text **TVs**, select a suitable image, click Insert, then close the Office.com Clip Art window.
   c. Position the image so that its top-left corner is at ¾" H / 3" V on the left page.
   d. Press and hold [Shift], then drag the lower-right sizing handle until the image is approximately 4" wide and 3" high.
   e. Save your work.

4. **Create a header and footer.**
   a. Open the header on the left master page, type **DVD Classics**, then make the text bold.
   b. Type **DVD Classics** in the header on the right master page.
   c. Right-align the text in the right Header text box, make the text bold, then save the publication.

5. **Add page numbers.**
   a. View the footer on the right page, then add page numbers to the footers on both pages, aligned at the outer margins.
   b. Close the master view.
   c. Delete the Page Number text boxes at the bottom of pages 2 and 3 (at 1" H / 7¾" V, and 9½" H / 7¾" V), then go to page 1.
   d. Prevent the page number from appearing on the first page, (*Hint*: Use the INSERT tab) then save the publication.

6. Edit a story.

a. Use the page icon button on the Pages pane to return to page 2.

b. Draw a text box at 1¼" H / 2½" V to 4¼" H / 6½" V.

c. Insert the text file PUB G-6.docx into the text box.

d. Add the following text in a matching font and text size as a new paragraph at the end of the story:

If we don't have what you're looking for, we can get it for you.

e. Add a three-line custom drop cap character to the first paragraph, then save the publication.

7. Modify a table of contents.

a. Select the text box at 6½" H / 2" V on page 3 (the table of contents text).

b. Delete the entries for pages 1–3.

c. Select the table of contents text, then change the tabs for the remaining entries to dot leaders.

d. Change the remaining entries using the information in **TABLE G-2**. Delete any unnecessary text.

e. Add a final entry to the table of contents that contains your name.

f. Save your work, then print pages 2 and 3. Close the publication, but do not exit Publisher.

TABLE G-2

page headings	page #
1930s	4
1940s	6
1950s	8
1960s	10
Award Winners	12
Independent Films	14

8. Create a label.

a. Create a label using the Video Face (Avery 5199A) Media design and the Aspect color scheme. (You will see the following text beneath the label: "This label is ready to print onto Avery Label #5199 (Face).")

b. Save the label as **PUB G-DVD Store Label** to the location where you store your Data Files.

c. Change the Video Title text to **Bell, Book, and Candle** and the font to Franklin Gothic Demi Cond.

d. Change the date text to the current date using a 7.1-point Times New Roman italic font.

e. Change the company name text to your name using a 9.5-point Times New Roman font.

f. Save your work, submit your publication to your instructor, then exit Publisher.

Independent Challenge 1

You are a member of a small theater group. You are asked to create the program for the next production.

a. Start Publisher, then use the BUILT-IN list and the Theater template in the Installed Templates category.

b. Use the Business Information set of your choice to enter appropriate information.

c. Save the publication as **PUB G-Play Program** to the location where you store your Data Files.

d. Use Master Page view to add a header displaying the name of the play. Choose any play with which you are familiar, such as *Rent, A Chorus Line*, or *Man of La Mancha*. Right-align the header on the right page.

e. Insert page numbers at the bottoms of the pages. If necessary, move any information so that your header and footer fit correctly and are visible.

f. Add any appropriate clip art to the master page, recoloring the clip art if necessary.

g. Return to the publication pages view, then make sure the page number, header, and footer do not appear on the first page.

h. Replace the placeholder text in the table containing the cast with the names of characters and cast members, as well as The Crew and Special Thanks To sections. Use the names of friends and family members or make up fictitious names.

i. Edit a paragraph describing the play in the existing text box on page 3.

j. Replace any placeholders so that all of the text in the program pertains to the play you chose.

k. Add your name as the author on page 1.

l. Rearrange and format any objects to create an attractive, effective design.

m. Check the spelling in the publication, save and print the publication, submit it to your instructor, then exit Publisher.

Independent Challenge 2

You have recorded several original songs and want to get feedback on your work from a friend who works in the music business. You decide to use a label template in Publisher to create a shipping label to send the CD to your friend.

a. Start Publisher, then create a new Mailing and Shipping label based on the Borders template (Avery 5164).

b. Use any Business Information set to enter appropriate information, including your name, then choose any color scheme that you like.

c. Save the publication as **PUB G-Personal Shipping Label** to the location where you store your Data Files.

d. Edit the mailing address information at 2" H / 2" V, using a fictitious name and address.

e. Create a DVD label using the Mosaic CD/DVD template (Avery 8931). (*Hint*: Choose the first instance of Mosaic (Avery 8931). There are two in the CD/DVD category.)

f. Save the publication as **PUB G-CD-DVD Label**

g. Add actual or fictitious information to the label placeholders, but use Your Name as the Performer's Name.

h. Delete any unnecessary objects, add artwork if you choose, then compare your work to **FIGURE G-23**.

i. Save your work and submit it to your instructor, then exit Publisher.

FIGURE G-23

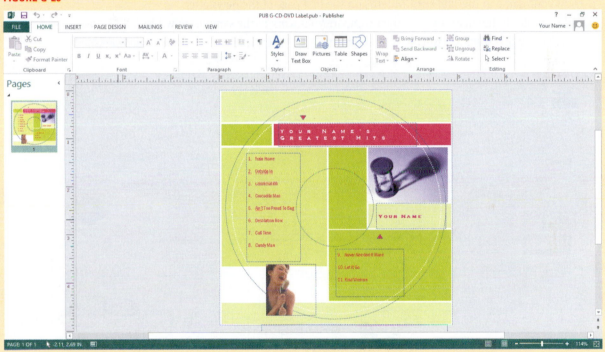

Image courtesy of Elizabeth Eisner Reding

Independent Challenge 3

A local elementary school asks you to design a newsletter for its staff and students. The staff and students will provide all of the stories except for one that you will write.

a. Start Publisher. Use the BUILT-IN list to create a new newsletter based on the Kid Stuff template in the Newsletters category.

b. Use any Business Information set to enter appropriate information.

c. Change the color scheme to a scheme of your choice.

d. Save the publication as **PUB G-School Newsletter** to the location where you store your Data Files.

e. Click the Calendars button in the Building Blocks group on the INSERT tab, select an appealing calendar, and place it in the upper-left corner of page 2.

f. Use the Reply Forms category in the Building Block Library to insert a response form of your choice in the lower-left corner of page 3. (*Hint*: Click the INSERT tab on the Ribbon, click the Page Parts button in the Building Blocks group, click More Page Parts at the bottom of the gallery, then make a selection from Reply Forms category.)

g. Replace the newsletter title with your elementary school's name, followed by the word **News**.

h. Make up your own headings and replace at least one story with your own original story on the topic of your choice.

i. Edit the story, then check the spelling in the publication.

j. Add your name in the Table of Contents on the first page of the newsletter.

k. Add a footer to the master pages, then compare your work to the sample shown in **FIGURE G-24**.

l. Save your work, submit it to your instructor, then exit Publisher.

FIGURE G-24

Independent Challenge 4: Explore

This Independent Challenge requires an Internet connection. You work at a computer camp during the summer and have been asked to teach a course on how to use Publisher. You decide to create a newsletter to inform the campers about the features of Publisher and show them what a great publication looks like.

a. Connect to the Internet and use your browser to go to www.microsoft.com. Find the home page for Publisher 2013.

b. Find information about Publisher's highlights and capabilities, then print out information pertaining to two topics of interest to you.

c. Start Publisher if necessary, then select a newsletter template of your choice.

d. Save the publication as **PUB G-Publisher Newsletter** to the location where you store your Data Files.

e. Use the Business Information set of your choice to enter appropriate information, then delete pages so that only two pages remain.

f. Create a title for the newsletter. Use the information you found on the Microsoft Web site to compose two stories for the newsletter: a lead story and a secondary story. You can copy and paste information from the Web site or write your own stories from scratch.

g. Add any clip art you feel is appropriate, then check the spelling in the publication.

h. Type your name in a text box on page 1, then compare your work to **FIGURE G-25**.

i. Save your work and submit it to your instructor, then exit Publisher.

FIGURE G-25

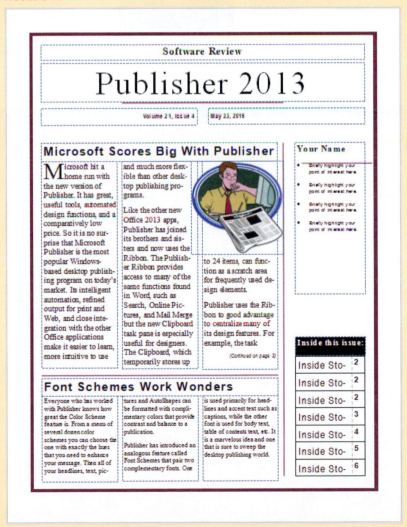

Visual Workshop

Open PUB G-7.pub from the location where you store your Data Files. Save the publication as **PUB G-Rug Collection Binder**. Modify the publication so that it looks like FIGURE G-26. (*Hint*: The image, PUB G-8.tif, which you need to add to the master page, is in the location where you store your Data Files.) Be sure to include your name where indicated. Save and print the pages. A sample of page 1 of the publication is shown in FIGURE G-26.

FIGURE G-26

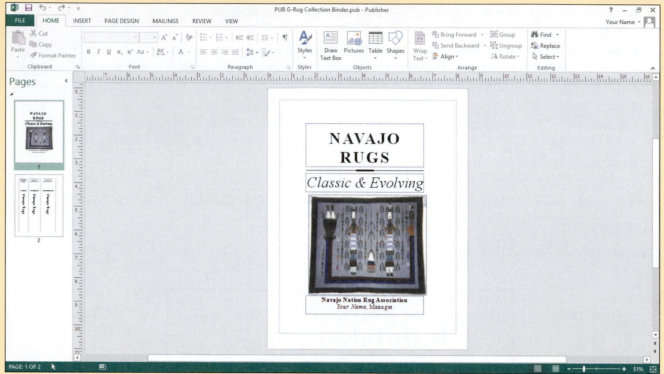

Image courtesy of Elizabeth Eisner Reding

Using Advanced Features

CASE — Design Diva has been hired to create a brochure for Piano Bravo, a company that sells and services pianos. You have created a draft of the brochure and are making final enhancements to it. In addition to your design work, the client also wants you to send the brochure to their customers. Your contact at Piano Bravo, Emma Rose, has given you a customer database you can use to address each brochure.

Unit Objectives

After completing this unit, you will be able to:

- Add BorderArt
- Design WordArt
- Wrap text around an object
- Rotate a text box
- Understand mail merge

- Create a mail merge
- Prepare for commercial printing
- Use the Pack and Go Wizard
- Capstone Project: Automotive Gift Certificate

Files You Will Need

PUB H-1.pub	PUB H-3.pub
PUB H-2.accdb	PUB H-4.pub

Add BorderArt

Attractive borders can add pizzazz to a publication. You can add borders to any object or text box. As with any design element, judicious use creates a smart, professional look; overuse distracts from the message. **BorderArt** lets you choose from a wide variety of decorative borders that come with Publisher. You can add a border to a text box, picture, or image using the BorderArt dialog box. You can choose a border style and modify the border's appearance. **CASE** ▶ *You want to add an eye-catching, imaginative border design to the first page of the brochure.*

STEPS

1. **Start Publisher, open PUB H-1.pub from the location where you store your Data Files, then save it as PUB H-Piano Brochure**

2. **Click anywhere in the text box containing the text Piano Bravo**

    To modify a frame or object, you must first select it. Compare your screen to **FIGURE H-1**.

3. **Press [F9], right-click the Piano Bravo text box, click Format Text Box on the shortcut menu, click the Colors and Lines tab in the Format Text Box dialog box if it is not already selected, then click BorderArt**

    The BorderArt dialog box opens. Borders can be simple lines of varying thickness or color, or they can be more elaborate designs that will help reinforce the theme of your document.

4. **Scroll the Available Borders list, then click Music Notes**

    FIGURE H-2 shows the BorderArt dialog box with the Music Notes border selected. When you click a border, the sample appears in the Preview box.

5. **Click the Always apply at default size check box to deselect it, then click OK**

    The BorderArt dialog box closes. The Format Text Box dialog box is open.

6. **In the Line section, select the number in the Width text box, type 12, then click OK**

    The BorderArt pattern appears in 12-pt characters on the edge of the text box, as shown in **FIGURE H-3**.

7. **Press [F9], then save your work**

Creating custom BorderArt

In addition to choosing a border style in the BorderArt dialog box, you can create your own custom borders using almost any simple clip art or graphic image. To do so, open the BorderArt dialog box, click the Create Custom button, then click Select Picture. You can choose from images in Online Pictures or elsewhere on your computer. You can also create BorderArt from your own images. Locate the image on your computer or SkyDrive, click the image, click Insert, choose a name for your border, then click OK.

FIGURE H-1: Text box selected

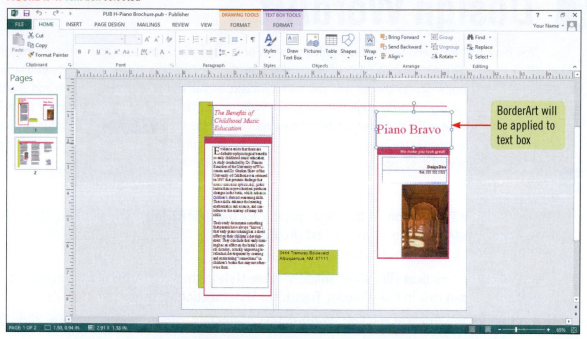

BorderArt will be applied to text box

FIGURE H-2: BorderArt dialog box

Available borders

Deselect check box to change the size of the border

Music Notes border

FIGURE H-3: BorderArt added to text box

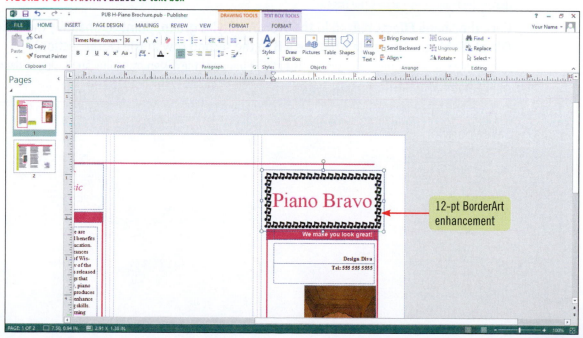

12-pt BorderArt enhancement

Design WordArt

Learning Outcomes
- Create WordArt
- Modify a WordArt shape
- Apply effects to WordArt

You have probably seen text that is highly designed, or in a specific shape, such as a circle or semi-circle. You can create this effect in Publisher by using **WordArt**. WordArt gives you a wide variety of text styles and effects from which to choose. You can transform text into all kinds of shapes, you can add shadows and patterns, and you can change text color. You want to add WordArt to the right panel of page 2 to identify the name of the store that will be on the back cover of the flyer. **CASE** ▶ *You want to emphasize the curve of the piano in the image at the bottom of the panel. You decide to change the shape of the WordArt once you've inserted it, so that the text curves in a way to complement the piano's shape.*

STEPS

1. **Click the Page 2 icon on the Pages pane, click the INSERT tab on the Ribbon, then click the WordArt button ▲ in the Text group**
   The WordArt Gallery displays WordArt styles.

2. **Click the Gradient Fill – Blue, Shadow, Wave style in the WordArt Gallery (second box in the second row in the WordArt Transform Styles section), as shown in FIGURE H-4**

3. **Type Piano Bravo in the Edit WordArt Text dialog box, click the Size list arrow, click 28, then click OK**
   The Piano Bravo WordArt object appears on the page in the default font of Arial Black, and the WORDART TOOLS FORMAT tab is displayed on the Ribbon. **TABLE H-1** describes some of the commonly used WordArt tools.

4. **Point to the WordArt object until the pointer changes to ⇖, then drag the object so that its upper-left corner is at 8" H / ½" V**

5. **Click the Change Shape button in the WordArt Styles group on the WORDART TOOLS FORMAT tab, then click Wave 2 (the last shape in the first row in the Warp category in the Shapes gallery)**
   The text takes on a different "wavy" shape.

6. **Click the Shape Fill list arrow in the WordArt Styles group, then click the Accent 3 (RGB (153, 255, 255)), Darker 25% color box (fourth column, third row)**
   The color of the WordArt has been changed to match the color scheme in use. It creates a focal point that draws the reader's eye across the page.

7. **Click the Shape Effects button in the WordArt Styles group, point to Shadow, then click Offset Right (the first style from the left in the second row in the Outer section)**
   The shadows appear in the text design. This addition improves the design by adding an illusion of depth.

8. **Click anywhere on the scratch area**
   The WordArt is deselected and the WORDART TOOLS FORMAT tab closes. Compare your page to **FIGURE H-5**.

9. **Save your work**

FIGURE H-4: WordArt Gallery

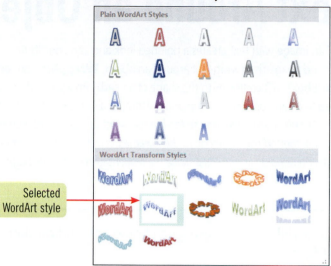

Selected WordArt style

FIGURE H-5: WordArt design in publication

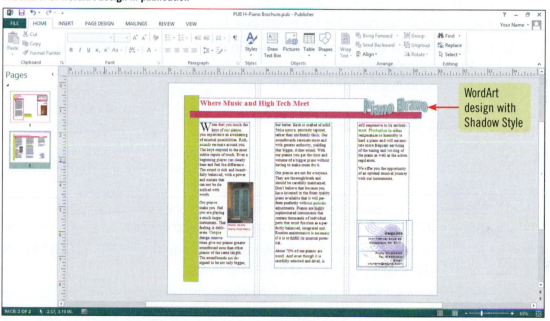

WordArt design with Shadow Style

TABLE H-1: WordArt Tools

button	name	description
	Insert WordArt	Opens WordArt Gallery (Located on INSERT tab)
	Edit Text	Opens Edit WordArt Text dialog box for modifying text in the current WordArt object
	Change WordArt Shape	Opens a gallery of available WordArt shapes for changing the current WordArt object
	Wrap Text	Opens a list of text wrapping options for the current WordArt object
	WordArt Even Height	Makes all letter heights equal
	WordArt Vertical Text	Places text on the vertical axis
	Align	Opens a list of options for modifying text alignment in the current WordArt object
	Spacing	Allows you to change the character spacing within the current WordArt object

Wrap Text Around an Object

Learning Outcomes
- Position an object on a page
- Edit wrap points surrounding an object

The careful integration of an image with text creates a polished look and can contribute to your overall design. One way to integrate text and images is to wrap text around an object. **Wrapping** text reshapes a text box (or just the flow of text in a text box) so it conforms to the shape of a nearby image or other object. Depending on an object's width, wrapped text can appear at the top and bottom, or along the sides, of the frame surrounding the object. **CASE** ▶ *You like what you have done so far, but you want to experiment with adding another image of a piano to page 2. You think that adding an image to the lower-left corner of the publication would create a new focal point, and wrapping text around an image could guide the reader's eyes across the page. The image of a piano will reinforce the subject matter of the brochure and direct the reader's eyes up and to the right.*

STEPS

1. With page 2 selected, right-click the grouped photograph and caption at 3" H / 4½" V, then click Delete Object

   The photo is deleted, and the text fills that space.

2. Click the INSERT tab on the Ribbon, click Online Pictures in the Illustrations group, type piano in the Office.com Clip Art search box, then press [Enter]

3. Locate and insert the piano image shown in FIGURE H-7 (if this image is not available, make a reasonable substitution)

   The graphic of a grand piano is placed on the page.

4. Right-click the picture, click Format Picture, then click the Layout tab in the Format Picture dialog box

5. Select the number in the Horizontal text box in the Position on page section, type 1.25, select the number in the Vertical text box in the Position on page section, type 5.5, then click OK

   The image moves to a precise location in the lower-left corner of the page, as shown in FIGURE H-7. There are times you may want to specify exact locations for an object rather than just dragging the object to a location.

QUICK TIP
Review text carefully after wrapping it to remove any awkward-looking hyphenation or isolated gaps of white space.

6. ▶ Click the Wrap Text button ▦ in the Arrange group on the PICTURE TOOLS FORMAT tab, click Tight, click ▦, then click Edit Wrap Points

TROUBLE
Your text may flow differently than shown. If so, create a different wrap point.

7. ▶ Position ✥ over the top-left corner of the object, then drag ✥ below the 'v' in innovations

   A second point is created. Each time a point is made, you can drag it to create a more form-fitting area.

8. Drag the top left point down toward the piano, drag the new point down toward the piano, press [Esc], then save your work

   Text is tightly wrapped around the image and slants upward along the lines of the image, as shown in FIGURE H-8.

Fine-tuning wrap points

You can fine-tune the way text wraps around a detailed object by editing the **wrap points**, the sizing handles that surround the object. To edit the points of an object that has already had its points modified, select the object, then drag the existing handles to fix specific areas. You can add or delete handles by pressing and holding [Ctrl] as you click an existing handle (to delete) or an empty spot on the selection border (to add). In FIGURE H-6, the handles surrounding the image can be moved to create an interesting effect.

FIGURE H-6: Text wrapped around points surrounding image

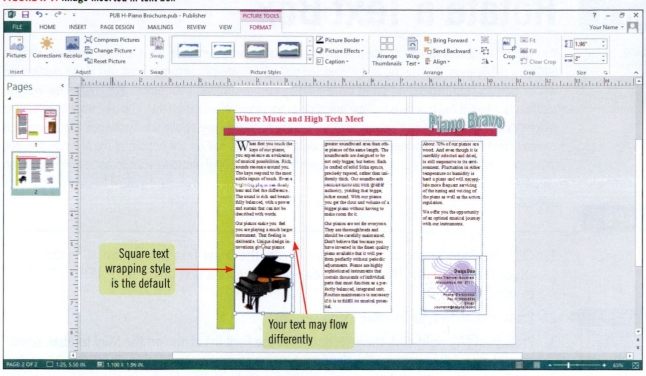

Square text
wrapping style
is the default

Your text may flow
differently

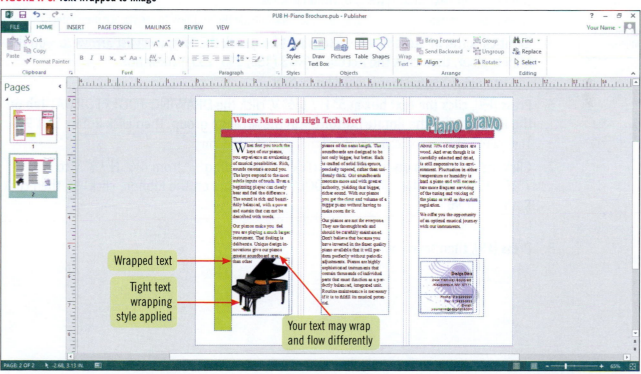

Wrapped text

Tight text
wrapping
style applied

Your text may wrap
and flow differently

Rotate a Text Box

You can rotate a text box to create interesting effects or to reorient text for a specific purpose, such as folding a publication. By rotating text in selected text boxes, you can ensure that all text in the publication will be easy to read depending on its placement in the final, folded publication. **CASE** ▶ *You want to rotate a text box in the brochure to draw attention to important promotional text. You also want to rotate the recipient's address and client's return address text boxes so they are "right-side up" when the brochure is complete and folded for mailing. You want to use a rotated text box on the bottom of the first panel to add important text. First, you will create a text box, enter the promotional message, then rotate it into position on the page. Next, you'll rotate the text box for the store's return address and create a rotated box for the recipient's address. These new text boxes will appear in the middle panel of the brochure.*

STEPS

1. Click the **Page 1 icon** on the Pages pane, click the **Draw Text Box button** in the Objects group on the HOME tab, then drag to create a text box from 7¾" H / 7¼" V to 10¼" H / 7¾" V

> **QUICK TIP**
> The promotional text should be brief but prominent; think of it as a visual sound bite.

2. Press **[F9]**, then type **In-Store Piano Lessons**

3. Press **[Ctrl][A]**, right-click the **selection**, click the **Font list arrow** on the Mini toolbar, scroll up and click **Arial Narrow**, click the **Font Size list arrow** on the Mini toolbar, click **18**, click the **Bold button** , click the **Center button** , then press **[Esc]**

   Compare your screen to **FIGURE H-9**.

> **QUICK TIP**
> You can drag the text box into different positions and use the rotation handle to fine-tune the positioning.

4. Right-click the **In-Store Piano Lessons text box**, click **Format Text Box**, click the **Size tab**, make sure that the height of the box is 0.5" and the width is 2.5", select the contents of the **Rotation text box**, type **–20**, then click **OK**

   The text box is rotated −20°. (You may have to click outside the text box to see the rotation effect.)

5. Right-click the **In-Store Piano Lessons text box**, click the **Shape Fill list arrow** on the Mini toolbar, then click the **Accent 3 (RGB (153, 255, 255)) color box**

   This text is more noticeable with the added fill color.

6. Press **[F9]**, click the text box at 5" H / 6½" V, click the **DRAWING TOOLS FORMAT tab** on the Ribbon, click the **Rotate button** in the Arrange group, then click **Rotate Left 90°**

   The return address is now correctly placed and oriented for printing.

7. Click the **HOME tab** on the Ribbon, click , then drag ╋ from 4½" H / 3" V to 7" H / 4½" V, click the **DRAWING TOOLS FORMAT tab** on the Ribbon, click , then click **Rotate Left 90°**

   Compare your work to **FIGURE H-10**.

8. Press **[F9]**, then save your work

FIGURE H-9: Completed text in text box

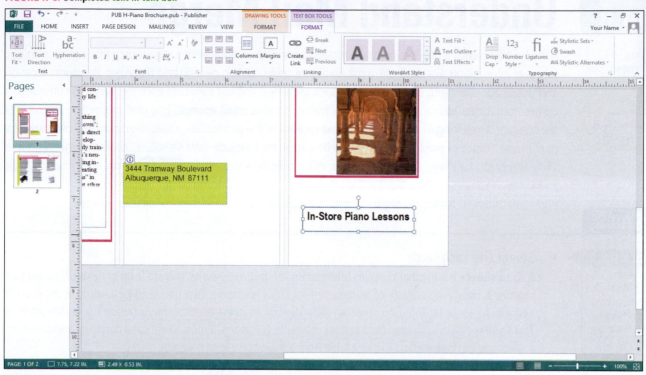

FIGURE H-10: Rotated text boxes

Understand Mail Merge

A mail merge blends a publication that contains generic information with a data source that contains unique pieces of information. For example, a gift certificate could contain generic text regarding the store's location and details about the gift, and unique text, such as the first and last names of each recipient. The unique text comes from a data source. In Publisher, this feature is called **mail merge**. In a mail merge two documents are combined, resulting in a set of customized versions of the publication. **FIGURE H-11** shows an overview of a mail merge. Types of publications that can be customized include sales literature, postcards, greeting and invitation cards, catalogs, award certificates, gift certificates, and labels. **CASE** *You know that once the publication is complete, Piano Bravo will want the brochure personalized with information it has collected about potential customers. Before you begin the mail merge process, you consider all the necessary steps.*

DETAILS

- ### Select the recipients

  A **data source** is a file that contains information about the recipients. It is made up of fields organized into records. A **field** is a category of information—such as last name, first name, address, state, or zip code. A **record** is a set of information about an individual or an item—for example, a person's complete address. **Data source files** can come from several programs, but you will most likely use a database, a spreadsheet, a Microsoft Outlook contact list, or a table from a word processing program.

  If you don't have a data source file from another program, or prefer to create a new one, you can create one using Publisher. The Mail Merge pane guides you through the main steps: creating or connecting to a recipient list, creating the merged publication, and preparing the merged publication. The Mail Merge pane offers choices as to the type of information you can collect for the data source file and even lets you add your own fields. Some commonly used mail merge information fields are address, city, zip code, country, e-mail address, and home phone. The Mail Merge command makes it possible to quickly create directories and product catalogs by automatically filling pages with text and images from a product database or list. A product list is merged into a desired format in a three-step process. To begin, click MAILINGS on the Ribbon, click the Mail Merge list arrow in the Start group, then click Step-by-Step Mail Merge Wizard.

- ### Create the publication

  A Publisher publication contains the generic information that appears in every merged publication. In the mail merge process, you insert a text box or a table frame that will contain the merge fields, where the unique information about the recipient is placed inside the publication. For example, you can insert the person's name in the Greeting line so that it will read "Dear John Smith." With the Mail Merge pane, it is easy to go back and edit the fields until you get exactly the publication you want.

- ### Consider options

  Using the mail merge capabilities, you can filter and sort a subset of records. **Filtering** allows you to print, preview, or merge a portion of qualifying records. **Sorting** allows you to change the order in which the merged publications are printed or viewed. You can sort and filter records using the Mail Merge Recipients dialog box.

- ### Preview the publication

  The ability to preview the merged publications allows you to look over the output before it is printed to catch any mistakes without wasting paper. This is particularly important because printing and mailing publications can be expensive. Paper, inks, envelopes, and even bulk postal rates are costly. Assuming all your merge fields are correct, Publisher offers a variety of ways to preview your work without printing. Using the Print preview link in the Create merged publications section of the Mail Merge pane, you can preview your merged documents prior to printing them.

- ### Print the publication

  The Publisher Mail Merge pane uses dialog boxes to guide you through printing your publications.

FIGURE H-11: Mail merge process

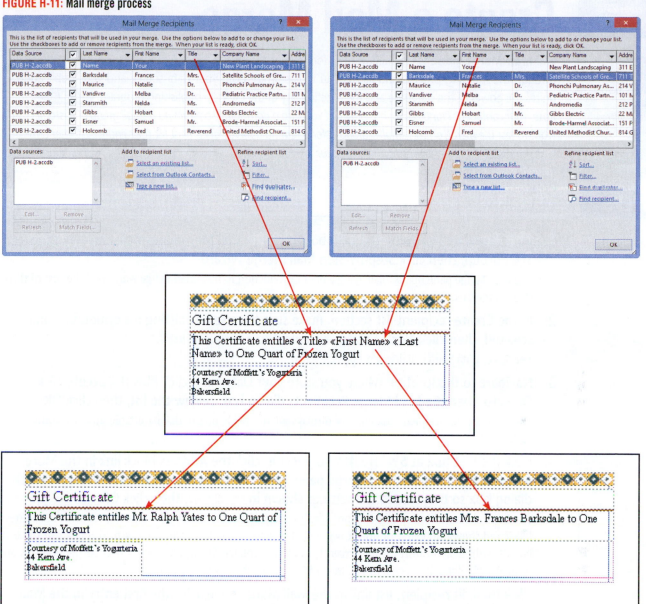

Catching costly errors

Several types of spelling errors demand your attention. The most obvious is the danger of misspelled words in a publication. Such errors make your company seem unprofessional. Another important error is the misspelling of a person's name. Errors in people's names and titles can offend them. A simple misspelling or a misuse of Mrs. or Ms. may annoy potential clients to the point that they will not do business with your company. When in doubt, find a way to verify a potential misspelling; the extra effort pays off. Bulk mailings are often a one-way communication, and you may never know that a recipient was offended.

Create a Mail Merge

The **Mail Merge pane** is an effective tool for creating personalized publications. This feature guides you through the merging process and allows you to customize both your data source and your publication. It unites the power of the database and the functionality of the desktop publishing program. **CASE** ▶ *Emma Rose, your contact at Piano Bravo, has provided you with a data source containing a small group of customers. You want to test the merge on this smaller group before creating a merge document for their entire customer base. You want the merged address information to appear in the recipient text box you created in the middle panel of the second page.*

STEPS

1. **Click the MAILINGS tab on the Ribbon, click the Mail Merge button list arrow in the Start group, then click Step-by-Step Mail Merge Wizard**

   The Mail Merge pane opens, displaying a brief introduction to how mail merge works and the first of three steps in the merging process.

2. **In the Create recipient list section, make sure the Use an existing list option button is selected, then click Next: Create or connect to a recipient list**

   The Select Data Source dialog box opens.

3. **Navigate to the location where you store your Data Files, click PUB H-2.accdb, click Open to open the Mail Merge Recipients dialog box, review the list, then click OK**

   The Mail Merge Recipients dialog box displays all the fields in the database table and the contents of each record.

4. **Click the text box at 5½" H / 4" V to select it, click the Address block link in the More items category on the Mail Merge pane, adjust the settings in the Insert Address Block dialog box so they match the settings shown in FIGURE H-12, then click OK**

   The Insert Address Block dialog box provides a variety of ways to insert the recipient's name in the address block and shows a preview of how it will look. On your screen, the address block field appears in the text box. It is difficult to read on the screen because it is rotated 90 degrees, but when the publications are printed and folded, the recipient's address will be in just the right spot for mailing.

5. **Click the Edit recipient list link in the Mail Merge pane, click the first entry in the Mail Merge Recipients dialog box if it is not selected, click PUB H-2.accdb in the Data sources box, then click Edit**

   The Edit Data Source dialog box opens. Compare your screen to FIGURE H-13.

6. **Press [Tab], type a preferred title, press [Tab], delete Your, type your first name, press [Tab], delete Name, type your last name, click OK, click OK to confirm the read-only cell, click Yes to update the database and save your changes, click OK to close the Mail Merge Recipients dialog box, then save your work**

   You replaced the first three fields in this record with your preferred title and your first and last names. Your name and title appear in the text box on the brochure. Compare your screen to FIGURE H-14.

7. **Click Next: Create merged publications in the Step 2 of 3 section at the bottom of the Mail Merge pane, click Print preview in the Create merged publications section of the Mail Merge pane, view the preview in Backstage view, make sure that the correct printer is selected, then print the first page of the merged document**

   Examine your publication.

FIGURE H-12: Insert Address Block dialog box

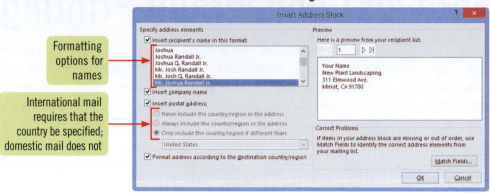

Formatting options for names

International mail requires that the country be specified; domestic mail does not

FIGURE H-13: Edit Data Source dialog box

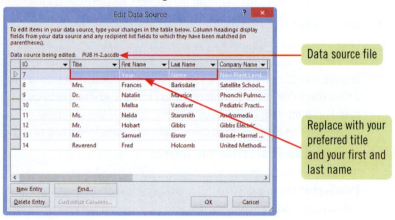

Data source file

Replace with your preferred title and your first and last name

FIGURE H-14: Preview of the Mail Merge

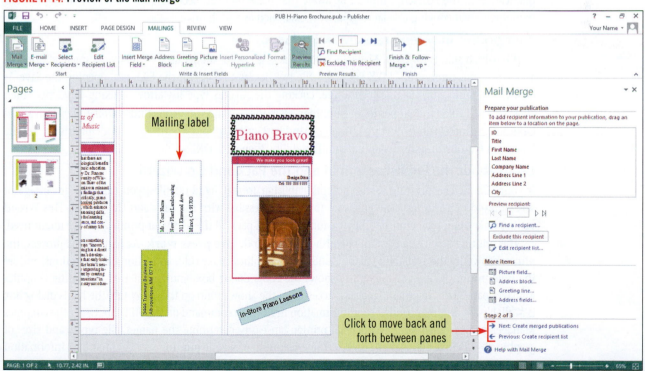

Mailing label

Click to move back and forth between panes

Using Advanced Features

Prepare for Commercial Printing

Learning Outcomes
• Learn about the printing process
• Discover printing options

Once your publication is completed, you can print it yourself or send the files to a commercial printer for bulk printing with high-quality options and results. For professional output, it is important to consult with the printer during the design process to save time and expense. **CASE** ▷ *You know that once the project is complete and successfully tested, Piano Bravo will want the brochure professionally printed. You examine the commercial printing options so you can start making arrangements.*

DETAILS

- **Consult printing professionals early in the process**

  Cost is important. You will need to know about quantity, quality, paper stock, binding, folding, trimming, and deadlines so that you can determine a budget and schedule. Ask your printer for recommendations on ways to reduce costs. For example, updating your graphics by doing your own scanning, or creating your own art files instead of relying on the printer's art services may reduce expenses.

- **Determine the file format**

  Once you select a printer, find out which hand-off format they require. The **hand-off format** is the final format the printer receives. Publisher can create files in the PostScript or Publisher formats. You can also prepare your files in the CMYK format (composite postscript files in the cyan-magenta-yellow-black format), which many commercial printers prefer. There are advantages to using the Publisher format, but this option may also limit your commercial printing options. You also need to know if your printer prefers to accept transferred files on disks, flash drives, CDs, by e-mail, by posting to an ftp site, or through some other means.

QUICK TIP
Once the file is saved as PostScript, you cannot make any changes to it.

- **Explore the PostScript file format**

  If your commercial printer doesn't accept Publisher files, or uses only Macintosh computers, you can use the **PostScript** file format. To do this, you must install a PostScript printer driver on your computer, then follow the steps to use the PostScript printer driver. **FIGURE H-15** shows the Save As PostScript dialog box. The Save As PostScript dialog box is opened automatically from Backstage view once you change the Save as type list arrow to PostScript in the Save As dialog box, then click Save.

  Ask your commercial-printing service if you need to apply any specific print settings, then save the publication in the PostScript format. Be aware that these files can become quite large. Try saving to your hard drive, then copying to a large-capacity media, such as a flash drive.

TROUBLE
You will receive an error message if you do not have a PostScript printer installed.

- **Your printer may require a CMYK PostScript file**

  CMYK, which stands for Cyan Magenta Yellow Black, is a color model used by many commercial printers. You can save a composite CMYK PostScript file by clicking Save As on the FILE tab, opening the Save As dialog box, supplying a name for the file, clicking the Save as type list arrow, clicking PostScript, then clicking Save. Click the Properties button, then click the Advanced button. Under *printer name* Advanced Options, expand Document Options, then expand PostScript Options. In the PostScript Options list, set the PostScript Output Options to Optimize for Portability, then click OK.

- **Learn about the Publisher format and the Pack and Go Wizard**

  If your commercial printing service accepts Publisher format hand-off files, you can take advantage of several important features. The Publisher format is accessible with the Pack and Go Wizard. This Wizard verifies linked graphics, embeds TrueType fonts, and will pack all the files your printing service might need.

  The printing service can use the Publisher format to do **pre-press work**. As part of this process, the printer can verify the availability of fonts and linked graphics, make color corrections or separations, and set the final printing options. **FIGURE H-16** shows the Fonts dialog box, and **FIGURE H-17** shows the Graphics Manager pane. The Graphics Manager is accessed in the Show group on the VIEW tab; the Fonts dialog box is available as part of Embedded Font Information in the Info command on the FILE tab. Using the Graphics Manager pane, you or your commercial printer can easily determine the names, file types, and sizes of graphic objects in a publication. Each of these features gives your printing service important information about elements that make up your publication, and any potential problems.

Using Advanced Features

FIGURE H-15: Save As PostScript dialog box

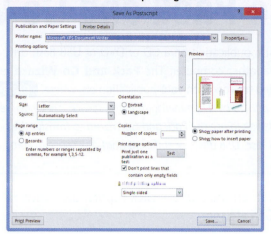

FIGURE H-16: Fonts dialog box

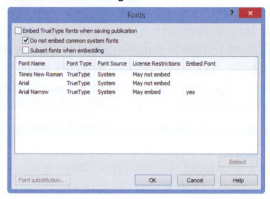

FIGURE H-17: Graphics Manager pane

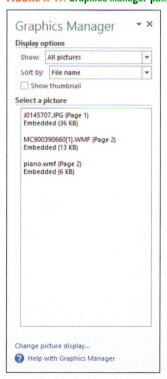

Use the Pack and Go Wizard

You may need to put a publication on a CD or DVD or USB flash drive to take to a commercial printing service or to use at another computer. The **Pack and Go Wizard** lets you package all the fonts and graphic images needed to work with your publication elsewhere. **CASE** ▶ *You have arranged to have the Piano Bravo brochure printed by a commercial-printing service. They have requested that you provide the file on a flash drive, so you decide to use the Pack and Go Wizard to transfer the publication. (You will need a writable CD, DVD-R or DVD+R disc, USB drive, or sufficient hard disk space to complete this lesson.)*

STEPS

1. Click the FILE tab on the Ribbon, click Export, then click Save for a Commercial Printer in the Pack and Go category

2. Click the Pack and Go Wizard button

   The Pack and Go Wizard dialog box opens, as shown in **FIGURE H-18**. The first Pack and Go Wizard dialog box defines the location where the packed file will be stored. As part of the packing process, the wizard also prints the publication, by default.

3. Select the Other location option button, if available, insert a flash drive in an empty USB port, click the Browse button and navigate to the flash drive or to a location where you want to store this file, click Select folder, then click Next

   The Pack and Go Wizard prepares your files. When it is done, you see a dialog box that tells you your publication was successfully packed.

4. Click the Print a composite proof check box to deselect it, as shown in **FIGURE H-19**, then click OK

   If you leave the check box selected, the Wizard prints the publication.

5. Exit Publisher

FIGURE H-18: First Pack and Go Wizard dialog box

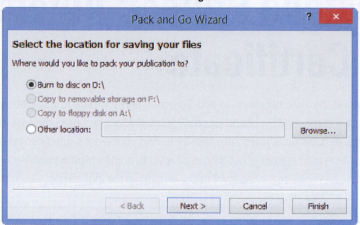

FIGURE H-19: Final Pack and Go Wizard dialog box

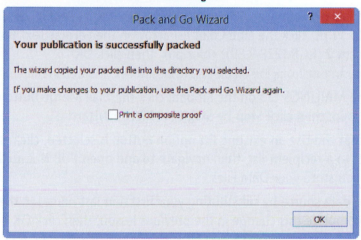

Sending a publication using e-mail

When you send a large number of e-mail messages that are nearly all identical, but contain some unique information, you can use the E-Mail Merge feature to create individually customized messages that contain personalized notes. You use this feature by creating or connecting to a recipient list, preparing a publication, then creating the merged publication. When you prepare the publication, you create the text that you want in every version of the message. When you create the merged publication, you can preview the individual messages and make specific changes. Click the E-mail Merge button list arrow in the Start group on the MAILINGS tab on the Ribbon, then click Step-by-Step E-mail Merge Wizard. You can also click the FILE tab, then click Share to see a variety of methods of sending publications using e-mail. See **FIGURE H-20** to see the available e-mail choices.

FIGURE H-20: Share with e-mail options

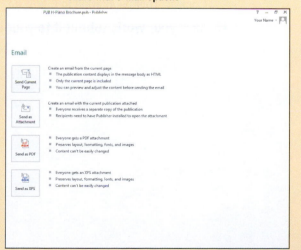

Using Advanced Features

Capstone Project: Automotive Gift Certificate

You have learned the skills necessary to add BorderArt and WordArt to publications. You have wrapped text around objects and rotated text boxes. You have learned about and used the Mail Merge feature and the Pack and Go Wizard, and the steps you should take for having your work printed commercially. **CASE** ▶ *You have been asked to create personalized gift certificates for select customers of an automotive service. You decide to enhance the certificate by adding thematic BorderArt before performing the mail merge.*

STEPS

1. Start Publisher, open **PUB H-3.pub** from the location where you store your Data Files, then save it as **PUB H-Automotive Gift Certificate**

2. Right-click the **text box at 5" H / 2" V**, click **Format Text Box**, click the **BorderArt button**, then click the **Coupon Cutout Dashes option**

3. Click the **Always apply at default size check box** to deselect it, click **OK**, change the Line width to **11 pt**, click the **Line Color list arrow** in the Format Text Box dialog box, click the **Accent 2 (RGB (228,0,89)) color box**, then click **OK**
   The BorderArt pattern appears on the edge of the text box, as shown in **FIGURE H-21**.

4. Click the **MAILINGS tab** on the Ribbon, click the **Mail Merge button list arrow** in the Start group, then click **Step-by-Step Mail Merge Wizard**

5. Verify that the **Use an existing list option button** is selected, click **Next: Create or connect to a recipient list**, then navigate to and open **PUB H-2.accdb** from the location where you store your Data Files

6. Edit the data source by **substituting your first and last names in the first record** if you didn't complete this change in the previous lesson, then click **OK**

QUICK TIP
If your work needs editing, click Edit recipient list or Previous: Create recipient list on the task pane to make corrections.

7. Click the **text box at 2½ H / 2" V**, click **Address block** in the Mail Merge pane, make sure the 'Joshua Randall Jr.' format is selected, deselect the **Insert company name** and **Insert postal address check boxes**, then click **OK**

8. Click **Next: Create merged publications** in the pane

9. Click **Print preview** in the Create merged publications section of the pane
   Compare your publication to **FIGURE H-22**.

10. Save your work, submit it to your instructor, then exit Publisher

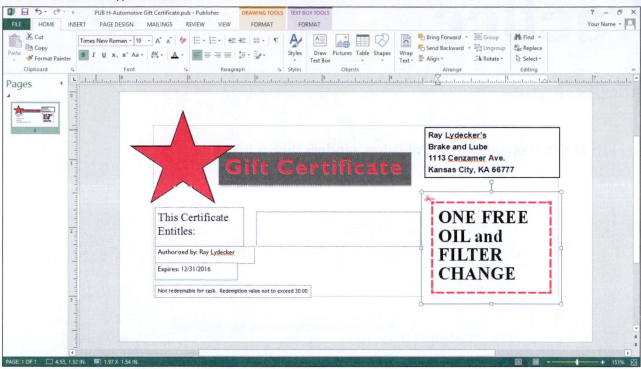

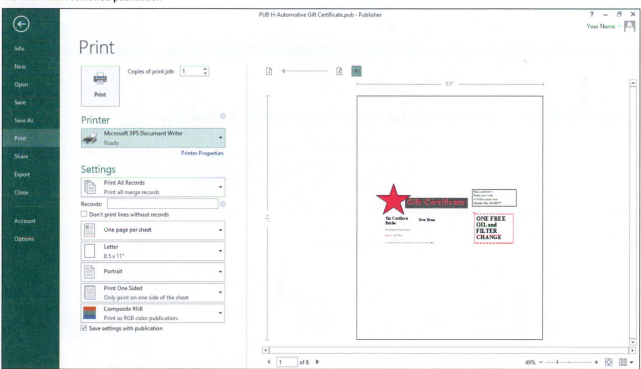

Practice

Concepts Review

Label each of the elements in the Publisher window shown in FIGURE H-23.

FIGURE H-23

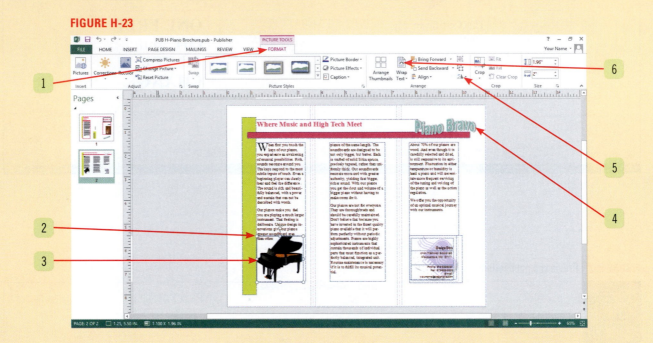

Match each of the buttons with the statement that describes its function.

7.   a. Formats WordArt
8.   b. Displays WordArt shapes
9.   c. Changes wrap text
10.   d. Rotates a selected object
11.   e. Changes fill color
12.   f. Edits WordArt text

Select the best answer from the list of choices.

13. Which button is used to insert stylized text?
    a.
    b.
    c.
    d.

14. Which button is used to change a stylized shape?
    a.
    b.
    c.
    d.

15. Which feature blends two information sources together?
    a. File Blender
    b. Mail Marriage
    c. Mail Merge
    d. WordArt

16. Each of the following is true about WordArt, except _____.
    a. WordArt has a text wrapping menu
    b. You cannot change character spacing in WordArt
    c. You can resize WordArt
    d. You can edit WordArt

17. A file that contains information about the recipients of a mail merge is called a _____.
    a. field
    b. record
    c. data source
    d. blend source

18. Which button is used to edit wrap points around a picture?
    a.
    b.
    c.
    d.

19. You can make the following changes to BorderArt:
    a. Customize the design.
    b. Change the color.
    c. Change the point size.
    d. All of the above

20. Which button is used to edit the content of WordArt?
    a.
    b.
    c.
    d.

Skills Review

Throughout these exercises, use the Zoom feature where necessary to work with the publication more easily.

1. **Add BorderArt.**
   a. Start Publisher.
   b. Open PUB H-4.pub from the location where you store your Data Files, then save it as **PUB H-Gym Flyer**.
   c. Right-click the blue text box at 1" H / 2" V, click Format Text Box, then click BorderArt.
   d. Scroll through the list of available borders, then click Hearts.
   e. Click the Always apply at default size check box to deselect it, then click OK.
   f. Change the line width to 15 pt, then click OK.
   g. Save your work.

2. **Design WordArt.**
   a. Click the WordArt button on the INSERT tab, then click the second box in the first row of the WordArt Gallery.
   b. Type **We want you back!** in the text box.
   c. Change the font size to 36 pt if necessary, make the text bold, then click OK.
   d. Reposition the WordArt so that the top-left corner is at 1½" H / 1½" V.
   e. Apply the Double Wave 2 WordArt shape (the second shape in the second row).
   f. Add the Accent 3 (RGB (224, 214, 245)) fill color to the WordArt.
   g. Save your work.

3. **Wrap text around an object.**

   a. Create an AutoShape using the Heart shape. The top-left corner of the heart should be at 1½" H / 5" V, and its dimensions should be 2½" H / 2½" V.

   b. Customize the wrapped text using the DRAWING TOOLS FORMAT tab.

   c. Experiment by moving the wrap points to alter the shape of the wrapped text, then click the Undo button.

   d. Click the Shape Fill list arrow, click More Fill Colors, then fill the heart with any shade of red you choose.

   e. Save the publication.

4. **Rotate a text box.**

   a. Draw a new text box anywhere that has the dimensions 1¾" H × ½" V.

   b. Type **We miss you!** in the text box, then change the font size to 20 pt.

   c. Use the Bring to Front command.

   d. Place the text box so that the top-left corner is at $1^5/_8$" H / 5¾"V (superimposed over the heart).

   e. Rotate the text box 25 degrees.

   f. Save your work.

5. **Understand mail merge.**

   a. Imagine that you are the owner of a health club. You are always looking for ways to communicate more effectively with your customers and distributors. Given these goals, what kind of mail merge documents might you want to create?

   b. What types of information might be in the data source files for your company?

   c. What programs would you be likely to use to create these data source files?

6. **Create a mail merge.**

   a. Display the Mail Merge pane.

   b. Select PUB H-2.accdb from the location where you store your Data Files as the data source, confirm that your first and last names and preferred title are in the first record, or make these changes, then click OK.

   c. Click the text box at 1½" H / 3" V to select it, press [F9], put the insertion point at the beginning of the text, then use the Insert Address Block dialog box to choose the Joshua Randall Jr. format and also choose to never include the country/region. (Deselect the Insert company name and Insert postal address check boxes.)

   d. Click Next: Create merged publications.

   e. Save your work, then print the first page of the merged document.

7. **Prepare for commercial printing.**

   a. Use the Web and your favorite search engine to research commercial printers and their requirements. Print at least one Web page that you find for a commercial printer.

   b. Make a list of requirements/suggestions from a commercial printer, or underline/highlight them on the Web page you printed.

8. **Use the Pack and Go Wizard.**

   a. Open the Pack and Go Wizard to take files to a commercial printing service.

   b. Use a blank flash drive, or other removable storage device, if necessary.

   c. Click Next in the first Wizard dialog box, then deselect the option to print a composite proof and click OK in the last dialog box.

   d. Close the publication.

   e. Exit Publisher.

Independent Challenge 1

As office manager for your company, you decide to make customized monthly calendars for the employees.

a. Start Publisher and use the BUILT-IN Templates list to create a calendar using the Layers design.

b. Use the Business Information set of your choice to add appropriate information, and apply the color scheme of your choice.

c. Save the publication as **PUB H-Monthly Calendar** to the location where you store your Data Files.

d. Add BorderArt of your choice, sized to 16 pt around the text box containing the month and year.

e. Use the WordArt feature to create text that reads **Go Team**. Change the font size to 40 pt.

f. Superimpose the WordArt over the filled text box to the left of the calendar.

g. Modify the fill color of the WordArt to Accent 3.

h. Type your name in the text box located at 2" H / 1½" V.

i. Delete the organization logo placeholder if necessary, save the file and submit it to your instructor, then exit Publisher.

Independent Challenge 2

The school band leader asks you to design a postcard announcing a concert.

a. Start Publisher and create a schedule using the Schedule template in the Event section of the All Marketing Postcards category of the BUILT-IN Templates list.

b. Use the Business Information set of your choice to add appropriate information, and apply the color scheme of your choice.

c. Save the publication as **PUB H-Band Postcard** to the location where you store your Data Files.

d. Add BorderArt around the Activities text box.

e. Modify the text at 2" H / 2" V with your own text.

f. Delete the object at 1" H / 1¾" V.

g. Delete the contents of the Activities text box but leave the title.

h. Write appropriate text in the text box.

i. Add your name as the contact person.

j. Change any text as necessary to fit the theme of a school band. Make up a suitable event title.

k. Use Online Pictures to add an image to the center panel.

l. Resize and move the object to illustrate that you know how to change the wrap text settings. Compare your publication to **FIGURE H-24**.

m. Save and print the publication, then exit Publisher.

FIGURE H-24

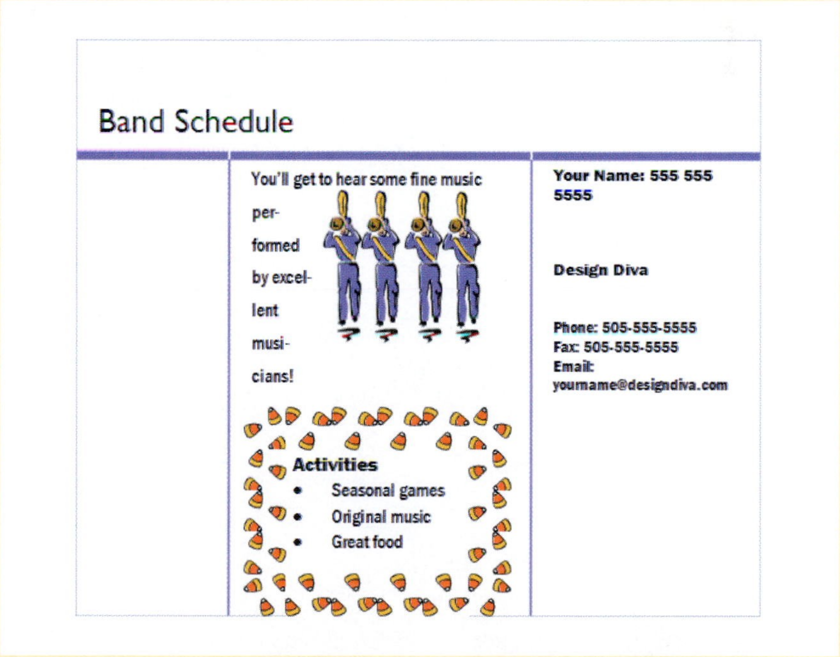

Independent Challenge 3

With your new Publisher skills, you'd like to open your own design shop called Design Center. First, you'll need business cards. You will use mail merge to personalize the cards for your employees and yourself.

a. Start Publisher, then choose a design in the Blank Sizes Business Cards category of the BUILT-IN Templates list.

b. Use the Business Information set of your choice to add appropriate information, and add any color scheme you like.

c. Save the publication as **PUB H-Design Center Business Card** to the location where you store your Data Files.

d. Open the Mail Merge pane, then select PUB H-2.accdb from the location where you store your Data Files as the data source.

e. Insert fields for your first and last name and company name where you want them to appear on your business card, and add a logo, title, business name, address, and phone, fax, and e-mail information.

f. Preview the business card to make sure that your name appears. Make any necessary corrections.

g. Use Backstage view to test print your business card.

h. Save the publication and exit Publisher.

Independent Challenge 4: Explore

A friend is celebrating her ten-year wedding anniversary and has asked you to create the cover of her anniversary party invitations. To do this, you'll use a Publisher template and BorderArt.

a. Start Publisher, then choose a template design in the Invitation Cards category of the BUILT-IN Templates list.

b. Use the Business Information Set of your choice to add appropriate information, and use any color scheme.

c. Save the publication as **PUB H-Wedding Anniversary Invitation**.

d. Add attractive BorderArt to a text box on the cover of the invitation, using any available style and size.

e. Create appropriate text for the cover, using your own name in the text. (You will add your friend's name once the invitation is approved.)

f. Change the BorderArt to a custom border using a piece of clip art.

Independent Challenge 4: Explore (continued)

g. Add a piece of clip art to the cover of the invitation.
Recolor the clip art. (*Hint*: Use the Adjust group in the PICTURE TOOLS FORMAT tab.) Compare your
publication to **FIGURE H-25**.

h. Save your work and print the publication, then exit Publisher.

FIGURE H-25

Visual Workshop

Use the BUILT-IN Templates list to create an Accessory Bar Informational Brochure as the initial design of a brochure for Rif's Toy Shop. Save this publication as **PUB H-Toy Shop Brochure** to the location where you store your Data Files. Use **FIGURE H-26** as a guide. The BorderArt around the text box at 5" H / 2" V has a Scared cat pattern. The style for the "Specializing In Model Airplanes" text comes from the WordArt Gallery—experiment to find the right style. Replace the e-mail address with your e-mail address. Save your work and submit it to your instructor.

FIGURE H-26

Working Efficiently

CASE > Design Diva is holding a two-day computer-training course for its employees. The training sessions will introduce employees to efficient methods of working with Publisher and other Microsoft apps. The training will also cover peripheral devices they can use to enhance and speed up their work. You have been asked to organize and create course materials for this event.

Unit Objectives

After completing this unit, you will be able to:

- Integrate with Office apps
- Import a Word document
- Use AutoCorrect
- Use digital images

- Embed and link objects
- Use Design Checker
- Understand speech recognition
- Capstone Project: Dinner Invitation

Files You Will Need

PUB I-1.docx	PUB I-6.pub
PUB I-2.pub	PUB I-7.pub
PUB I-3.pub	PUB I-8.docx
PUB I-4.docx	PUB I-9.docx
PUB I-5.pub	

©Alena P/Shutterstock

Integrate with Office Apps

All Microsoft Office apps are designed to work together, sharing files and data. Because Word, Excel, PowerPoint, Access, Publisher, and Outlook have a similar look and feel, your familiarity with one app makes it easier to use others. Office apps make it possible to easily transfer information or objects created in one app, such as Excel, to another app, such as Publisher. **CASE** ▶ *One of the goals of the training course is to familiarize employees with business productivity software and advise them on which apps are best suited to particular tasks. To make the training interactive, you decide to ask co-workers familiar with specific apps to speak about how they use them at Design Diva.*

DETAILS

- ### Microsoft Word

  Almost everyone at Design Diva uses Word, a **word processing** program, to create letters, memos, reports, and stories. But not everyone is as familiar with Publisher as you are. You plan to teach employees how they can import a Word document, such as the one shown in **FIGURE I-1**, into a publication. You will explain how this allows them to take advantage of some features in Word, such as advanced formatting or word count, that aren't available in Publisher.

- ### Microsoft Excel

  Many employees use Excel, an **electronic spreadsheet** program that automatically calculates and analyzes data and creates powerful charts. A **chart** is a graphical representation of data. Ricardo Fernandez, Design Diva's office manager, uses Excel to create budgets and financial statements, and to track customer billing and invoices. **FIGURE I-2** shows an Excel worksheet with data and a chart. This chart is also shown in **FIGURE I-3**, after it was pasted into a Publisher publication.

- ### Microsoft PowerPoint

  When the staff needs to present information to a group of people, they create professional visual presentations using PowerPoint. A **presentation** is a series of projected slides and/or handouts that a speaker refers to while delivering information. Together, Publisher and PowerPoint can make for an impressive and cohesive presentation using a slide show from PowerPoint and supporting documents from Publisher that share similar fonts and colors. Maria Abbot, Design Diva's president, will use PowerPoint to create a slide show summarizing the company's growth and financial performance; she will give the presentation during the training session and later at an annual meeting of investors, creditors, and clients.

- ### Microsoft Access

  Complex data can be organized, tracked, and updated using an Access database. A **database** is a collection of related information that is organized into tables, records, and fields. Information in a database can be sorted and retrieved in a variety of ways, and then used to make business decisions. Access databases can be used as a data source for Publisher mail merges. Nancy Garrott, Design Diva's marketing manager, uses Access to create and maintain a customer information database. She shares this information with the accounting department so it does not have to re-enter information about new customers and sales.

- ### Microsoft Outlook

  All Design Diva employees use the Outlook personal information manager to keep track of business and personal contacts and to schedule appointments. Outlook contact lists can be used as data sources for mail merges in Publisher.

- ### Office tools

  All Office programs include **online collaboration**, the ability to share information over the Internet. Employees can schedule online meetings and have discussions over the World Wide Web. The **Speech Recognition** feature lets them enter data and give commands verbally using a computer microphone. You can use the Research task pane to obtain online information from reference sources such as the Encarta Dictionary, Thesaurus, HighBeam™ Research, Factiva iWorks™, and Bing.

FIGURE I-1: Word document

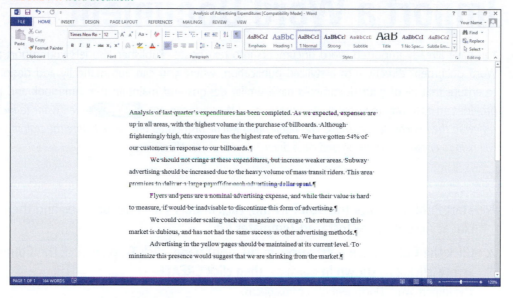

FIGURE I-2: Excel worksheet containing a chart

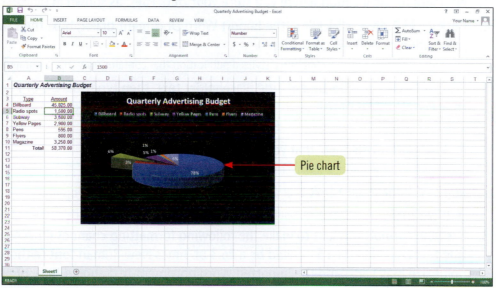

FIGURE I-3: Excel chart and Word story in publication

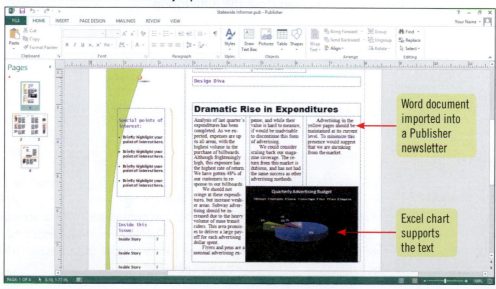

Import a Word Document

Learning Outcomes
• Use a template to create a publication with an imported Word document

You have already imported Word documents into text boxes. Publisher also lets you import an existing Word document directly into a stylized publication, where you can automatically add design elements to ensure that all of your documents have similar designs and maintain the same look and feel. It also provides an easy way to enhance an unformatted Word document. **CASE** ▶ *You want to include a book review in the pre-course materials. This publication will be distributed one week before the training session and will help to encourage thinking and class discussion about job effectiveness.*

STEPS

TROUBLE
If you get a warning box that you need a converter, contact your instructor or technical support person.

1. Start Publisher, click the **BUILT-IN tab**, click **Import Word Documents**, and then click **Linear Accent** in the Installed Templates list

2. Click the **Color scheme list arrow** in the right pane, click **Tropics**, click the **Columns list arrow**, click **2** as shown in **FIGURE I-4**, then click **CREATE**

   The Import Word Document dialog box opens.

3. Navigate to the location where you store your Data Files, as shown in **FIGURE I-5**

4. Click **PUB I-1.docx**, click **OK** in the Import Word Document dialog box, then save the publication as **PUB I-Book Review**

   The Word document is imported into a stylized publication that contains only this document.

5. Press **[F9]**, click the **Document Title placeholder text**, then type **Sources of Power: How People Make Decisions**

   The title of the book review is inserted, but it looks too small.

6. Right-click the **Title text** (that you just typed), then click **Best Fit**

   The font size of the title is now larger and fills the text box.

7. Right-click the **Page 1 text box** at **1" H / ½" V**, then click **Delete Object**

   Page numbers are not necessary because this is a single-page publication. Compare your page to **FIGURE I-6**.

8. Use your formatting skills to make the following formatting changes if necessary: the title text (typed in step 5) should be a **26.3 pt Times New Roman** font (although your point size may vary) and the imported Word document text should be a **10 pt Times New Roman** font

9. Press **[F9]**, save your work, then close the publication

---

Publishing HTML

Using the Export command in Backstage view, you can publish your publication as a web page. To do this, click the FILE tab to open Backstage view, then click the Export command. Click Publish HTML in the center pane. In the right pane, click the Web Page (HTML) arrow to choose between the two options: Web Page (HTML) or Single File Web Page (MHTML).

The Web Page option creates an HTML file with fixed objects and their supporting images and sounds. The Single File Web Page creates an embedded HTML file that contains no supporting files or folders. Once you've selected the type of HTML version you want to save, click the Publish HTML button in the right pane.

FIGURE I-4: Import Word Documents templates

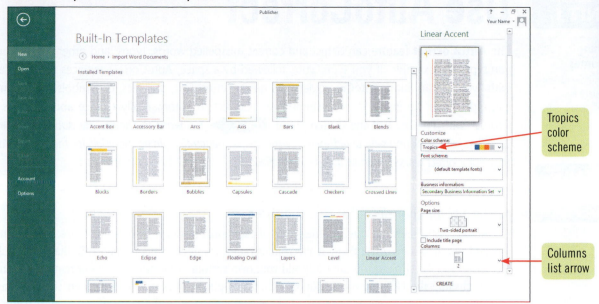

FIGURE I-5: Import Word Document dialog box

FIGURE I-6: Imported Word document

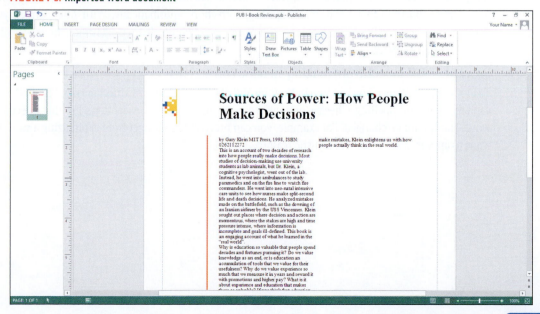

Use AutoCorrect

The **AutoCorrect** feature can detect and correct misspelled words, typos, and other common errors as you type. For example, if you type "yuo" followed by a space, AutoCorrect replaces the incorrect word with "you." In addition, AutoCorrect lets you quickly insert text, graphics, or symbols. For example, you can type "(tm)" to insert ™, or customize AutoCorrect to automatically replace abbreviations such as "potus" with President of the United States. **CASE** *You want to change the AutoCorrect settings to speed up your work and help avoid spelling errors as you generate training materials for the course. You review how AutoCorrect works and how it can be modified.*

DETAILS

• **Add to or change AutoCorrect entries**

AutoCorrect uses AutoCorrect entries, a list of commonly misspelled words and typos, to detect misusages and automatically correct them. It also contains some common symbols, such as ©, that can be substituted for specific keystrokes. You can easily add your own custom AutoCorrect entries or remove unwanted ones by clicking the FILE tab on the Ribbon, clicking Options, clicking Proofing, then clicking AutoCorrect Options. You can make additions or changes to AutoCorrect in the AutoCorrect: English (United States) dialog box. You can add an entry to AutoCorrect by typing the text you want replaced in the Replace text box, and the text that will replace it in the With text box. Once you create your entry, click Add, and the new AutoCorrect entry will be in effect. **FIGURE I-7** shows a new entry added to AutoCorrect. You can delete an AutoCorrect entry by clicking the entry you want to delete, then clicking Delete. You can also use AutoCorrect to format as you type. By clicking the AutoFormat As You Type tab in the AutoCorrect dialog box, shown in **FIGURE I-8**, you can set this feature to automatically apply bullets and numbers to lists of text.

• **Use AutoCorrect to correct capitalization errors**

AutoCorrect recognizes words that are commonly capitalized and corrects them when they are entered incorrectly. For example, the first word in a sentence, or the days of the week, are recognized and corrected if they are not capitalized. AutoCorrect also recognizes when the first two letters of a word have been capitalized incorrectly and makes the second letter lowercase. You can also add names or words that you want capitalized or set in lowercase to the AutoCorrect entries.

• **Use AutoCorrect to correct spelling errors**

AutoCorrect works differently than the Publisher Spell Checker. The Spell Checker does not automatically correct all of your spelling errors. After it identifies potential misspellings, it underlines the words with a red wavy line. As you edit your publication, you can decide whether the underlined words are truly misspelled. AutoCorrect, on the other hand, makes spelling corrections automatically. With AutoCorrect, you enter your common misspellings and the proper replacement spellings. It then identifies the misspellings and makes the replacements as you type.

• **Prevent AutoCorrect from making specific corrections**

To modify AutoCorrect, you can turn options on and off, or edit the AutoCorrect entries. For the AutoCorrect capitalization and Spelling Checker options, you can also create an exceptions list that specifies which words should not be changed. For example, you can prevent AutoCorrect from capitalizing a word that you want to appear in lowercase for stylistic reasons.

FIGURE I-7: Entry Added in AutoCorrect dialog box

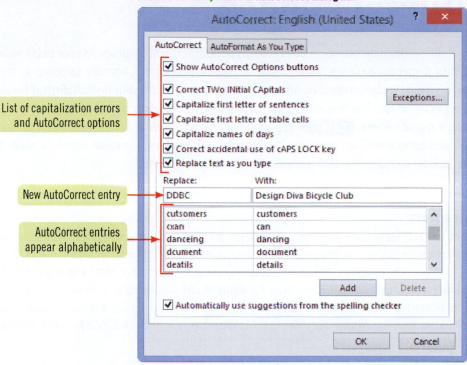

List of capitalization errors and AutoCorrect options

New AutoCorrect entry

AutoCorrect entries appear alphabetically

FIGURE I-8: AutoFormat As You Type tab in the AutoCorrect dialog box

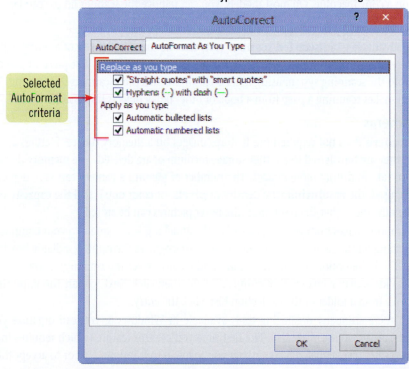

Selected AutoFormat criteria

Using tools wisely

AutoCorrect is a powerful tool. However, like all tools, it is important to recognize appropriate uses and limitations. There may be occasions when, for design or literary reasons, you want to turn off AutoCorrect features. Consider how the works of Mark Twain, James Joyce, e. e. cummings, Lewis Carroll, and other English-speaking authors would have been altered by the tools found in software products. Knowing how and when to use a tool is vital. Knowing when and how to dispense with a tool is important, too.

Use Digital Images

Publisher is a powerful program because of its ability to handle both text and graphics. As your publications become targeted to a specific audience, your choice of graphic images will become targeted as well. Instead of relying on digital images created by others, you may wish to create your own. A **digital image** is a picture in an electronic file. The two most common methods of creating digital images are using a scanner and using a digital camera. **CASE** ▶ *You want the training materials to foster a sense of inclusion and help all employees get to know each other. You decide to ask each employee to provide a favorite photo for you to scan, or to pose for a photograph that you will take with a digital camera.*

DETAILS

- ### Types of scanners

  Many kinds of scanners are in use today, and each type has advantages and disadvantages. By far, the most popular scanners are the flatbed and sheet-fed variety. Both types of scanners come with their own software that must be loaded on the computer, and they must be connected to a computer. Most scanners come with **optical character recognition (OCR)** software for scanning and translating text documents. Assuming your computer is attached to a scanner, you can scan an image using Windows Fax and Scan, which is supplied with Windows. Press the Windows key 🪟 on the keyboard, type sc, then click Windows Fax and Scan.

- ### Flatbed scanners

  A **flatbed scanner** has a flat surface from which the image is scanned, and it is the best type for creating digital images from photos and printed materials. To scan an item, place it face down on the scanner's glass surface, as on a copy machine. On most models, you can remove the scanner lid to scan large objects.

- ### Sheet-fed scanners

  The biggest advantage of a **sheet-fed scanner** is its size. Commonly the size of a portable printer, it takes up little space on a crowded desktop. Instead of placing a document on a flat piece of glass, you feed the document into the scanning system using rollers. This limits sheet-fed scanners to scanning single sheets of paper, which makes scanning a page from a book or other bulky objects impossible.

- ### Digital cameras

  A **digital camera** does not require film; it stores images on a memory device. Pictures are stored on the device until they are transferred to another storage medium or are deleted. The memory device can then be used again to take and store more images. The number of pictures a camera can save depends on the file format being used, the **resolution** (the density of **pixels**, or color dots), and the capacity of the memory device. Generally, the higher the resolution, the fewer pictures can be stored.

  You can import images from your digital camera by attaching your camera to your computer using a USB cable and turning on the camera. When your computer recognizes the camera, a dialog box for that camera will display. Click the option to Import pictures and videos, select the option you want from the Import Pictures and Videos dialog box, as shown in **FIGURE I-9**, then click Next to start the importing process. To insert an image from a folder in the Collection List, click the entry.

  Although there are many organizing tools available in Windows 8, you can organize your images in Photo Gallery, as shown in **FIGURE I-10**. The first time you use this feature (which requires Internet access), you may encounter several dialog boxes asking you to log in to Windows Live or to accept the types of files Windows Live can open.

- ### Copyright laws

  Images that you take with your own camera are your property to use as you want. However, images from other sources, including magazines, books, and the Internet, are the **intellectual property** of others and may be copyrighted and have limitations placed on their use. Permission for you to use an image may be granted by the copyright holder; sometimes permission is received just by asking, and other times you may be required to pay a fee. It is your legal and ethical responsibility to only use images that belong to you or that you have permission to use.

FIGURE I-9: Import Pictures and Videos dialog box

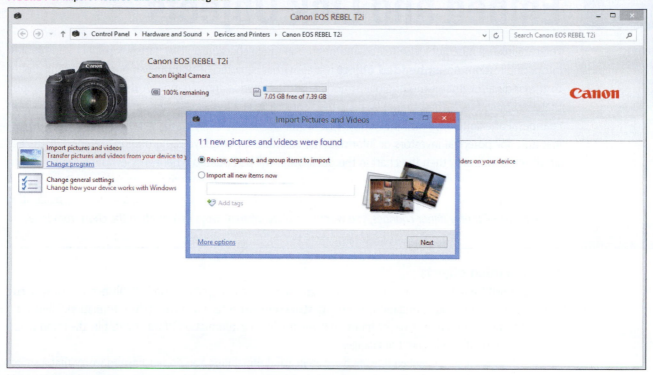

FIGURE I-10: Photo Gallery

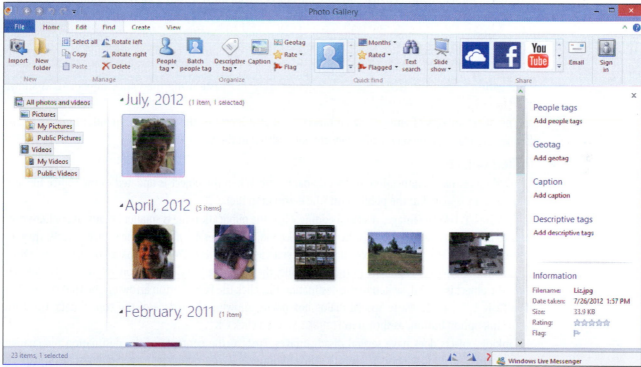

Images courtesy of Elizabeth Eisner Reding

Studying color

Color is one of the most difficult areas of design to master, for a variety of reasons. Because the human eye can detect several million hues, color perceptions and descriptions are subjective. In addition, language is limited in its ability to describe and define so many shades of color. Also, between five to eight percent of males have some defect of color vision (females are much less affected because color-blindness is a male dominant trait). Considering the limitations of language and perception, a good way to study color is by using a color wheel. A **color wheel** teaches color relationships by organizing colors in a circle so you can visualize how they relate to each other.

Embed and Link Objects

Learning Outcomes
- Know the difference between embedding and linking
- Determine when to use a linked object

You can link or embed objects created in other programs, such as graphics, charts, worksheets, and tables, into a publication. An **embedded object** is a copy that is pasted into a publication. It maintains no ties to the original, so that if the original is modified, the copy does not change. A **linked object** is a copy that is connected to the original. When the original is modified, the copy is updated to reflect those changes. For example, you might want to include an Excel chart that shows quarterly sales in promotional literature for potential investors or informational literature for employees. If you link the chart instead of simply embedding it, then the chart in the publication will be updated whenever new data is entered into the Excel workbook. **CASE** *As part of the training literature, you want to include a chart of Design Diva's growth in a publication that documents the history of the company. Because you anticipate using the publication in the future with only minor changes, you want to explore different ways of importing the chart from Excel.*

DETAILS

- ### Embedded objects

  An embedded object is created in another program and copied to a publication in Publisher. The **source file** contains the original information, and the **destination file** is the recipient of the information. There is no connection between the two programs, so if you modify the information in the source file, the information in the destination file does not change.

  The advantages of embedding are permanence and portability. You do not have to worry that a source file will be deleted, moved, or renamed, which would render the link between the files useless, or that its contents or formatting will change. Because the object is contained within your publication, it will stay the same unless you change it. An embedded object can always be edited (unless you use the Picture option) using its original program by double-clicking it, but once the editing is done, the connection is again severed. To embed an object in an Office document, select the object in the source file, click the Copy button 📋 in the Clipboard group on the HOME tab, switch to the destination file, then click the Paste button 📋 on the HOME tab. You can also copy and paste using the Office Clipboard, as shown in **FIGURE I-11**.

  The disadvantages of embedding an object are that it increases the size of the publication, and if any changes are made to the source file, they are not updated in the destination file.

- ### Linked objects

  A linked object has a connection to the original object. When the object is updated in the source file, it is automatically updated in the publication (the destination file).

  Linking has two advantages over embedding. First, the publication file is smaller because it contains only links to the objects, not the objects themselves. Second, if changes are made to the source objects, they are automatically reflected in the publication when you view the objects. You can link an object in any Office document by selecting the object in the source file, then clicking the Copy button 📋 on the HOME tab. Once the object is copied, switch to the destination file, click the Paste button arrow on the HOME tab, then click Paste Special. The Paste Special dialog box opens, showing the source of the copied data. Click the Paste Link option button, as shown in **FIGURE I-12**, then click OK.

  Linking objects does have several disadvantages. First, as the contents of the destination file change, those changes may not be reflected in the surrounding text. For example, an article may state a quarterly sales figure that differs from the updated Excel chart. In addition, the formatting of a linked object may change and be disruptive to your design, and if you move, delete, or rename the source file, the link will be broken.

FIGURE I-11: Objects in the Clipboard pane

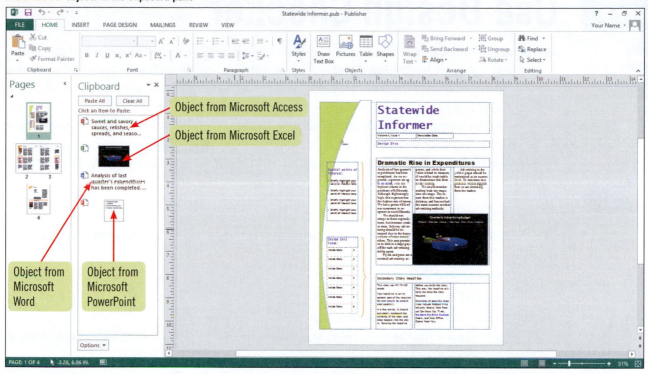

FIGURE I-12: Paste Special dialog box

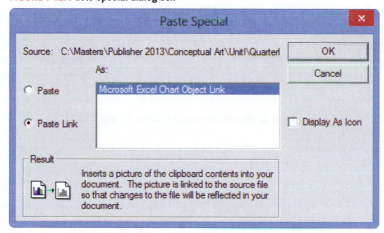

Using Publisher e-mail

Publisher contains a wide variety of e-mail templates that can be used to create electronic publications such as a letter, an announcement of an event, a product list, or a newsletter. These publications are found in the BUILT-IN list when you open a new publication and are designed to contain hyperlinks. If you use Microsoft Outlook or Windows Live Mail, you can send a single publication page as the body of an e-mail message. You can use any of the provided templates to keep your e-mail messages consistent with your publication designs.

Use Design Checker

Learning Outcomes
- Check a publication for design flaws
- Correct flaws in design

Most publications contain multiple text and graphic elements, making it easy to miss design problems during a casual review. You can use **Design Checker** to objectively review your publication and identify potential general design problems, commercial printing issues, web site design issues, and e-mail text problems. Design Checker looks for layout errors, alerts you, and suggests changes, but it does not fix the problems automatically. Sometimes your design choices may cause you to reject the Design Checker suggestions, but often it can help find areas of your publication that you can improve. **CASE** ▶ *You created a flyer containing intentional errors that can be used to demonstrate the capabilities of the Design Checker feature. You want to use this publication so others can see how Design Checker works.*

STEPS

1. Open **PUB I-2.pub** from the location where you store your Data Files, then save it as **PUB I-Training Flyer**

   The flyer appears on the screen. It has two areas of color on the page.

2. Click the **FILE tab** on the Ribbon, click **Info** if it is not already selected, then click **Run Design Checker** in the center pane

   The Design Checker pane opens on the right side of the screen. By default, it will check all pages as well as the master page.

3. Click **Design Checker Options** at the bottom of the Design Checker pane, click the **Checks tab** in the Design Checker Options dialog box, read all the selected features that Design Checker can examine, then make sure all the check boxes contain a check mark

   See **FIGURE I-13**.

4. Click **OK** in the Design Checker Options dialog box

   The errors found by Design Checker do not have to be addressed or fixed in any particular order. Design Checker finds that part of the e-mail address went into the overflow area (item 2). Design Checker makes suggestions about possible remedies in the task pane. Two errors are listed in the Design Checker task pane. The first error listed reads "Page has space below top margin." Design Checker also finds that the address box text in the lower-left corner has a text-overflow. In order to go to a specific item listed in the task pane, you position the pointer over the item, then click the list arrow that appears to the right of the item.

   TROUBLE
   Design Checker results may vary with different printer installations.

5. Click the **Story with text in overflow area (Page 1) list arrow** on the Design Checker pane

   See **FIGURE I-14**.

6. Click **Go to this Item**

7. Point to the **lower-middle handle of the selected text box** until the pointer changes to ↕, drag the border to **10½" V**, then click **anywhere in the scratch area** to deselect the text box

   One item remains in the Design Checker pane; as corrections are addressed, items are erased from the pane.

8. Click the **Page has space below top margin (Page 1) list arrow** on the Design Checker pane, click **Go to this Item**, press **[↑]** until the selected objects are at the top of the page at the blue guide and the icon for the current item is automatically removed from the task pane, then press **[Esc]**

   There are no more items in the Design Checker pane. (*There are no problems in this publication.* displays in the Select an item to fix box in the Design Checker pane.)

9. Type **your name** in the e-mail address in the lower-left text box, save your work, submit your work to your instructor, then exit Publisher

FIGURE I-13: Design Checker Options dialog box

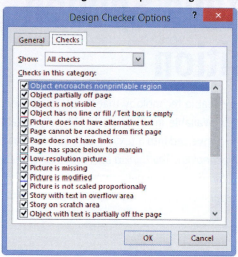

FIGURE I-14: Results of Design Checker

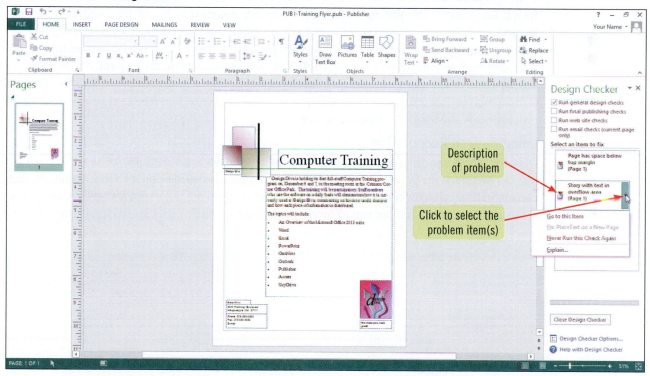

Working with Design Checker

Design Checker is a helpful tool, but it is crucial to recognize its limitations. For example, Design Checker recognizes WordArt as an object, not as text, and does not recognize WordArt when it is placed on an otherwise empty text box. Design Checker does not recognize color clashes or insufficient white space in a publication. You can work around these limitations by visually inspecting a publication in addition to running Design Checker. In addition, there may be occasions when you wish to ignore the Design Checker suggestions in order to achieve a design goal. For example, you may want to change the proportions of an image to create an interesting visual effect or simply to fill a space.

Understand Speech Recognition

Speech recognition is valuable technology that translates spoken language into computer commands or text. The technology is available in Windows 8. When you talk into a microphone connected to a computer, your words are converted into a text file by a software package. **CASE** *You have heard a lot about speech-recognition technology. You think a brief overview of the technology would interest employees at the training session and foster discussion about improving work practices at Design Diva. You consider some key issues related to speech recognition that you want to bring up at the training session.*

DETAILS

- **Installation**

  Installation of the Speech Recognition component may require some additional hardware, such as a microphone, and requires answering some simple questions in several dialog boxes.

- **Training sessions**

  To set up Speech Recognition on your computer, press the Windows key [■], type sp, then click Windows Speech Recognition. The first time you start the Speech Recognition feature the Welcome to Speech Recognition dialog box opens, as shown in **FIGURE I-15**. Training involves reading a series of paragraphs into your computer's microphone. The training sessions teach the software's speech module to recognize your voice, and teach you the correct speed and clarity that are understandable to the program. **FIGURE I-16** shows a dialog box that lets you set up the type of microphone you want to use. **FIGURE I-17** shows the dictation training process. Training sessions can be completed more than once, and repetition results in improved performance of the Speech Recognition module.

- **Using Speech Recognition**

  Once the Speech Recognition component is installed in Windows 8, it is available for all Office programs and can be turned on by pressing the Windows key, typing co, clicking Control Panel, typing sp, then clicking Start speech recognition. With Speech Recognition turned on, the Speech Recognition bar appears at the top of the screen. You can turn off Speech Recognition by clicking the Close button on the bar.

Choosing a microphone

Many newer computers come with a microphone already installed, allowing you to easily use the speech-recognition feature. If your computer did not come with this accessory, use the web to research manufacturers and styles and to learn which models work best with your system. Connect to the Internet, then use your browser and your favorite search engine to search on "PC microphones" or "PC sound systems."

FIGURE I-15: Welcome to Speech Recognition dialog box

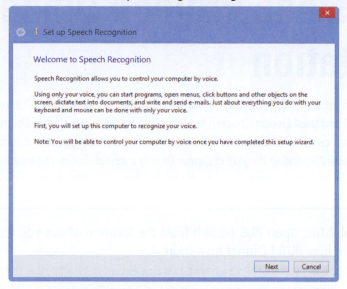

FIGURE I-16: Select the type of microphone you would like to use dialog box

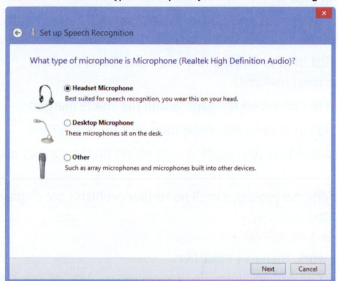

FIGURE I-17: Adjust the volume of (*your microphone*) dialog box

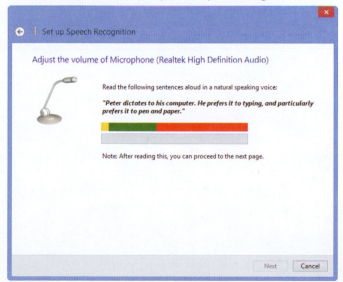

Capstone Project: Dinner Invitation

You have learned the skills necessary to transform Word documents into Publisher publications. You have learned about and used Design Checker. You have also learned about using alternative input devices, such as scanners, digital cameras, and speech recognition, as well as linking and embedding objects. **CASE** *The corporate president is inviting the staff of Design Diva to a formal dinner. The invitations will be engraved, so you want them to be perfect when you hand the file over to the printer. You decide to use Design Checker.*

STEPS

1. **Start Publisher, open PUB I-3.pub from the location where you store your Data Files, then save it as PUB I-Dinner Invitation**

   The invitation appears on the screen with two elements of color alongside the text at the top and bottom.

2. **Click the FILE tab on the Ribbon, click Info if it is not already selected, then click Run Design Checker**

   The Design Checker pane opens, as shown in **FIGURE I-18**. By default, it will check all pages as well as the master page.

3. **Click the first item to fix list arrow, then click Go to this Item**

   The problem object is selected.

4. **Reposition the object on the page within the visible margins**

5. **Click the first item to fix list arrow, then click Go to this Item**

6. **Press the arrow keys to reposition each object on the page as needed within the visible margins**

7. **Fix any additional problems until no further problems are displayed in the Design Checker pane**

   Compare your work to **FIGURE I-19**.

8. **Save your work, then exit Publisher**

   Examine your printed page. If you find any mistakes, go back and correct them. If necessary, print the pages again.

FIGURE I-18: Design Checker task pane

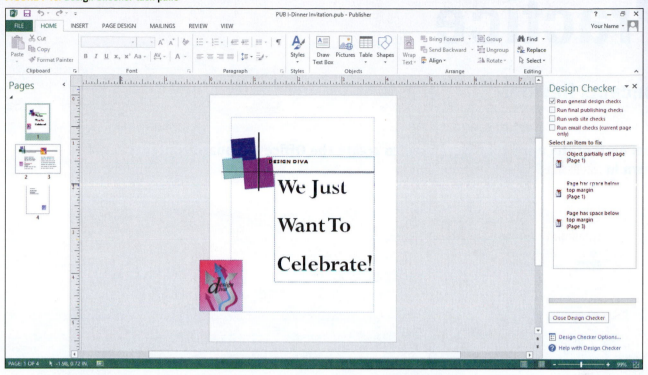

FIGURE I-19: Completed Dinner Invitation

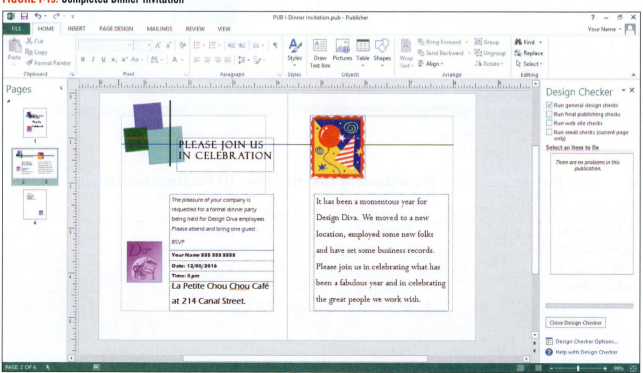

Practice

Concepts Review

Label each of the apps that were used to create the Office Clipboard contents shown in FIGURE I-20.

FIGURE I-20

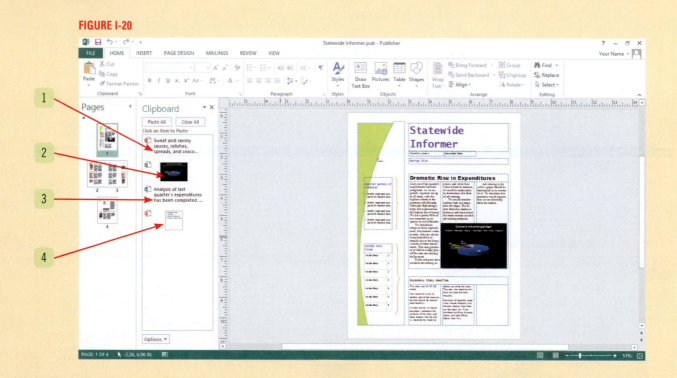

Match each of the features with the statement that describes its function or attribute.

5. **Embedded object**
6. **Design Checker**
7. **Digital camera**
8. **AutoCorrect entries**
9. **Linked object**
10. **Flatbed scanner**

a. List of common misspellings
b. Transforms images or text into electronic files
c. Finds problems such as an object in nonprinting areas of the page
d. Maintains a connection to the source file
e. Creates your own images
f. Must be double-clicked for editing

Select the best answer from the list of choices.

11. **You can use Design Checker to _____.**
    - **a.** correct misspelled words
    - **b.** find and correct typos
    - **c.** correct errors in capitalization
    - **d.** correct layout and design errors

12. **Which Microsoft product can you use to organize data into tables, records, and fields?**
    - **a.** Access
    - **b.** Excel
    - **c.** Outlook
    - **d.** PowerPoint

13. **You can use Microsoft Excel to _____.**
    - **a.** create presentations
    - **b.** create charts
    - **c.** write e-mails
    - **d.** All of the above

14. **You can use a copyrighted image in a publication if _____.**
    - **a.** you ask permission of the copyright holder
    - **b.** you copy it from the World Wide Web
    - **c.** you credit the copyright owner in a footnote
    - **d.** you receive written permission from the copyright holder

15. **Design Checker can check for _____.**
    - **a.** text in the overflow area
    - **b.** blank pages
    - **c.** subject-verb agreement
    - **d.** clashing colors

16. **AutoCorrect is used to do all of the following, except _____.**
    - **a.** correct misspelled words
    - **b.** find and correct typos
    - **c.** correct errors in capitalization
    - **d.** correct layout and design errors

17. **A linked object _____.**
    - **a.** can never be updated
    - **b.** is updated when the source file is changed
    - **c.** is updated by double-clicking on the object
    - **d.** has to be removed from the publication for updating

18. **An embedded object _____.**
    - **a.** can never be updated.
    - **b.** is updated automatically
    - **c.** is updated by double-clicking on the object
    - **d.** has to be removed from the publication for updating

19. **Which Microsoft product can you use to exchange e-mail across the Internet?**
    - **a.** Access
    - **b.** Outlook
    - **c.** Excel
    - **d.** PowerPoint

20. **Each of the following is true, except _____.**
    - **a.** Word documents can be imported directly into Publisher
    - **b.** Word can be used to edit stories written in Publisher
    - **c.** stories written in Word are created in text boxes by default
    - **d.** import Word documents into Publisher publications to maintain design consistency by adding design elements.

21. **To detect and correct misspellings, AutoCorrect uses _____.**
    - **a.** a list of AutoCorrect entries
    - **b.** the main dictionary
    - **c.** the custom dictionary
    - **d.** a thesaurus

Skills Review

1. Integrate with Office apps.

   a. You work for a chain of restaurants and are responsible for creating menus, advertisements, business plans, and monthly specials flyers. List at least three ways in which you could integrate Office programs to create these materials on a regular basis.

   b. You work for a nonprofit organization dedicated to pet adoptions. What tasks could you perform using Office programs?

   c. You work for a small, family-owned plumbing company. How could you use Office products to make this business more efficient?

2. Import a Word document.

   a. Start Publisher, then select the Bars template in the Import Word Documents category in the BUILT-IN list.

   b. Choose 2 columns and the color scheme of your choice, then click CREATE.

   c. In the Import Word Document dialog box, select PUB I-4.docx in the location where you store your Data Files, click OK, then save the publication as **PUB I-Astronomy Story**.

   d. Press [F9].

   e. Replace the Document Title placeholder text with **Enjoying Astronomy Correctly**.

   f. Change the title font size to 18 point.

   g. Save and then close the publication, but do not exit Publisher.

3. Use AutoCorrect.

   a. Examine the list of default AutoCorrect entries. Are there any entries missing that you think you will need?

   b. Will any of the default entries cause problems in your everyday use?

4. Use digital images.

   a. Find two images, then scan them.

   b. Open a new, blank publication, then save it as **PUB I-Scanning Practice** in the location where you store your Data Files. Insert the two images, place your name somewhere on the page as well as the title **Scanning Practice**, print the page, then save and close the file.

5. Embed and link objects.

   a. Think of a real-world situation in which linking an object, such as financial data, would be advantageous. One example might be a book distributor working with several warehouses across the country. How could linking help to keep inventory reports in this sort of business up to date?

6. Use Design Checker.

   a. Open PUB I-5.pub from the location where you store your Data Files, then save it as **PUB I-New Design Diva Newsletter**.

   b. Start Design Checker.

   c. Ignore the items **Object partially off page (Page 1)** and **Object is not visible (Page 2)** if they appear in the list.

   d. Fix items 2, 3, and 4 (although your items numbers may vary) that say **Object is not visible (Page 1)**.

   e. Fix the remaining problems by either deleting empty text boxes, moving objects, scaling objects proportionally or bringing objects forward. (Your results using Design Checker may vary.)

   f. Print page 1 of the publication.

   g. Save the publication and exit Publisher.

7. Understand speech recognition.

   a. If you have a microphone and speakers attached to your computer and you completed the Speech Recognition training in the lesson, make a list of two simple tasks in which you could use speech recognition. (*Hint:* You could create a text box, then use the Speech Recognition feature to fill it. Or, you could select a text box, then use the Speech Recognition feature to open the Format Text Box dialog box.)

   b. Write down what tasks you accomplished, then try each task and rate the feature's effectiveness.

Independent Challenge 1

As the office manager for your local Chamber of Commerce, you decide to spend time working with employees to improve their skills. One of the employees needs help with a postcard announcing an upcoming event. You will use Design Checker to find and fix problems.

   a. Start Publisher, then open the file PUB I-6.pub from the location where you store your Data Files.

   b. Save the publication as **PUB I-Potluck Supper Postcard**.

   c. Use Design Checker to find and correct any problems. (Some problems are printer-dependent. Your files may get different results.)

   d. Adjust the text point size (you may use Best Fit) so that all of the text is visible.

   e. Make any necessary adjustments such as cropping, or changing the way the text wraps around the image, then compare your work to **FIGURE I-21**.

   f. Include your name in the e-mail address.

   g. Save and print the publication, then exit Publisher.

FIGURE I-21

Independent Challenge 2

Some friends from an art school are giving a party with the theme "Bad Taste in Your Face." You agreed to make a flyer in the worst taste you can imagine announcing the party.

   a. Start Publisher, then open the file PUB I-7.pub from the location where you store your Data Files.

   b. Save the publication as **PUB I-Party Flyer**.

   c. Use Design Checker to find and correct any problems it identifies in the flyer.

   d. Correct any text spacing problems not found by Design Checker.

   e. Correct any typos or misspellings.

   f. Substitute your name for the e-mail address.

   g. Save your work and submit it to your instructor, then exit Publisher.

Independent Challenge 3

You have been researching the topic of color psychology in preparation for a talk you are giving to graphic designers later this month. You wrote up a summary of your notes in a Microsoft Word document, and have decided that you want to provide a hard copy of the summary to people attending the talk. You decide to import the document into Publisher so that you can create a sharp-looking publication to hand out to attendees.

a. Start Publisher, then click Import Word Documents in the BUILT-IN list.

b. Click the Blocks template using the color and font options of your choosing, then click CREATE.

c. In the Import Word Document dialog box, open the file PUB I-8.docx from the location where you store your Data Files, click OK, then save the publication as **PUB I-Color Psychology Story**.

d. Press [F9].

e. If necessary, adjust the spacing between paragraphs and change the font size of the imported text to 12, then delete the page number text box.

f. Click the Document Title placeholder text, right-align it, type **The Psychology of Color, by**, then type your name.

g. Select the document title, change the font to a 20 pt Rockwell Condensed font (or something similar) and adjust the size of the text box if necessary.

h. In the Columns dialog box, change the number of columns to 2.

i. Create shapes for some of the colors mentioned in the publication, then arrange and group them.

j. Compare your publication to FIGURE I-22. (*Hint*: The length of your name and the font used will make your publication look different from the sample shown.)

k. Save your work and submit it to your instructor, then exit Publisher.

FIGURE I-22

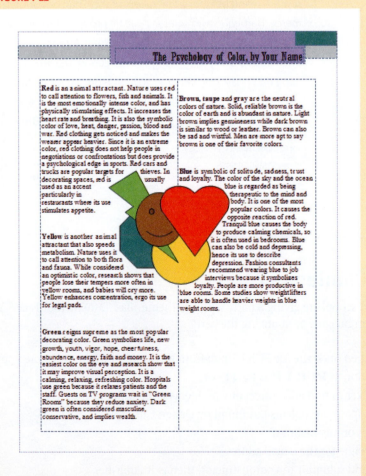

Independent Challenge 4: Explore

This Independent Challenge requires an Internet connection. You consider yourself artistic with good instincts about design, but wish you knew more about colors and how to choose them. Use your browser and search engine to explore articles about color wheels on the web. Create a brief description of color wheels in Word, then import it into Publisher.

a. Connect to the Internet, then use your browser and favorite search engine to explore the term "color wheel."

b. Find out the key features and benefits of color wheels and print out any information that will help you write a brief Word document about the subject.

c. Use the information you gathered online to write a short Word document about color wheels, then save it as **PUB I-Color Wheel Story** to the location where you store your Data Files.

d. Use the BUILT-IN list to pick the Word document template of your choice in Publisher.

e. Import your Word document into Publisher.

f. If possible, find an image of a color wheel and insert it into the publication.

g. Save the publication as **PUB I-About the Color Wheel** to the location where you store your Data Files.

h. Change the title to **About The Color Wheel, by**, then type your name.

i. Select the one-sided printing option.

j. Compare your publication to **FIGURE I-23**, save your work and submit it to your instructor, then exit Publisher.

FIGURE I-23

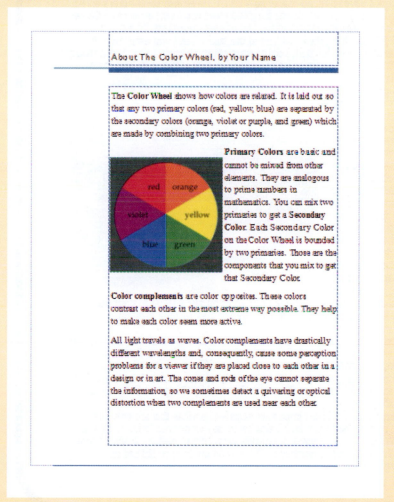

Visual Workshop

Use the BUILT-IN list to create the Studio publication (found in the Import Word Documents category). This is the initial design of a story you are importing from Word. Import the file PUB I-9.docx into the publication, and then save the publication as **PUB I-Presenting Designs**. Use FIGURE I-24 as a guide for enhancing the publication and including or removing additional elements such as your name. Move any of the objects on the page to make the publication easier to read, and use the Best Fit AutoFit feature. The color scheme used is Tropics and clip art shown in the sample can be found by searching, using "meeting" as the keyword. Save your work, then print the first page and submit it to your instructor.

FIGURE I-24

PRESENTING DESIGNS, by Your name

When I started designing, I was embarrassed to present bad ideas. I kept a sketchpad and wrote down ideas when I was in front of the TV, doing hobbies, at meetings, or traveling by bike to work. I never let anyone see it. Many of my ideas were bad. But with each concept I developed, no matter how bad, it illustrated some other way of thinking about design. Each bad idea highlighted some important aspect of a design problem that I hadn't thought about before. Out of every ten ideas, I'd have one or two that might be OK. Sketching the ideas helped me, and when I was away from the computer it was all I could do. Still, I didn't want others to know I sketched. I thought people would think I was a lousy artist or a poor designer if they saw how many sketches I made.

When it came time to present ideas to my boss, I'd lead with my best idea. I'd invest a lot of time in making it as perfect as possible. He was always dissatisfied and I soon started looking for ways to keep him from "messing" with my concept. I would throw in some spelling errors or some neologisms to divert him away from the meat of my ideas. It didn't work. There are so many variations for a design that if you only show one idea, anyone who thinks they can design (that is everyone) will give you alternatives to your design, and ask why the idea you're going with isn't the one they just put forward.

After many anxiety-provoking meetings, and hearing my boss's advice, *ad nauseum*, I learned the best way to present design ideas. Show the worst ones first, in order to help support the good ones. I began presenting five different ideas, selecting three of the most meaningful designs and two that I considered just odious. I don't avoid my boss anymore and I don't throw in those gratuitous misspellings. I talk boldly about the key trade-offs.

When discussing ideas, I cull out important negative qualities that are only answered by the idea I'm recommending, which helps set up my recommendation to be well received. Sometimes I'll get a good suggestion for taking something from the first design and adding it to design number 5. That would not happen if I had only presented a single idea.

Glossary

Align To arrange two or more items along an edge.

Asymmetrical balance Designing a page to balance elements to achieve a more dynamic and informal appearance than symmetrical balance; provides more visual interest than a symmetrically balanced page.

AutoCorrect A feature that automatically corrects misspellings and grammatical errors as you type.

Autoflow A feature that automatically places text that does not fit in a text box into the next available text box.

AutoShapes Ready-made design elements, including lines, connectors, basic shapes, flowchart elements, stars and banners, and callouts.

Available Templates An area of the Backstage view that contains categories of publication types, such as newsletters.

Backstage view The display accessed by clicking the FILE tab, which contains commands needed to perform actions common to most Office programs.

Balance The symmetrical arrangement of design elements on a page.

Baseline guides A set of layout guides that help align text to the baseline, and add equal line spacing so the text appears balanced along columns.

BestFit A feature that automatically resizes type and manipulates text to fit within a text box.

Booklet A multi-page publication that is folded or bound.

Border The edge or boundary line of an object.

BorderArt Decorative borders that come with or can be created using Publisher for placement around most objects.

Branded publications Those publications that have a similar look to them, giving your company or organization instant recognition.

Bring to front A command that places the currently selected object in front, or on top, of other objects.

Building Blocks A group on the INSERT tab that gives you access to a library of design elements that contain text or graphic images that can be edited for size, shape, and content.

Bulleted list Used to illustrate items that can occur in any order or that are of equal importance.

Business Information Sets An unlimited number of distinct sets of information that can be used to store frequently used information such as names, addresses, and phone numbers, which can be placed automatically in publications.

Camera-ready artwork Graphic illustrations that have been fully prepared for the printing of a publication.

Catalog A publication that presents a list or display of items.

Chart A graphic representation of numerical information.

Clip art Electronic artwork available for use free of charge or for a fee.

Clipboard A temporary holding area in Office apps into which as many as 24 objects can be copied and pasted. (The Windows Clipboard holds a single copied or cut item.)

Color schemes Coordinated sets of matched and complementary colors that may be applied to a publication.

Color wheel A circular illustration used to teach color relationships, where primary and intermediate colors are arranged so that related colors are next to each other and complementary colors are opposite one another.

Continued on/Continued from notices Text that tells on what page a story is continued on or from, and automatically updates if the story is moved.

Copyfitting To make text fit into a space within a publication.

Crop To conceal portions of an image.

Database A collection of related information arranged for easy search and retrieval.

Data source A file in which names, addresses, and other contact information is stored for use in a mail merge.

Design A consistent *look* contained within a publication.

Design Checker A feature that searches publications for specific layout problems.

Designs Stylized publications in which you choose the layout, colors, fonts, and artwork.

Desktop publishing program A program that lets you combine text and graphics, as well as worksheets and charts created in other programs, to produce typeset-quality documents for output on a computer printer, or for commercial printing.

Destination file The file into which an object is embedded or linked.

Digital camera A camera that captures and stores images as digital electronic information on a storage medium instead of on photographic film.

Digital image A pictorial representation generated, stored, or displayed electronically.

Drag and drop A moving or copying technique in which an object, or a copy of an object, is dragged to a new location using the mouse.

Drawing tools Commands that let you create geometric designs.

Drop cap A formatting feature that lets you draw attention to the beginning of a story by changing the size and appearance of a paragraph's initial character.

Electronic spreadsheet Software in which data is arranged in rows and columns and mathematical operations and charting functions are performed.

Embedded object An object created in a source file that is inserted in a destination document, becoming part of the destination file.

Field An element of a database record that contains one piece of information, such as a zip code or first name.

Fill To add a color, pattern, or texture to a design element.

Fill color The hue added to shade a design element.

Filtering Allows you to print, preview, or merge a portion of qualifying records in a mail merge.

Flatbed scanner A type of digital scanner that has a sheet of glass where the page is placed to be scanned.

Footer Text that repeats on the bottom of each page in a publication.

Formatting tools Commands that display in the Font and Paragraph groups of the HOME tab and contain buttons for frequently used text formatting such as bold, italics, or underlining.

Graphic image A piece of artwork, a graph, or a drawing in electronic form. (Also called a *graphic*.)

Grid guides On screen lines that appear as column and row guides and are used to position objects.

Group Selection of multiple images that can be moved or resized as a single unit.

Grouping The process of combining several objects into one: an easy way to move or manipulate multiple objects.

Handles Small hollow circles displayed around the perimeter of a selected object.

Hand-off format The final digital electronic format of a publication that is conveyed to a commercial printer.

Header Text that repeats on the top of each page in a publication.

Help A feature that gives you immediate access to definitions, explanations, and useful tips on working in Publisher.

HOME tab The first white tab on the left edge of the Ribbon that contains buttons for the most frequently used Publisher commands.

Horizontal ruler Measuring guide that appears above the publication window.

Intellectual property Digital materials, including images, magazines, books, and other material available on the Internet, that may be copyrighted and have limitations placed on their use. Permission is required for the use of such materials.

Kerning A form of character formatting that adjusts the spacing between character pairs.

Keywords Text or characters used to search for specific pages, objects, or images within applications.

Layer To change the position of objects in relation to one another so that one appears to be on top of or in back of another.

Layout guides Horizontal and vertical lines positioned on a publication's Master Page and visible on all pages to help you accurately position objects: includes margin guides and grid guides.

Leaders Dots, dashes, or lines in a row that make it easier to read a table of contents or other information by guiding the eye across the page.

Linked object An object created in a source file that is shared in a destination file. The object retains its connection to the source file.

Logo A distinctive shape, symbol, or color that visibly identifies a company, organization, or product.

Mail merge A feature that combines a destination document, such as a personalized brochure, with a data source, such as an Access file containing names and addresses, using an interactive set of dialog boxes that guides the user in creating a mail merge.

Mail Merge pane A tool that guides you through the merging process and allows you to customize your data source and your publication.

Margin guides Lines that display on the top, bottom, left, and right, and repeat on each page, separating the margins from the other design elements.

Margins The space between the edge of a design element and the edge of a page, as well as the space that surrounds any boundary.

Mask An object designed to hide a specific area.

Master page The background of a publication page where repeated information such as a pattern, header, or footer can be stored, viewed, and edited.

Masthead The arrangement of text and graphic elements found at the beginning of a newsletter with its name, volume, issue, and date, which remains consistently formatted from issue to issue.

Matte A colorful shape positioned behind an object to make it stand out.

Measurement pane A context-sensitive pane that lets you more precisely move, resize, or adjust text point size, distance between characters, and line spacing as well as an object's height, width, length, and rotation.

Microsoft Office Online A Microsoft Web site that continually offers new downloadable resources for creating publications.

Mirrored guides Layout guides and margins on left and right facing pages that appear to be mirror images.

Mirrored image A type of two-page layout where either page appears as if viewed in a mirror, with right and left reversed.

Nudge To move a selected object a defined distance by pressing one of the arrow keys.

Numbered list Used to list items that occur in a particular sequence.

Object An element such as a table, text box, geometric shape, clip art, or picture frame that can be resized, moved, joined, or layered.

Object shadow Gives an object the illusion of depth by adding a shadow behind it.

Office Collections The artwork library shared by all Microsoft Office applications.

Online collaboration Participants working together on a project across the Internet.

Optical center The point around which objects on the page are balanced, approximately 3/8" from the top of the page.

Optical Character Recognition (OCR) A software application that transforms scanned images of text into digital electronic documents.

Orientation The direction in which paper is printed; options are landscape and portrait.

Pack and Go Wizard A feature that compacts all the files (fonts, graphics, and essential design elements) needed by a commercial printing service onto your choice of media.

Page indicators Located on the left side of the status bar and show you the numbers of pages in a publication and indicate which page is active.

Page navigation icons Located at the bottom of the workspace, one page icon displays for each page in the publication. You click a navigation icon to go to a specific page.

Page numbers The numbers assigned in sequence to pages of text in a publication.

Pages pane The area that shows you how many pages are in the current publication, which pages are active, and allows you to navigate the pages.

Pane The area of the Publisher window that is a visual gallery and appears alongside your publication.

Pixel A color dot: the fundamental unit of an image on a television screen, computer monitor, or similar display.

Placeholder A design element provided by Publisher that you can replace with your own information to customize a publication.

Point size The measurement of the height of a character. 1/72 of an inch equals one point.

Postscript A page description format developed by Adobe Systems that is widely supported by both hardware and software vendors.

Pour To move text that will not fit in a text box to an empty text box.

Pre-press work The process in which a commercial printer verifies the availability of fonts and linked graphics, makes color corrections or separations, and sets the final printing options.

Presentation A series of projected slides and/or handouts that a speaker refers to while delivering information.

Printing Creates output from a publication into paper form.

Proof print An approximation of how your final publication will look when printed.

Publication A document created in Publisher.

Pull quote A short statement extracted from a story (the wording does not have to be exact) and set aside from the body of the text.

Record A group of related fields, such as the name, address, and title of a customer.

Resolution A measure of the fineness of detail that can be distinguished in an image.

Reversed text Formatting effect that displays text so that it appears in a light color on a dark background.

Ribbon The area in the Publisher window that contains tabs grouped by tasks.

Rotate Changes the position of an object in degrees from a horizontal plane.

Rotation An object's position measured in degrees from a vertical plane.

Ruler guidelines *See* Ruler guides.

Ruler guides Green horizontal and vertical lines that appear on the screen to help you position objects on a page, but do not print.

Rulers Horizontal and vertical measurement guides located beneath the Ribbon and to the left of the workspace that let you precisely measure the size of objects and place objects in exact locations on a page.

Sans serif font A typeface that has no small strokes at the end of the main stroke of the character.

Scaling A formatting effect that stretches or shrinks the widths of characters.

Scanner Hardware that enables you to convert information on paper into an electronic file format.

Scratch area The gray area surrounding the publication page that can be used to store objects such as design elements.

ScreenTip A label that displays when the mouse pointer hovers over a button and describes its function

Send to back A command that places an object behind other objects.

Serif The small decorative stroke added to the end of a letter's main strokes. They help distinguish one character from another and serve as an aid to comprehension.

Serif font A typeface that has a small cross stroke at the end of the main stroke of the letter.

Sheetfed scanner A digital scanner that uses rollers to pull a single sheet of paper past the optical scanning device.

Sidebar Information in a publication that is related to the main story, but not vital to it; placed to the side of the regular text to create interest.

Signature A section of a large publication, such as a book or catalog, consisting of a large sheet of paper that is printed with eight pages (four on each side). The publication is entirely made up of these multiples of eight pages.

Smart objects An object category in the Design Gallery that can be modified by clicking the associated Wizard button.

Snap To command When turned on, this feature has a magnet-like effect that pulls whatever is being lined up to an object, a guide, or a ruler mark.

Sorting Allows you to change the order in which the merged publications are printed or viewed.

Source file When linking, the file that contains the information you want to share with another document. Once linked, the shared information will be updated if the source file is updated.

Speech recognition Software used to transform human speech into computer commands or text.

Spelling checker Used to check a story or publication for spelling errors.

Start screen A landing page that appears when you first start an Office app.

Status bar Located at the bottom of the Publisher window; provides information relevant to the current task.

Story Text in a publication.

Style A defined set of text and formatting attributes used to make pages easily recognizable and consistent.

Style by example To name an existing set of (perhaps unknown) text attributes as a style.

Symmetrical balance Objects are placed equally on either side of an imaginary vertical line.

Tab A defined location that the insertion point advances to when you press [Tab].

Tab bar Area that displays tabs that contain buttons that are organized in task-based categories.

Table Collection of information stored in a grid of columns and rows.

Table AutoFormat Pre-existing designs used to quickly format an existing table.

Table of contents A sequential list of the contents and associated page numbers of a publication.

Template A specially formatted publication of your own design with placeholder text that serves as a master for other, similar publications.

Text box An object in which text is typed, that can be resized and repositioned on a page.

Text overflow Text that does not fit within a text box.

Text wrapping The automatic placement of text around design elements.

Title bar The area at the top of the window where the program name and the filename of the open publication appear.

Tracking The spacing between characters.

Two-Page spread A view that enables you to see two pages at once.

Ungroup To turn one combined object into individual objects.

Vertical ruler A measuring guide that displays to the left of the page.

Washout A faint, lightly shaded image that appears behind other images. Also known as a watermark.

White space Also known as negative space, describes the open space between design elements.

WordArt An object containing stylized text that is shaped and has colored borders and fills.

Word processing program A software application used to generate and edit electronic documents.

Workspace The area where a new or existing publication appears and its surrounding scratch area.

Wrapping Text that is reshaped so it conforms to the shape of a nearby image or other object.

Wrap points The points on the edges of a text box that surround an object that which are used to fine tune the position of the wrapped text.

Zero point The location of zero on both the vertical and horizontal rulers that can be moved and lets you make precise measurements.

Zoom To make the page scale larger or smaller so that you can move in or away from page objects.

Index

Note: Page numbers in boldface indicate key terms.